Masculinities, Care and Equality

Genders and Sexualities in the Social Sciences

Series Editors: **Victoria Robinson**, University of Sheffield, UK and **Diane Richardson**, University of Newcastle, UK

Editorial Board: **Raewyn Connell**, University of Sydney, Australia, **Kathy Davis**, Utrecht University, The Netherlands, **Stevi Jackson**, University of York, UK, **Michael Kimmel**, State University of New York, Stony Brook, USA, **Kimiko Kimoto**, Hitotsubashi University, Japan, **Jasbir Puar**, Rutgers University, USA, **Steven Seidman**, State University of New York, Albany, USA, **Carol Smart**, University of Manchester, UK, **Liz Stanley**, University of Edinburgh, UK, **Gill Valentine**, University of Leeds, UK, **Jeffrey Weeks**, South Bank University, UK, **Kath Woodward**, The Open University, UK

Titles include:

Niall Hanlon
MASCULINITIES, CARE AND EQUALITY
Identity and Nurture in Men's Lives

Sally Hines and Yvette Taylor (*editors*)
SEXUALITIES
Past Reflections, Future Directions

Victoria Robinson and Jenny Hockey
MASCULINITIES IN TRANSITION

Yvette Taylor, Sally Hines and Mark E. Casey (*editors*)
THEORIZING INTERSECTIONALITY AND SEXUALITY

S. Hines and Y. Taylor (*editors*)
SEXUALITIES: PAST REFLECTIONS, FUTURE DIRECTIONS

Genders and Sexualities in the Social Sciences
Series Standing Order ISBN 978-0-230-27254-5 hardback
978-0-230-27255-2 paperback
(*outside North America only*)

You can receive future titles in this series as they are published by placing a standing order. Please contact your bookseller or, in case of difficulty, write to us at the address below with your name and address, the title of the series and one of the ISBNs quoted above.

Customer Services Department, Macmillan Distribution Ltd, Houndmills, Basingstoke, Hampshire RG21 6XS, England

Masculinities, Care and Equality

Identity and Nurture in Men's Lives

Niall Hanlon
Dublin Business School, Ireland

palgrave
macmillan

First published 2012 by
PALGRAVE MACMILLAN

Palgrave Macmillan in the UK is an imprint of Macmillan Publishers Limited, registered in England, company number 785998, of Houndmills, Basingstoke, Hampshire RG21 6XS.

Palgrave Macmillan in the US is a division of St Martin's Press LLC, 175 Fifth Avenue, New York, NY 10010.

Palgrave Macmillan is the global academic imprint of the above companies and has companies and representatives throughout the world.

Palgrave® and Macmillan® are registered trademarks in the United States, the United Kingdom, Europe and other countries

ISBN: 978–0–230–30021–7

This book is printed on paper suitable for recycling and made from fully managed and sustained forest sources. Logging, pulping and manufacturing processes are expected to conform to the environmental regulations of the country of origin.

A catalogue record for this book is available from the British Library.

A catalog record for this book is available from the Library of Congress.

10 9 8 7 6 5 4 3 2 1
21 20 19 18 17 16 15 14 13 12

Transferred to Digital Printing in 2012

For Emily, Hazel and Rowan

Contents

Preface and Acknowledgements

It is probably no exaggeration to say I began writing this book long before it was ever conceived as a research project. The central role of care in social life, the way it is organised and practiced, how it affects our lives, and especially its gendered nature, have occupied me since my youth. The process of writing this book has proven a cumulative reflective process that has challenged me academically and personally. Growing up in Irish society with five brothers, one of whom was severely physically and intellectually disabled, within the context of a conservative and patriarchal society wherein women were expected to be primary carers, and men to be primary breadwinners, left me with the strong sense of how closely interrelated that personal domain of care is with social justice. Personally I recall an overwhelming sense of how isolated, overburdened, and powerless women could find themselves feeling when faced with the imperative to care in the absence of equal rights and opportunities. However, this appreciation of the gender oppression could never obliterate the sense that men too, despite the system supporting their higher status, power, and access to resources, could be trapped by gendered expectations and prohibitions.

The last three decades of the twentieth century saw major social transformations in the political and social climate in Ireland as key battles over sexual morality and intimate family life convulsed the established gender order. Pressed by irrefutable demands for change from within the society as well as the external carrot-and-stick approach of the European economic project, an intensely conservative gendered society slowly and reluctantly began to liberalise by granting greater rights and freedom to women. Many women entered the world of paid work but there was, however, little political will among society at large to seriously consider how care-work between men and women might be redistributed. Yet greater gender-equal working relations raised questions about the private sphere and who would fill the care gap. Certainly, men were not rushing to do so! In fact, in marked contrast to any semblance of new man discourse, insidious revelations began to creep into the public domain about the puritanical authoritarianism, moral hypocrisy, and sexual crimes of the patriarchal Catholic Church which, since the foundation of the Irish state, had monopolised a moral and political hold on the caring institutions of society. The relationship between men and care became increasingly problematic as men seemed to be either absent from care or abusive when doing so! For its part, the State appeared to be complicit with oppression or at least incompetent or inept at meeting the goals of gender equality. It seemed clear to me how the State on the whole represented the views and values of conservative men.

These issues raised profound questions about the nature of care in Irish society. Why should men not be expected to undertake a fair share of care-work and why should they not reap the emotional benefits that can be gained from doing so? My initial attempt to find answers led me to pursue a career in the female-dominated world of social care. Out of 40 or so undergraduates three of us were men, and although I felt quite comfortable in this grouping among women I recall one of these men clinging to me with trepidation, desperately needy for male company and affirmation. Experiences like these made me realise how social care-work was gendered just like society at large and after spending four years studying Applied Social Studies I had learned virtually nothing about the relationship between gender and care. My hunger to find answers directed me towards a Master's and eventually a PhD programme in Equality Studies at the School of Social Justice in University College Dublin. Here I learned about gender, feminism, and masculinities and found conceptual tools to name care as a social good and a generative source of inequality itself. Every angle from which I have studied gender has brought me back to the intersection between power and care, dominance and emotions, the political and the personal. Feminism, and critical studies of men and masculinities, has alerted me to the power relations embedded in social life. It made me realise how this way of studying gender is both fundamental and incomplete. This book is an exploration of the relationship between masculinities, care, and equality and above all how men think and feel about care and equality as men. I hope it can make a small contribution to a complex and often controversial debate.

The reflective process of writing this book was at least as insightful as the analysis of the data itself. Although I had plenty of experience of working in the care field before embarking on the book, during its production I became the parent of two children. And, despite having read hundreds of texts on care, my belief that reading is no compensation for experience has been much strengthened. It has also reminded me of how much work and sacrifice my own parents made in raising me and my brothers and for that I am truly grateful. My personal faithfulness to gender equality in personal life has been challenged by the intense commitment and dedication of time that paid work expects, which increasingly requires us to revise our educational goals and reconstruct a self depending on shifting labour market expectations. This is true for academic work and the intense education upon which it relies. Writing about men and masculinities as a man is necessarily a reflection on self, on my own subjectivity, and social location. The personal experience of many of the men in the study have resounded with experiences I have had myself even including hegemonic practices, the hidden privileges, rewards, encouragements, and acknowledgements, from which I have personally benefited. Writing this book itself is an act of public recognition and self-affirmation, part of the contradictory experiences of being male, as it also is an attempt to challenge hegemonic masculinity and promote new nurturing ways of being male. Moreover, it is important to acknowledge that my treatise on men and care should not be taken as a personal moral judgement on other men (although it is a political one with personal implications for all men who take gender equality seriously).

I am deeply indebted to Kathleen Lynch, whose abundant energy, intellect, and moral persuasion spurred me to write this book. It was Kathleen's belief in me that gave men the confidence to feel that I could do it. Moreover, her scholarship on equality has proven an enormous source of inspiration, and, in particular, her perspective on affective life has enabled me to make connections between issues which are intrinsically personal as well as intensely political and theoretical. Very special thanks also to Jeff Hearn and Anne Cleary and Jack Kahn, who offered their invaluable insights and theoretical feedback on my drafts. Thanks to Ann Lynch, Dunia Huchinson and my wife Emily Doherty for their excellent editorial work. Many other people helped me in different ways including Maureen Lyons, Maggie Feeley, John Baker, Ernesto Vasquez Del Aguila, Bernie Grummell, Carlos Bruen, Mary Daly, John Bissett, Katherine O'Donnell, John Evoy, Conor Dervan, Edel McGinley, Keith Styles, Ann McWilliams, Fergus Comerford, and Jan Pettersen.

I would like to thank the series editors Diane Richardson and Victoria Robinson, the editorial board Raewyn Connell, Kathy Davis, Stevi Jackson, Michael Kimmel, Kimiko Kimoto, Jasbir Puar, Steven Seidman, Carol Smart, Liz Stanley, Gill Valentine, Jeffrey Weeks, and Kath Woodward. Thanks also to the publisher and the production team at Palgrave Macmillan, including Philippa Grand, Andrew James and Vidhya Jayaprakash. Although not named for the purposes of confidentiality, I am indeed most indebted to all those who participated in the study, for sharing their personal intimate stories and giving me their social and political perspectives. I am very grateful to Dublin City Council, University College Dublin, and the Irish Research Council for the Humanities and Social Sciences (IRCHSS) for grant and scholarship funding for the original research.

Like everything else in social life, this book is the product of care invested in me. It would not be possible without the emotional, intellectual, and financial support of my wife and soulmate Emily. The book is dedicated to her, our daughter Hazel and son Rowan, and our lives together. Finally, I would like to thank all those who appreciate the centrality of care in human life and to those who ceaselessly promote a more caring and equal society.

1
Care in Masculinities Studies

Prevailing images of masculinity are equated with power, physical strength, aggression, toughness and resilience, whilst prevailing images of femininity are associated with sexuality, emotion, nurture, sensitivity, compassion, and care. These antagonistic, binary representations (De Beauvoir 1949) have implications for the way gender is constructed as oppositional, and they can overlook the extensive variability of gender in social life. Just how inflexible or malleable gender has become, and to what extent gender equality has been achieved, remains a major topic in gender studies (Ranson 2001; Segal 2007; Delamont 2001). Unquestionably gender relations have been subject to considerable change in much of the Western world over the past fifty years. This was certainly true in the Ireland of my youth, during the 1970s and 80s where I grew up. Within the context of a sustained economic depression, and a desire to embrace social, political, and economic liberalism, Irish society began shaking off much of its conservative patriarchal heritage. The conservative gender order was undermined by increasing secularisation and the decline of the power and influence of Roman Catholicism (Inglis 2007, 1998a, 1998b). The women's movement in particular was at the forefront in battling for equal rights to contraception, abortion and divorce, to services for abused women, to childcare and children's rights, and to antidiscrimination protection in the workplace (Bacik 2004). Women in Ireland have caught up on men in many domains of social life especially in education and workplace participation and by international standards Ireland fairs favourably among the leading countries globally (Hausmann, Tyson, and Zahidi 2011). Both men and women have experienced greater sexual freedom and gay rights have gained more recognition (Rose 1994). Women have successfully entered a male-dominated public sphere competing with men in the media, the professions, in education and cultural life and to a lesser extent in politics and business (Galligan 1998: 28; Kennedy 2001; Barry 2008; Baker et al. 2004: 207–11).

However, in many respects Ireland remains 'a man's world' (O'Connor 2000). Fifty years on, despite significant advances for women in Ireland, even when defined in moderate liberal terms, women are still grossly under-represented in politics and are disadvantaged in paid work (Barry 2008; Crowley 2006; CSO 2010), and they continue to shoulder the burden of caring and unpaid labour (Lynch and Lyons 2008; McGinnity and Russell 2007, 2008). These patterns are mirrored in many other Western societies (Scott, Crompton, and Lyonette 2010).

Many problems of gender equality persist in Western societies in traditional forms with new forms arising under the guise of sexual and economic liberation (Walter 2011; Ging 2009; Banyard 2010). The remarkable achievements of second wave feminism have been overshadowed by the rhetoric of post-feminism which asserts 'that equality is a *fait accompli* and that feminism's work is done'; such views are espoused by neo-liberal ideology which proposes that gender equality was delivered by the free-market, with feminism positioned as an outdated oppressor while the market is 'packaged in a discourse of progress, empowerment and free choice' (Ging 2009: 56–7).

Despite feminist advances, the moral and structural imperatives on women to care along with women's subordination in the public sphere remain foremost obstacles to gender equality in economic, cultural, and political life (Baker et al. 2004: 60–4). Caring is now one of the most important equality issues facing Irish society in terms of how it is organised, supported and how the burdens and benefits of caring work is distributed (Cullen, Delaney, and Duff 2004; The Equality Authority 2005). The increasing care gap in Irish society has heightened the roles, rights, and responsibilities of men to share caring on an equal basis with women (Fanning and Rush 2006). Other European societies are similarly concerned about care where between a quarter and one-third of citizens provide unpaid care for either elderly, disabled, or child dependents within the context of women engaging in paid work (Daly and Rake 2003: 168). The question of who does the caring, and under what conditions, is also a major global issue as it interconnects with a series of complex social problems related to care migration, labour market supply, gender equality, and social justice more broadly (Zimmerman, Litt, and Bose 2006; Hochschild, Hutton, and Giddens 2000).

Gender and care

The analysis of care has at best been assigned a marginal position within the social sciences, which by and large have focussed on the outer spaces of life, centred on economic, cultural, and political affairs (Baker et al. 2004). The core assumption of many social sciences is that the prototypical human being is a self-sufficient rational economic man (Folbre and Bittman 2004; Folbre 1994; Ferber and Nelson 2003). The social sciences have given little serious attention to the reality of dependency and vulnerability for all human beings, either in childhood or at times of illness and infirmity (Fineman 2008; Badgett and Folbre 1999). Care is rarely defined as a core dynamic of social life and when it is studied it is generally confined to professional care studies (such as social work, social care, childcare, youth and community work, and nursing) or family studies (Fine 2006).

By exception, feminist scholars from various traditions have taken a keen interest in care and identified it as a major social good (Sevenhuijsen 1998; Tong 2009). They have revealed how we are relational beings, emotional and intellectual, social and individual (Gilligan 1995) and demonstrated how caring is a basic human capability related to satisfying our basic human needs (Engster 2005; Kittay 1999; Nussbaum 1995a, 1995b, 2000). Feminists have given care a social context not only derivative of psychological experience but upon which economic, cultural, political, and social life is made possible. They also have contested the devaluation of care in purely economic terms and have shown how economic flourishing depends on it (Pettinger et al. 2005). They have confirmed women's unpaid caring work as central to gender inequality within both the private and public sphere and have shown how advances towards gender equality are stalled by the obstinacy of the gender division of caring work (Hochschild 1989). Moreover (and contesting the latent idea that feminists are only concerned about women's lives), care-focussed feminists across the social sciences have rejected the concept of citizenship deplete of care, challenging us to redefine citizenship in a manner that respects emotionality, dependency and interdependency for all (Fineman 2004; Fisher and Tronto 1990; Held 1995; Hobson 2000; Kittay and Feder 2002; Tronto 1993; Williams 2004; Dean 2004).

The impressive contribution of feminism to gender studies has been, in recent decades, complemented by scholarship on men and masculinities (Elmore 2007; Connell 2003a; Brod 1987). Men's interest in gender was from the beginning criticised by many feminists (Heath

1987; Campbell 2003), who felt gender studies risked being colonised, dominated and ultimately de-gendered (Hanmer 1990; Canaan and Griffin 1990) while in the process de-radicalising women's studies and undermining its relevance (Richardson and Robinson 1994). They alleged that men would reinforce the already competitive, misogynist and homosocial academic culture within social science (Morgan 1981: 86; Skeggs 2008; Witz and Marshall 2003; Oakley 2005). The history of social science suggested that male privilege was invisible to men; men were defined as the norm and their interests were researched with the gender-blind perspectives developed by men and for men (Oakley 1998; Harding 1991; Kimmel 1993, 1990). Even within gender studies, where gender could hardly be lost entirely, the danger was that men would focus on men's pain and the oppressive experience of gender for men, rather than maintain a critical focus on men's power privilege (Morgan 1981; May 1998).

The controversial shift from women's studies to gender studies (Evans 1990; Richardson and Robinson 1994) and the development of men's studies hostile to feminism (Foundation for Male Studies 2010) perhaps support these fears. However, it can also be argued that many feminist fears about men's studies have not been realised. Perhaps as a result of feminist criticisms, masculinities researchers have asserted a strong commitment to the critical analysis of gendered power (Kimmel 1990, 1987; Carrigan, Connell, and Lee 1985; Hearn and Pringle 2006; Davis, Leijenaar, and Oldersma 1991). Masculinities scholars have been very conscious in developing research practice that takes on board feminist concerns and criticisms of traditional masculinist research methodologies chiefly by presenting an anti-oppressive position and by making gender visible in the research process (Kimmel 1990). Ironically as Beasley (2005) notes, this focus on male domination and men's power may at times have inadvertently exaggerated the power of white-hetero-sexual-middle-class Western men and overlooked the agency of women and marginalised and minority men, though this does not discount the importance of male researchers continually and explicitly making connections between feminist thought and masculinities theories (Robinson 2003).

Despite these theoretical disputes masculinities studies remain committed to gender equality, and though varieties of feminism hold differing implications for men (ibid.), critical gender scholarship depends on engaging with feminist insights in ways that complement rather than displace feminist academics. Men can become effective allies with women when they acknowledge male privilege, develop self-reflective skills, confront hegemonic masculinities, and pursue social justice (Kahn 2010). This has led masculinities scholars to develop concepts and methodological approaches to study men's lives (Hayward and Mac án Ghaill 2003), generally from a pro-feminist standpoint (Harding 1998; Hearn 1989; Jones 1996; Levin 1996; Leyland 1987; May 1998; Morgan 1981; Schwalbe and Wolkomir 2001; Pease 2000; Messner 1990). Feminist standpoint theory, which initially foresaw a direct correlation between one's social location (as women) and one's consciousness, implied that women alone should research gender based on their tacit and experiential knowledge of oppression. Contemporary approaches to standpoint theory have, however, taken greater cognisance of the diversity and intersectionality of social life and the complex role of ideology in shaping consciousness (Harding 2004). This has encouraged masculinities scholars to explore how contradictory experience of masculinity at the intersection of multiple identities can be harnessed as sources of insight and inspiration for egalitarian values (Ashe 2004; Hearn 1987: 5; Harding 1998, 1991, 1989; Connell 2011). Men's experiences of privilege thus can provide a valuable socially situated source of knowledge that allows researchers to reflect on their own and other men's complicity and dominance, and at the same time examine the contradictions and tensions embedded in the hierarchies of social relations (Fawcett and Hearn 2004; Pease 2000). Standpoints may be situational yet remain grounded within multiple social hierarchies, be they gender, class, race/ethnicity, disability, religion or age (Pease 2000; Hartstock 1998). Emphasis is on reflexivity in research practice to take account of the affect of one's gendered social location on research choices, processes, practices, and outcomes (Hopkins 1998; Pease 2000; Ashe 2004; Kimmel 1998). Standpoint epistemologies

> offer opportunities for men to develop distinctive subject positions as socially situated men who have learned to think through feminist theories, descriptions, and practices that themselves started from women's lives. They, too, can come to think about their lives, and about the rest of natural and social relations from a gap between how their lives are shaped by their concerns as feminists and how the dominant conceptual frameworks perceive and shape men's lives. (Harding 1998: 192)

A critical reflection on one's masculinity exposes the 'ambiguities', 'contradictions', and 'patriarchalism' that form men as a class as well as the complex subjectivity, internal contradictions, and tensions inherent

in the experience of being male; the privileges and the pains as a consequence of men's positioning within gender hierarchies (Hearn 1989: 3).
Privileged experiences can 'give rise to patriarchal identity' but men's
emotional pain can generate both pro- and anti-feminist positions
(Ashe 2004: 191). Men can identify with women's lives based on gender
injustices inflicted on female loved ones whether it is their wives, partners, sisters, daughters, or close friends (Connell 2003b). Care relations
expose important contradictions and tensions in men's lives: between
the hegemonic dictates of masculinities, and the intimate, compassionate and empathetic experience of our inherent human vulnerability.
Men's emotional–relational identifications with women and feminism
are sources of intellectual, emotional, and experiential knowledge from
which men can draw strength and guidance in resisting inequality and
oppression.

Masculinities scholars have made a valuable contribution to gender
studies and the deconstruction of men's power and dominance, yet
they have not shown widespread interest in care (Hanlon and Lynch
2011). One possible explanation for this is the historical tension within
masculinities studies arising from the focus on men's power and privilege and an oftentimes-competing emphasis on men's pain and oppression. Those who emphasise men's power tend to be critical of the view
that men are oppressed by their gender and often see this as a cloak
for a reactionary politics. Certainly the history of men's studies alerts
us to this danger, but the result I suspect is that many researchers with
pro-feminist sentiments have avoided researching issues and contexts
that could be perceived as identifying with men's vulnerability and,
therefore, powerlessness. The interest masculinities researchers have
taken in men in the public sphere may simply reflect the fact that these
spaces are important gendered locations that men occupy. It makes
sense, therefore, that scholars committed to feminism would seek to
deconstruct men's hegemonic practices within these spaces, but this
focus may also reflect the gendering gaze and interests of male scholars.
Nonetheless, the ongoing deconstruction of men's power in public
life is a valid and important goal for masculinities studies. To be fair,
men's affective relations have not been entirely ignored by the cannon.
Intimate personal aspects of men's lives have been addressed under a
number of themes, including an extensive literature on fatherhood (e.g.
Duindam 1999; Ferguson, McKeown, and Rooney 2000; Barker 1994;
Edwards, Doucet, and Furstenberg 2009) men as caregivers (paid and
unpaid) (e.g. Kramer and Thompson 2005), and on friendships and
intimacy (e.g. Messner 2001; McKay, Messner, and Sabo 2000), and

especially in relation to men's violence, sexuality, and sexual relations (e.g. Kimmel 2005; Metcalf and Humphries 1985; Hearn and Pringle 2006). However, the field overall has not sufficiently deconstructed the relationship between masculinities and care, both within public and private spheres, and within different cultures and societies. It is encouraging to see recent scholarship beginning to take a greater interest in care although the direction this takes is unclear at this point.

Gender and hegemonic masculinity

Masculinities studies took their cue from systemic approaches to patriarchy within feminism by offering a critique of sex/social role theory and other sociological and psychological traditions that ignored men's power in their analyses (Carrigan, Connell, and Lee 1987; Brittan 1989). Initially, masculinity was understood in terms of a structure of patriarchal power wherein all men collectively as a sex-class gain a patriarchal privilege or 'dividend' from the operation of capitalism–patriarchy in the form of higher incomes and other privileged access to resources, superior status against a cultural background that endorses and validates men's interests, and power and control in public and private life (Hearn 1989; Stoltenberg 1989; Connell 1987). Some scholars continue to hold the view of men's categorical role in gender domination as men (Hearn 2004) and there is an ongoing tension within the field between men's role in gender inequality and the existence of diverse men and masculinities. These disputes are evidenced in arguments about the use of the terms men, masculinity or masculinities in how they address men's relations with other men, with women and to power and inequality. R. W. Connell has been especially influential within the field by proposing that masculinities are multiple, conflicting, and hierarchical. Forming part of a wider acknowledgement of intersectionality within critical gender studies (Davis 2008; Valentine 2007; Spade and Valentine 2007), Connell develops a concept of multiple masculinities. As originally formulated, all men were perceived as holding power individually and collectively over women although the existence of hierarchical relations among men produces several configurations of masculinities and results in men benefiting differentially from the gender order related to their class, race/ethnic, religious, sexual, and other statuses (Connell 1995). Connell (2002, 2000) is particularly concerned with gender relations 'on the large scale', which she argues operate in terms of four dynamic systemic relations: production, power, symbolic, and emotional. This gender order operates globally but contains a dynamism that changes historically and cross-culturally as different systems interact with local gender orders and gender regimes (institutions) (Connell 1998, 1993).

Connell combines a structuralist and macroscopic analysis of gender with microscopic, ethnographic and voluntaristic dimensions which highlight gender is constructed on the small scale through dynamic interactional performances (e.g. West and Zimmerman 1991). Masculinities are theorised as the product of men's investments in social practices. Men actively take positions or actively respond to the positions in which they are placed within the gender order, including its discourses, institutional practices, and political, sexual and affective dynamics of daily life. Connell gives bodies a central role in this position-taking in the first instance in how men engage active bodywork through bodily reflective practices (e.g. bodybuilding and dieting). Typically bodily reflective practices involve negating bodily similarities and exaggerating and naturalising differences. While Connell principally stresses the social exploiting the biological, bodies are also active in the construction of gender because they have a material reality that binds and empowers them. Bodies are for Connell both 'objects and agents of practice' (Connell 2005: 61). Shilling (1997: 65) takes a similar position claiming that bodies are shaped and shaping of social differences with embodiment defined as ' ... how the bodily bases of people's actions and interactions are socially structured in different ways'. Thus, bodies have an experiential reality with potentials and limitations which react and interact with the social. From this point of view men can also be negatively affected by the pressure they experience to perform masculinity and through their investments in oppressive social practices such as excessive risk-taking, aggression, and violence which can at times result in men's bodies and emotions becoming sites of crisis when bodies reach their somatic limitations (Connell 2005: 54).

The concept of hegemonic masculinity is central to Connell's theory, defined originally as ' ... the configuration of gender practice which embodies the currently accepted answer to the problem of the legitimacy of patriarchy, which guarantees (or is taken to guarantee) the dominant position of men and the subordination of women' (Connell 1995: 77). Hearn (2004) explains hegemony as the operation of material and symbolic forms of power that produces, by force or consent, historically, practices of male domination. Beasley (2005: 229) describes Connell's concept of hegemonic masculinity as ' ... a socially dominant ideal of manhood which consolidates solidarity among men for the maintenance of masculine authority'. Hegemonic masculinities encourage men to identify with dominant practices that ward off any association with femininity including homophobia, heterosexuality, and misogyny (Donaldson 1993; Kimmel 2003). These practices embody patriarchal legitimation and female subordination allowing men to monopolise positions of power and wealth and to normalise their positions and silence dissent (Connell 2005; Connell and Messerschmidt 2005; Carrigan, Connell, and Lee 1987). Hegemonic masculinity draws attention to processes within the gender order that secure the consent of men for a male-dominated society by making sure men's privileged position and superior status appear so normal that it is effectively invisible to them.

Hegemonic masculinity is not necessarily easy for men to realise or live up to its ideals. For most men it is elusive and aspirational yet held up in various ways as a social measure of their masculinity. Men, therefore, relate to hegemonic masculinity in various ways, in terms of dominance, alliances and subordination, and to a lesser extent resistance. There are then multiple configurations of masculinities (Connell 2005: 35–7). The majority of men are *complicit* with hegemonic masculinity; they may not reap all the 'rewards' but gain enough (e.g. higher pay and social power) to easily ignore injustices to women. There again, other men remain *marginalised* from accruing hegemonic rewards because they are disadvantaged by race/ethnic, class, disability, or other minority statuses. Subordinated masculinities – men perceived by hegemonic norms as less masculine – are the most loathed of all within this hierarchy of masculinities. Women are not left out of this picture and hegemonic or emphasised femininities are proposed as those forms of femininity which support and complement hegemonic masculinities. More recently the notion of hegemonic masculinity a model of how men hold categorical power over women has been increasingly challenged by assertions that gendered power is more nuanced and relational understanding, that multiple masculinities and femininities operate dynamically and that subordinated or marginalised genders may influence hegemonic masculinity. This more complex model of hegemonic masculinities emphasises the agency of women, diverse geographies of men and masculinities, a more specific treatment of the embodiment of gender with the context of men's privileges and power, and the internal contradictions for men and the prospect of change in the direction of equality (Connell and Messerschmidt 2005: 846).

Connell's theory helps us to appreciate how numerous forms of masculinities can coexist within any given culture and how different historical eras give rise to different masculinities. Yet, though the performances of masculinities are ubiquitous and destabilised (Butler 1990), they are performances that are situated in social hierarchies. Masculinity is constructed against the backdrop that normalises male privilege as an entitlement; men are structurally positioned to defend privilege rather than embrace change (Bourdieu 2001; Connell 2005; Kimmel 2000), including more egalitarian care relations (Bubeck 1995; Giddens 1992; Segal 2007; Delamont 2001). Summing up decades of research on masculinities Connell (2000: 216–19) argues that masculinities are multiple (varying historically, culturally and geographically), hierarchical and hegemonic (relate to each other in terms of domination and subordination), collective (not only individual and relational but also structured institutionally and collectively), involve bodies as arenas of practice, actively constructed using the resources available within a given environment, internally complex giving rise to tensions and contradictions for individuals, and finally created dynamically and historically and are subject to change and contestation.

In recent years, Connell's concept of hegemonic masculinity has been subject to an extensive critique in several respects: because it dilutes men's collective power over women and the naming of men as men (Hearn 2004; Clatterbaugh 1997); because it overemphasises men's collective power and denies women agency and non-hegemonic masculinities agency (Beasley 2008a, 2008b; Connell and Messerschmidt 2005: 847); because it overlooks the complex fluidity and intersectionality of masculinities (Mac án Ghaill and Hayward 2007); and because it is used imprecisely to refer to several variables including character traits, ideologies, and institutional processes (Beasley 2008a, 2008b; Hearn 2004; Connell and Messerschmidt 2005; Howson 2008). Beasley (2005) claims the ascendancy of Connell's theories within the field has resulted in a rather unitary and unhealthy dominance of moderate socialist social constructionism. She proposes that masculinity studies have been reluctant to reconceptualise power in regulative/discursive terms compatible with post-structural and postmodernist thought as, she claims, has occurred within feminist theory and sexuality studies (see also Schippers 2007).

Gender and symbolic domination

As part of the challenge to Connell's theory, there has been an increasing interest in the writings of the late Pierre Bourdieu even though his consideration of masculinity has been more of an afterthought than a central theme in his writing. Bourdieu developed several concepts to explain social relations. Bourdieu's subject is deeply gendered and classed by what he refers to as the '...somatization of the social relations of domination' (the internalisation of class and gender structures) through a long and continuous 'labour of socialisation' (Bourdieu 2001: 23 and 49). Bourdieu (2001: 61) claims that '[c]ollective expectations, positive or negative, through the subjective expectations that they impose, tend to inscribe themselves in bodies in the form of permanent dispositions'. Social actors embody a disposition or *habitus* by internalising the particular rules or logics operating within different institutions or *fields* of social life. Fields are competitive systems of social relations each with their own specific rules and logic (Moi 1991: 1021). As we operate as social actors in different fields we adjust our disposition or *habitus* to the competitive game of the *field* in order to achieve *legitimacy*.

Legitimacy involves imbuing our habitus with various material and cultural resources that have symbolic currency within that field. Bourdieu highlights three sets of resources or *forms of capital* for which actors compete. *Economic* capital refers to material resources and social goods, *social* capital refers to social connections and network resources, and *cultural* capital refers to status bearing resources including education credentials, cultural knowledge, and embodied mannerisms (Bourdieu 1997). To achieve legitimacy we must be in a position to play the *game* – to trade different forms of capital such as prestige for wealth, or money for influence. To successfully play the game and to achieve legitimacy, however, one must acquire the capitals which have symbolic value. *Symbolic capitals* are those forms of capital (cultural, economic, or social) which have symbolic value within a given field. Being in possession of large amounts of symbolic capital places one in a dominant position within that field.

Bourdieu (2001, 1997) shows how lives are lived out as embodied dispositions bearing symbolic capital. Masculinity can be understood as the habitus adjusted to the game of differently gendered fields as men engage in social practices that seek out forms of capital with symbolic value. Like Connell, Bourdieu's gendered subject is deeply embedded in the social order. Bourdieu (2001: 30) sees gender as '...two different classes of habitus, in the form of opposed and complementary bodily hexis and principles of vision and division...' that make up social practices of distinction (legitimate taste). The symbolic hierarchies of the gender order place the feminine below the masculine. In the relational world, the feminine becomes inferior; it is part of what a man is not to be. For men this process of distinction involves writing out femininity since '[m]anliness...is an eminently relational notion, constructed in front of other men and against femininity, in a kind of fear of the female, firstly in oneself' (ibid.: 53).

Bearing some resemblance to Connell's concept of hegemony, Bourdieu employs the concept of *symbolic domination* to explain the way that patriarchal power becomes inscribed in bodies as a gendered habitus; an intensive socialisation process that strips masculinity of the feminine. Masculinity becomes inscribed in bodies in a way that is entirely unreflective, deeply held and unconscious as '...[b]eing a man...imposes itself in the mode of self-evidence, the taken for granted' (Bourdieu 2001: 49 and 64). The naturalised character of gender divisions makes it intensely difficult for actors to recognise their own roles in the practice of domination (ibid.: 23 and 37). The internalised gendered subject is generally not reflexive; she just is, and that lack of reflexivity allows power and powerlessness to be embodied and practised, often without dissent.

Bourdieu's most comprehensive treatment of gender, *Masculine Domination*, is critiqued for presenting a highly dualistic and deterministic reading of gender that denies reflexivity, change and agency to women (McLeod 2005; Mottier 2002; Chambers 2005). Nonetheless, many feminists have found grounds to develop Bourdieu's work because it offers an alternative to perspectives which overemphasise the fluidity and malleability of gender (Butler 1990). They are interested in Bourdieu's emphasis on the practical rather than the purely rationalistic embodiment of gender, his focus on symbolic aspects of power, and the dialectical relationship between agency and complicity (Lovell 2000; Mottier 2002). To date masculinities scholars have been slow to take up on Bourdieu, but those who have, have found ideas that undermine Connell's theory (Thorpe 2010), as well as concepts that develop them (Coles 2008, 2009). Connell (2007: 41) herself is highly critical of Bourdieu's overall theory remarking how it extends a 'market vision into apparently non-market fields of social life, including cases where the market logic is systematically denied by the people themselves'. She also argues that Bourdieu offers merely a theory of social reproduction where 'history is frozen'. Connell (2007: 42) also dismisses Bourdieu's analysis of gender on the grounds that it universalises an 'absolute dichotomy' of gender relations in Kabylie society onto other gender formations. She claims that he not only overlooks feminist theory but moreover claims 'Because of Bourdieu's fame as a social theorist, this badly outdated formulation is now having a considerable influence on some areas of gender studies.'

Much of the criticisms of Bourdieu are well founded but not so much to dismiss the important contribution his concepts have made. In my view, the work of Pierre Bourdieu is powerful because it provides a complex theory that challenges many postmodern assumptions about the subject and the relationship between structure, agency, and the body. Bourdieu attempts to explain beyond essentialist and culturalist divisions, and his theory enables us to link a micro theory of power in everyday life with macro theory by showing how agents internalise dominant social values and how field and habitus are deeply interdependent (Moi 1991). Bourdieu's theories are, therefore, attractive to scholars who remain sceptical of the voluntarism, fluidity, and malleability implied by postmodern gender theory, yet they acknowledge the symbolic nature of social life whilst not accepting that gender is enacted independently of social structure (Lovell 2000).

The theories of both Bourdieu and Connell inform the concept of gender I employ in the study. Both have limitations especially in some of the rigidity of Bourdieu's binary formulation of gender. Nevertheless, their explanation of gender as a social practice represents a theoretically sophisticated way to conceptualise gender, with holding both symbolic and material relations to account for how gender domination operates, and in how gender practices become embodied. They do, however, place a different emphasis on the acquisition of gender and on social change. The concepts of hegemony and symbolic domination differ in so far as the former refers to a conscious consent in domination, whereas the latter refers to the unconsciousness of domination (Burawoy 2010). Nevertheless, in many respects both concepts both grapple with this tension. Regardless, they both also acknowledge the materiality of social life, the role of class, and other hierarchical relations among men and between men and women, and they both consider bodies of central importance. Several questions remain, however, about the deterministic or reflexive acquisition of gender, about the dualistic or pluralistic nature of masculinities, and how social change is to be conceptualised (Costa 2006) and how men can resist hegemonic masculinities psychologically and socially (Wetherell and Edley 1999; Speer 2001; Connell and Messerschmidt 2005). As sociological theories that privilege a macro analysis, both views lack a more detailed appreciation of the idiosyncratic nature of gender in everyday life and how actors consciously and unconsciously locate themselves within social discourses (Yates, Taylor, and Wetherell 2001; Wetherell and Edley 1999; Kahn, Holmes, and Brett 2011).

Care conversations with men

The research data for the book was generated by in-depth qualitative interviews with 31 men (referred to as care conversations). The conversations comprised of two distinct sets of interviews with 21 men and 10 men respectively lasting between 1.5 and3 hours each. The purpose of the interviews was to explore how the men defined masculinity in relation to care. Qualitative interviews were used because they offer respondents a chance to tell their story and provide access to respondents' subjective definitions, sense-making, and experiences of social life, especially when research questions cause difficulty or introspection (Schwalbe and Wolkomir 2001; McCracken 1988; Lee 1997; Owens 1996; Fontana and Frey 1994; May 2001; Clifford 1994). These interviews were not about positivist fact-finding or trying to define reality unambiguously, nor about attempting to be free of interpretation as some postmodernist researchers' desire. The interviewer–interviewee relationship provides an environment where knowledge is interactively constructed (Arendell 1997; Mason 2002) with the interviewer's personal and social attributes, their social identities, and their interviewing style, all contributing to the interview dynamic (Williams and Heikes 1993). The interview dynamic itself shows the way people construct their lives, how they manage and negotiate contradictions and dissonance, and how they are positioned, and locate themselves, within multiple realities and identities (Campbell 2003).

The first set of interviews was framed as political care conversations. Their purpose was to include in the data a range of male political voices and their perspectives on care in men's lives. The intention was to understand the ways that masculinity can be activated and politicised around particular concerns in solidarity with other men (see Bradley 1997; Pease 2000; Kimmel 1995; Clatterbaugh 1997; Messner 2002; Seidler 1991). Therefore, I decided it is useful to locate these male political voices through a variety of diverse men's groups because men's interests are activated in these settings. On the one hand they may encourage homosocial and heterosexist gender practices that maintain hegemonic masculinity '... by supporting meanings associated with identities that fit hegemonic ideals while suppressing meanings associated with non-hegemonic masculinity' (Brid 1996: 121) and thus they allow for the presentation of perspectives that represent a backlash against gender equality and the reaffirmation of male privilege (Hantover 1998: 150; Remy 1990; Brid 1996; Connell 2002; Gosine 2007). On the other hand, even reactionary patriarchal men's groups can contain contradictions

Table 1   Political care conversations sample frame[a]

Principal solidarity aim	Pseudonym	Men's group
1. Rights	Paul	Fathers' Rights Group
2. Inclusion	Eddie & Tom	Community Development Group
3. Inclusion	Peter	Traveller Advocacy Group[b]
4. Well-being	Geoff & Alex	Gay Men's Support Group
5. Well-being	Fran	Catholic Religious Order
6. Well-being	Paddy	Older Men's Support Group
7. Rights	Declan	Construction Workers Trade Union
8. Networks	Denis	Male Secret Society

Notes: [a] Travellers are an indigenous, traditionally nomadic, ethnic minority in Ireland and they experience widespread discrimination, marginalisation and racism; [b] All of the groups were exclusively men's groups except Group 3, which was a advocacy group for both male and female Travellers. Tom from Group 2 was also a community worker with male Travellers.

with some emphasising aspects of ' ... men's emotionality and of shared (non-sexual) bonds between men' (Beasley 2005: 181). There again, some men's groups including gay, pro-feminist, and social justice groups can emphasise progressive gender politics antagonistic to reactionary masculinities (Pease 2002b; Kimmel and Mosmiller 1992).

Ten men were selected from a sample of eight diverse groups advocating for or supporting men in the following ways: fathers' rights (Group 1), social inclusion (Groups 2, 3, and 6), gay men's well-being (Group 4), spiritual well-being (Group 5), employment rights (Group 7), and elite social networks (Group 8) (see Table 1). All of the interviews represent the opinions of the interviewees, and they were not acting as the official voice for their organisations. The majority of the interviews were conducted with one respondent from each group, but two of the interviews are conducted with two group facilitators upon their request (Groups 2 and 4). The conversations therefore reflected the interests and perspectives about care of gay men, marginalised men based on their class, ethnicity/race or disability, working-class men and upper-class men, older men, religious men and single fathers. The interests of wealthier men were under-represented because of the difficulty encountered in getting wealthy or elite men's groups to participate. Elite men's groups have grown significantly in Ireland in recent years (Gallagher 2008), and several attempts were made to include them in the research as a way of reflecting the voices of more wealthy men. Dozens of phone calls, e-mails, and letters were sent to several elite social and business men's clubs but only one club was willing to participate. Many groups would not provide reasons for not participating or did not return my communications.

The second set of interviews with twenty-one men was designed to complement the political conversations by exploring the meaning of care in men's personal care stories (Table 2, page 17). A relatively heterogeneous purposeful sample (see Curtis et al. 2000) selected men on the basis of key social inequalities in Irish society related to age, gender, sexual orientation, ethnicity, family and civil/marital status, disability and religion (Government of Ireland 2004). Additionally, they considered social class differences by taking into account diversity in terms of the men's housing status, unemployment, occupation and education levels as indicators of social class. The personal care conversations included one very wealthy businessman (Adam, 73), eleven men with broadly middle-class occupations (Dave, Liam, Dessie, John, Douglas, Pascal, Simon, Rory, Conor, Cathal, and Nevan), six men with broadly working-class occupations (Fionn, Graham, Charlie, Jamal, Tommy and Greg), and two men who were unemployed (Cian and Dermot), as well as one full-time home carer (Angus). The men ranged in age from 25 to 74. Seven men were rural dwellers, four suburban, and ten urban; one was protestant, one Jewish, and one Muslim and although the remainder were Catholic at least half of these men identified as lapsed or non-religious. All the men were permanent residents in Ireland and all were Irish national except for Charlie who was British, Jamal who was African-Irish, and Adam who was Polish-Irish. Ten were married, four were either separated or divorced and seven were single; and three identified as gay men (Pascal, Simon, and Angus).

The care status sample is understood as a person's care responsibility for either child or adult dependents. Since the focus of the research was not about men as caregivers per se, only a minority of the men were selected for the study because they were primary carers (Angus, Cathal, Simon, Tommy, and Angus); some of them had no care responsibilities (Liam, Charlie), but the majority had shared or secondary responsibilities in varying amounts. Fourteen men were fathers including ten from intact families and four who were separated/divorced fathers (Graham, Simon, Tommy, and Cathal). Of the separated/divorced fathers, Tommy and Cathal were sole primary carers and Simon was a shared primary carer, while Graham was a non-custodian secondary carer. One man (Angus) was a primary carer for his elderly parents and a number of the men (Dave, John, Douglas) had secondary care responsibilities for elderly parents in varying amounts while Conor had secondary responsibilities for his disabled brother.

Table 2 Personal care conversations sample frame[*]

Pseudonym	Age	Occupation	Care and marital status	Sexuality	Religion	Ethnicity	Location
Fionn	25	Financial services	Married, shared carer for 2-year-old daughter	Heterosexual	Catholic	Irish	Suburban
Graham	26	Technician	Separated, secondary career of 4-year-old daughter	Heterosexual	Catholic	Irish	Suburban
Charlie	28	Retail	Cohabitating, no care responsibilities	Heterosexual	None	British	Suburban
Jamal	32	Professional care	Married, secondary carer of infant daughter	Heterosexual	Muslim	African-Irish	Urban
Dave	34	Social researcher	Cohabitating, secondary carer of mother with disability	Heterosexual	Catholic	Irish	Suburban
Dermot	35	Unemployed	Cohabitating, secondary carer of 8-year-old step-daughter	Heterosexual	Catholic	Irish	Urban
Liam	36	Accountant	Single, no care responsibilities	Heterosexual	Catholic	Irish	Urban
Angus	43	Home carer	Full-time primary carer of frail and disabled elderly parents	Homosexual	Catholic	Irish	Rural
Dessie	46	Farmer	Married, secondary carer of 2 children; one with disability	Heterosexual	Protestant	Irish	Rural
John	47	Civil servant	Married, shared carer of 3 young children & secondary carer for mother	Heterosexual	Catholic	Irish	Urban
Douglas	48	Farmer	Married, secondary carer of 6 children and elderly mother	Heterosexual	Catholic	Irish	Rural
Pascal	48	Management	Single, occasional secondary carer of 'god' children	Homosexual	Catholic	Irish	Urban
Simon	48	Academic	Separated, shared primary carer of 2 children	Homosexual	Protestant	Irish	Rural
Tommy	49	Community worker	Separated, primary carer of 4 children	Heterosexual	Catholic	Irish	Urban
Cian	49	Unemployed	Single, disability, no care responsibilities	Heterosexual	Catholic	Irish	Rural
Greg	51	Retail	Married, primary carer of 2 children, one with a disability	Heterosexual	Catholic	Irish	Urban
Rory	55	Management	Married, secondary carer of mother-in-law	Heterosexual	Catholic	Irish	Urban
Conor	57	Farmer	Married, secondary carer of 5 children	Heterosexual	Catholic	Irish	Rural
Cathal	58	Self-employed	Separated, was primary carer of 4, now-adult, children	Heterosexual	Catholic	Irish	Urban
Adam	73	Business/executive	Widowed, no care responsibilities, 3 adult children	Heterosexual	Jewish	Polish-Irish	Urban
Nevan	74	Management	Married, 3 adult children	Heterosexual	Catholic	Irish	Rural

Note: Some details have been altered to preserve anonymity.

The distinctions between primary and secondary carer are somewhat artificial because care relations are not necessarily bounded in this way at all times. The study also takes a broad focus on care rather than analyse very particular care contexts and relationships. Contextualised studies of specific contexts of men's caring are illuminating because they can compare the experiences of men in respect of these precise care relations and highlight their distinct challenges for men. Nonetheless, whilst the identity of the carer and the nature of the care work provided are contingent on whether the recipient is a child dependent, ill, disabled or elderly, and on the nature of the relationship, it is also valuable to consider care as an overarching concept because of how central care is to all human relationships (see Lynch, Baker et al. 2009; Daly 2001b: 35; Sevenhuijsen 2000). The broad focus on care limits a more detailed analysis of men's identities in respect of specific care contexts, but it has the advantage of permitting a wider analysis of how men understand care generally, and this is the specific focus of this book. The concept of care itself has limitations. For a start, the term does not in every case translate easily from English (Fine 2006). Moreover, the meaning of care is criticised by disability scholars because of its association with passivity and dependency (Fine and Glendinning 2005; Shakespeare 2000). I would argue, however, that care is a useful concept that can be reclaimed and politicised because it also captures the immensely human and personal.

Researching men and care

Generating good data from the interview situation relies on the quality of rapport, trust, and dialogue between the interviewer and interviewee. The interviewer wants the interviewee to reflect, disclose, and converse honestly and openly within a context where the questioning may be personally and politically challenging and perhaps threatening for the interviewee. The disclosure in-depth interviewing requires can be difficult to achieve when researching men about personal and emotional life because it exposes men to a degree of vulnerability and emotionality that contradict dominant norms of masculinity (Jones 1996; Delamont 1996; Hanmer 1990; Morgan 1981; Lohan 2000; Lee 1997; Leyland 1987; Schwalbe and Wolkomir 2001; Way 1997; Donaldson 1997; Owens 1996; Padgett 1998; Carter and Delamont 1996; May 2001; Warren 1988; Messner 1990). The fact that men are so accustomed to relating to other men in ways that shore up masculinity can limit the possibilities for open disclosure if the researcher is also a male. Women's traditional positioning as attentive and empathetic emotional listeners on the other hand is said to allow male interviewees to disclose without feeling that their masculinity has been compromised (May 2001: 136–7; Finch 1984; Lohan 2000). There is certainly practical truth in this but with a notable caveat that other variables also impinge open communication making the interview situation more complex (McKegany and Bloor 1991: 197). Sexuality, class, race/ethnicity, and age all can impact the construction of masculinity in interview situations. Respondents spoke with me not only as a 'man' but also as an older man, or a younger man, or a Dublin, or an academic man and so forth, and each of these factors contains its own complexity.

Rapport is not the only goal of effective interviewing in critical gender research. Empathetic interviewing styles, a hallmark of feminist interviewing techniques, may help the researcher in creating the rapport conducive to openness and revelation, but at the same time it risks colluding with dominant constructions of masculinity if such representations are left uncontested (Lohan 2000: 177). This is true of both male and female researchers who are capable of using relational techniques that may lure required data such as the use of flirting (Campbell 2003; Lohan 2000; Arendell 1997) and complicity with sexist camaraderie (Flood 1997). A balance needs to be achieved between the advantages of good rapport and trust and a critical dialogue with respondents. Therefore, as a way to balance the competing techniques of empathy and confrontation I choose a style of interviewing equating closely with what Patton (1990) refers to as the 'informal conversational interview'. Though the conversations were recorded and ordered with a semi-structured guide, most of them took place within the informality of the participants' homes or workplaces, and there was an open and adaptable, free-flowing dialogue. The approach facilitated rapport and helped to establish honesty, empathy, and respect between the researcher and the participant (Holloway and Jefferson 2000: 100–103).

Both sets of interviews took a conventional semi-structured approach to questioning. In the political care conversations the men were questioned about the purpose of the respective men's group, their experiences and involvement in the group, the needs, interests and concerns of other men involved in the group, the problems experienced by the men involved with the groups and how they coped with their problems, their friendships and work lives, and finally about men's beliefs about caring and their involvement in caring. A life-story approach was used in the personal care conversations. Narrative styles provide useful ways to research gender and sexuality in men's personal lives (Ryan 2006; Oakley 2005; Connell 2000), because they help to open up 'temporal realities' and 'complexities' in how men relate to hegemonic masculinities (Gray et al. 2002: 43). Narrative interviews focus on identities and are useful in tracing 'storied' trajectories and engaging with context, complexity, and contradiction (Mason 2002; Somers and Gibson 1994). These personal interviews began with a series of general questions about the men's current occupation/socioeconomic status, where they lived, and about their lifestyles. The questioning then followed a chronological trajectory by asking them about the care they had received as children and subsequently about significant care relations in their life to date, including important friendships, their relationship with their parents, and, where appropriate, relationships with children and partners. Interviews were concluded with a series of questions about the men's attitudes to gender equality in care work.

The data was managed with the MAXqda software package and was analysed thematically (Braun and Clarke 2006). Following verbatim transcription, a process of familiarisation began by reading and rereading the interviews. Preliminary descriptive (imic) codes were then applied to data segments which were then recoded over several weeks. Codes deepen the analysis by simplifying or reducing some data sections and by opening the data generally to allow for more complex coding and analysis (Coffey and Atkinson 1996: 27). Imic knowledge, as Bourdieu (1990) regards, is about understanding the logic of practice by drawing on participants' own language descriptions that orient their lives. The quality of the coding was tested by checking samples with colleagues and, as Arksey and Knight (1999: 163) suggest, a number of questions are asked of the codes: (a) Do they cover all the data that are relevant to the research aims? (b) What new categories are required? (c) Do categories need to be split into sub-categories? (d) Are there too many categories? and (e) Are there categories suggested in the literature that are not being used? Codes were eventually grouped into larger categories and 'sensitising' themes constructed in relation to the research question, current debates in the literature, and the insights of informants (Arksey and Knight 1999). Themes amount to patterns constructed from the data about the research question and connect the data to the research question (Braun and Clarke 2006: 82).

Similar to feminist approaches, masculinities researchers' have developed techniques as aids to reflexivity (Seidler 1989; Hearn 1989; Pease 2000. Reflective methodology is characterised by systematic reflection, careful interpretation, awareness of the political aspects of the research, and reflection on the problem of representation and authority (Alvesson and Skoldberg 2000). Researchers turn the spotlight of the research on self by scrutinising personal values and making visible ones complicity with oppressive relations, by acknowledging the social domain of the researcher and clarifying the researchers 'Other' (Harding 1989; Lohan 2000; Fawcett and Hearn 2004). The researcher should remain critical of these categories and assumptions, sensitive to hidden structures, gender processes, and collusion in the production of meaning (Alvesson and Skoldberg 2000: 17). Personal experience can be a source of both 'insight' and 'blindness' and critical reflection requires the maximisation of insight and the reduction of blindness (McCracken 1988). Reflecting on the data researchers ca: match their experience with that of the researched (ibid.: 19). Even when the experiences of the interviewee appear alien, the researcher can imagine what the respondent's world view is like, based on their underlying assumptions and categories (McCracken 1988). The approach I adopted firstly involved asking of myself the same questions that I posed to others: principally how my masculinity is defined in relation to care, and moreover, why the issue of care has become such a focus in my life personally. This process was not without personal anguish and confusion and so I chose individual psychotherapy (see Jackson 1990) as a method to help me unravel my thought and feelings. For all this, I also chose not to make the 'self-revelation' the central focus of the research (see Skeggs 2002) and so I have not written this into the project here.

Outline of the book

This book explores how men define masculinity in relation to care, the ways in which they reflect on care, think about care, and feel about care in respect of their identities as men. My interest was in how men make sense of care, what it means to them personally and politically, within the context of it being primarily defined as feminine. In doing so it investigates the ways men embrace aspects of care, value care and give it meaning, as well as how they resist it, devalue it and reject it.

The book is divided into 11 chapters. Chapters 2 and 3 address the substantive literature on care and masculinities respectively while Chapters 4–10 analyse the care conversation data. Chapter 11 briefly returns to some of the issues raised from the outset and offers some conclusions and afterthought.

Chapter 2, 'Gendered Care Practices', outlines how care has been considered in gender studies. Care is firstly explored as both work and identity; a relation between how we feel and what we do. Secondly, a distinction is drawn between emotional and nurturing work and the boundary between care and love is discussed. Thirdly, the nature of care as sets of intimate relational obligations is discussed in respect of the moral imperative on women to care. Finally, the relationship between care and multiple inequalities in terms of power, resources, respect and recognition and working and learning is highlighted. The concept of affective inequality is presented as a way to understand the interrelation between love/care, as a major social good that is unequally distributed in terms of the benefits and burdens it generates, and other more established inequalities in economic, cultural, and political life. Affective inequality is not only construed as determined and consequential but as generative of inequality itself, and a topic that masculinities studies have not sufficiently explored.

Chapter 3, 'Masculinities and Care', begins by outlining two broad perspectives about men's care practices within gender studies. One view presents the rather positive perspective that men are slowly embracing change in care relations whilst a second is largely negative in its outlook. Despite these different emphasises, on the whole there appears to be considerable agreement in the literature that men are not caring on an equal basis as women. Men would appear to be relatively care-free in most societies, if not all, compared to women, although importantly men are not equally care-free in all societies. Although other explanations exist, and wider socio-structural forces are crucial, the reason why men are unequal participants in caring primarily addresses arguments within gender studies that imply a complex interrelationship between gender identity and care. Three quite broad and somewhat overlapping perspectives are outlined with each containing a number of theories. Care is explained to be written out of men's lives firstly drawing on the sociological argument that instrumental definitions of masculinity results in men pursuing public goals at the expense of caring ones. The second perspective is founded on psychodynamic arguments that gender identification is socialised through early childcare practices resulting in oppositional gendered personalities that see men repress the feminine qualities necessary for caring and consequently avoid caring work throughout their lives. The third perspective focuses on micro-sociological perspectives that have broadly influenced contemporary gender studies which emphasise the reflexive nature of gender in conjunction with the operation of power and hegemony. On the whole the argument in this chapter is that care and emotional relations have not featured as central concerns within contemporary masculinities theory. There is reluctance to theorise the emotional lives of men in gender relations. The theory of hegemonic masculinities (as it is variously formulated) rightly considers the dynamic operation of power in men's lives, but it fails to fully account for how hegemonic practices amongst men are also about being care-free.

Chapter 4, 'Masculinities and Emotions', is the first of six chapters analysing the care conversations. Chapter 4 explores the relationship between male dominance and affective relations. The chapter begins by considering the role of having a socially valued masculinity in men's lives and how not realising it, or feeling it, relates to feeling inferior. This sense of inferiority derived from men's failure to realise hegemonic ideals of masculinity is embroiled in writing out care from men's lives. Four contexts are identified in the care conversations. Firstly, to be recognised as a valuable man is to have status, power and the command of resources and the pursuit of this capital feeds a powerful competitive dynamic among men. Secondly, to lack these characteristics equates with 'failure' to realise a socially valued masculinity, which all too often is projected as inferiority onto others through misogyny, gender-based violence and homophobia. Thirdly, warding off feelings of inferiority involves performances of careless masculinities, 'proving' one's masculinity through machismo and risk-taking practices, denying vulnerability and the need to care for self or look after one's health and welfare. Fourthly, men avoid primary caring because to do so risks one's legitimacy as a man, especially when to do so is also to opt out of practices which define manhood. Men's caring is further marginalised because the heteronormative definition of men's roles in care still prevails even if it is weakened and this denies men access to care relations outside of these norms. The relationship between masculinity and dominance is not uncomplicated. In fact it is highly conflictual and contradictory because hegemonic masculinity may be care-free and care-less but men are certainly not; men have intimate and reciprocal care needs and desires. Debates about masculinities and emotions within the field of masculinities studies have not been as fruitful as they might and this remains a challenge to the study of men's lives from a pro-feminist perspective.

Chapter 5, 'Nurturing Femininities', analyses the meanings that the men assign to love and caring work. Caring is found to be highly valued with the attributes of carers idealised in terms of a feminine ethic of care. Carers are expected to possess a gendered caring habitus that is warm, trustworthy, devotional, and selfless and not possessing this habitus is presented as reason to choose not to care. This archetype of nurturing femininity that implicitly defines the ideal carer for these men is a form of emphasised femininity because it supports the ambitions of hegemonic masculinity defined in terms of dominance in public life. Yet men are apprehensive that nurturing capital and the caring habitus upon which it is built is declining and being encroached by an increasing self-serving instrumental rationality of the public sphere. In other words, the men are sensing the 'care gap' but are uncertain about how it is to be filled and how their masculinity is changed when filling it.

Chapter 6, 'Breadwinner Masculinities', explores how the men in the study define masculinity in relation to traditional breadwinner 'caring' expectations. Some men describe male breadwinning as an imperative; a prescribed role about which they felt they had little choice, while in contrast others explained dual-breadwinner arrangements as the ascendant norm. Either way, far from irrelevant in the lives of these men, breadwinning continues to operate as a master discourse; a referent against which their relative involvement in both paid work and caring is imagined, rationalised, and legitimated. Though men are subject to greater expectations to be involved nurturers, some men still consider they are failing to care when they are unable to construct themselves as breadwinners or are the main earners within traditional heterosexual breadwinner relationships. Traditional and conservative men who reify male breadwinner roles are one form that care-free masculinity takes. Even these men, however, can experience a tension between their investment in paid work and nurturing, something they tended to mitigate by proposing that paid work was either a sacrifice for their families and that it amounted to caring itself as providing. Additionally some men assured themselves that they are caring in their work by stretching the definition of care to include how they care for colleagues, employees, customers, and others in their work role. Apart from the older men in the study, few men felt the pressure to be sole breadwinners, but men are subject to neo-liberal expectations to be highly committed, flexible, and competitive care-free workers and these expectations also have an affinity with beliefs that men are natural breadwinners. Though some welfare states seek to accommodate care in order to support women's fuller participation in the labour market, neo-liberal expectations are premised on masculine norms because they typically (with some exceptions) reinforce care as women's responsibility, and even when they do not, the model they espouse reifies the care-free worker. The notion, therefore, that men are symbolically dominated by norms of nurturing is dubious against the background of neo-liberal work imperatives that especially privatise caring obligations for men.

Chapter 7, 'Nurturing Masculinities', explores how the men account for, and feel about, men's involvement in nurturing caring work. Most men claim to be involved in nurturing in some respects although a minority admit that it is not a feature of their lives whatsoever. While most men feel positive about their involvement in nurturing in that they enjoy and value it especially in respect of their relationships with their children, a significant theme related to the burdens of caring in terms of the emotional demands, responsibilities and time constraints it places on caregivers. Moreover, nurturing masculinities are not only about whether men are involved in caring or not; men's involvement is also relational because it involves a negotiation with partners or ex partners as well as care recipients. The relational context of care negotiations involves care itself, and as such can present a challenge to men's roles and masculine identity. More than other issues it is men's ambivalent relationship with emotional labour that raises the most detailed discussion in the conversations. Again, some men feel comfortable with expectations that men should be emotionally intimate and sensitive emotional communicators whereas others find this expectation a threat to their masculinity.

Chapter 8, 'Childhood Care Stories', explores the men's personal recollections of both the care that they received as children and the care responsibilities that they held (or not) as children on their gendered care identities. The care experiences of the men were diverse and generational issues are important in how men perceive care, but for all men the care they received was highly gendered. A central conclusion is that the experience of a traditional gender division of labour within one's family of origin becomes the default model from which men construct their caring identity and model care practices in their lives, be they conformist or oppositional. When men did not receive care as children because, for various reasons, this gender order was disrupted, the default model becomes less assured. This is related to men constructing a more caring masculinity as adults even if, at times, this is mediated through a conventional masculinity. That said, although childhood care experiences are highly influential, they are also very complex because they involve an intricate and dynamic interaction involving several forces including those internal to the particular care–family dynamic as well as the wider social, cultural, and economic climate. This involves different parental caring styles, gender expectations, and emotional identifications with both parents and other caring figures. Moreover, these relationship dynamics occur in the context of the cultural and social milieu of that time. The men's caring orientations were also related to the way they identify with and admire their parental or substitute parental figures and the extent that they identify with their caring practices either as breadwinners or as hands-on carers. The men's stories demonstrate their reflection on the meaning of care in terms of both what it meant historically and what it means for their lives in the present.

Chapter 9, 'Care-Free Masculinities', identifies how care is rhetorically written out of masculinity by the men through the deployment of four care-free discourses. These discourses define primary caring as unnatural, impractical, dysfunctional, or abnormal for men. In other words, men's primary caring is perceived as going against men's evolutionary and biological nature, against dominant social norms and conventions, against a properly functioning social order, and against practical economic considerations. However, men draw on these discourses differently when defending male privilege and when managing tensions that arise between the ideology of equality (of access and opportunity) and the persistence of the gender division of caring labour depending on the amount of sharing or caring that they undertake. Broadly the care-free understanding of masculinity is based on the belief that men are either innately or socially construed with identities, interests, and capabilities at odds with those necessary for primary caring work. The fact that some men experience caring to be difficult and demanding, not least because it begins to deconstruct often deeply held beliefs and unravel repressed feelings about what makes for legitimate masculinity, makes it sensible that caring should be a free choice because to do otherwise can feel like losing one's identity as a man.

Chapter 10, 'Care-Full Masculinities', explains how the men in their personal care conversations construct themselves in terms of holding a *Conservative, Sharing* or *Caring* identity. *Conservatives* define their caring most in terms of breadwinning; *Sharers* define their caring in terms of their involvement and sharing of care work as well as breadwinning whilst *Carers* define their masculinity in terms of primary caring. All three basic configurations of masculinity are, however, constructed against the dominance of the two dialectical narratives of *Nurturing Femininities* and *Breadwinner Masculinities*. Regardless of individual men's attitudes towards gender equality, men have affective relations, needs, and aspirations. It is not that power is a less significant force in men's lives; it is highly significant, but hegemonic masculinity coexists with a conflicting desire for change among men. Hegemonic masculinities need to be understood as having a care-free dynamic as well as being power-pursuing, because men's power is limited when men recognise and embrace affective relations; when care needs and inherent vulnerability are recognised and when the need and responsibility to care for others are embraced. This is obvious in the men's stories about how caring has changed their masculinity. To really understand masculinity, therefore, we need to appreciate the role of love and caring in men's lives in constructing domineering practices and in theorising how men and masculinities can change.

Chapter 11, 'Towards Affective Equality', offers a short reflection on the findings and advances the importance of affective equality and the broadening of the concept of citizenship to include the right to provide and receive care as ways to envision a more (gender) equal society.

Reading the text

This book is a qualitative exploration of the particular experiences of a small number of men in Ireland. My academic and professional background is drawn principally from interdisciplinary social sciences including social work and social care, applied social studies, equality studies and gender studies and from within each area I have been more heavily influenced by critical and sociologically informed perspectives. While researching for this book I have also found companionship in critical discursive psychology (e.g. Edwards and Potter 1992) and more recently dialogical self-theory (Hermans and Hermans-Konopka 2010; Kahn, Holmes, and Brett 2011), and I have become more aware of the interesting contribution of fields such as social history and geography. Most of my sources are drawn from Western (and indeed Anglophone) social science and I acknowledge the limiting rich-world and linguistic bias this demonstrates (Connell 2007).

Like many sociologists I believe how we define the social world as real has real consequences (and not all intended), but I also believe there are multiple complex cultural, individual, interactional, and institutional intervening factors shaping our social practices. The concept of gender employed is influenced by scholars like Connell and Bourdieu because they acknowledge the interrelation between our material bodies, social structures, and symbolic systems, as well as the relationality of small-scale interactions. Nonetheless the major concern is with gender identity as a concept that addresses our every day meaning-making through an internal-external dialectic constructed dynamically through social interaction (Jenkins 2004). This is not to discount the problems posed by the use of the term nor the fact that gender is more than an idea we carry in our heads (Connell 2002), but it does suppose that gender identity is a significant dimension to gender focussed on the active, everyday, intimate and personal that speaks back at us through social classifications (Wagner 2001).

The concept of hegemony has been employed because it offers a way to describe a complex political dynamic and process operating within social (gender) relations. I have tried to use it in a way that avoids confusion and slippage between related concepts including hegemonic practices, ideals, identities, and characteristics and to make a distinction between singular and plural forms. Therefore, at times I use the phrase *hegemonic practices* to imply actions which men undertake that are hegemonic in contrast to *hegemonic ideals* as images or models, or *hegemonic identities* to suggest how men identify with them. I have used *hegemonic masculinity* in places where I suggest one ideal is ascendant, but I recognise that hegemonic masculinity is subject to change, contestation, and is culturally diverse. Therefore *hegemonic masculinities* are also used in places to signify diversity between local, regional, and global versions. My use of hegemony, however, does no suppose to resolve the tensions between meanings. Whether using men or masculinity(ies), I have tried to avoid the essentialist impression that masculinity is unitary, fixed or trait based, but this stands at times in tension with the sense of gender as embodied and resistant to change.

In the text I have tried to do justice to the men's accounts and reflections by presenting their worlds here honestly and clearly using detailed exemplary quotations. Nonetheless oversimplification can occur in attempting to get close to complex lives. The text should not be read in a positivist way – it is based on how specific men have constructed gendered meanings with me in a particular conversation at a precise point in time. It is more appropriate to consider the conversations not as facts about men's lives or fixed beliefs but as situational constructions in relation to the topic of care. This is not to say that they have no general relevance beyond these situations. Our lives are governed by patterns and regularities and more than individual or idiosyncratic experiences. Small studies of this sort make for at best modest generalisations (Williams 2002: 138) and although findings can be extrapolated beyond the study this is not on the basis of statistical probability (Sarantakos 1988: 26; Fine 2006; Silverman 2000). The data illustrates different levels and versions of reality and the complexity of social reality (Denzin and Lincoln 1994: 353), and as such will have a high degree of transferability to different contexts (Denscombe 2002). Therefore, the contribution I make here is necessarily modest but given the global issues of care I believe it will resonate widely. If my call for masculinities studies to explore care is taken upon then the task I have set is achieved.

2
Gendered Care Practices

Caring defies neat definition. In one sense caring can be understood as socially constructed in so far as what counts as care, good or bad, and how societies organise, reward, and regulate care is historically and culturally contingent (Fine 2006; Chapman 2004). These variable meanings of care, and the enormous cultural relativity of caring practices at different times and places, are nonetheless rooted in a universal material reality of the human condition (Nussbaum 2000, 1995). Human social life is impossible without care; we are born entirely dependent on the care of others, and although we may achieve a degree of independence at different points in our life, we can never escape the reality of our inherent vulnerability (Badgett and Folbre 1999; Bowlby, McKie, and Gregory 2009). Most of us will also be called on to provide care to others in various ways, but even those who live relatively care-free lives, as social and emotional animals we necessarily subsist within webs of emotionally reciprocal relations.

The intrinsic nature of care in social life has only relatively recently emerged as a concern of social scientists. Feminists have been most vocal about care as a major social problem that affects everyone, if not all equally; they have addressed the fact that private care troubles (typically women's) are public issues, and they have exposed the invisibility of care in academic and political discourse. The focus on care within academic feminism addresses several problems including what is care and what does caring entail, why do women undertake a disproportionate amount of societies' caring, why is caring undervalued, what are the affects of caring on carers and care recipients, what is the relationship between caring work and identity, and inequality, and how are the meanings and practices of caring negotiated between individuals and within households. But the overriding interest in care from a feminist perspective is focussed on the fact that caring is prototypically and archetypically feminine. Caring is socially constructed as feminine within both the private and the public sphere because women comprise the majority of society's carers and because caring is defined as feminine (Reskin 1991). Despite the fact that caring is sometimes idealised and valorised in itself, to be a carer is to be materially and symbolically subordinated (Lynch, Baker et al. 2009).

Care work and identity

At its most basic level caring can be thought of as a set of activities or tasks related to helping people to meet daily personal needs and desires (Cheal 2002: 92). Any discussion of care must, however, recognise that the satisfaction of universal human needs take a multitude of forms specific to different cultural and historical epochs giving rise to a great variability of desires and types of activities designed to realise them. Common everyday care-related activities within contemporary Western societies consist typically of specific practices related to meeting dietary and nutritional requirements, incorporating grocery shopping and food preparation, cooking, feeding and clean-up. Additionally caring may include meeting protection and security needs such as attending to, supervising, minding, and teaching. Care is perhaps most often associated with the provision of personal care needs, which can include grooming, toileting, bathing and dressing, but it can include the ferrying between home and public places (to schools, workplaces, and leisure pursuits). Caring might also involve meeting environmental needs that could embrace maintaining domestic spaces, potentially incorporating a wide variety of domestic chores and routine cleaning such as polishing, hovering, cleaning kitchens, bedrooms and bathrooms, and everyday laundry and sewing. The intensity of caring may vary from time to time, including not only direct, intensive, continuous and predictable in nature but also occasional, unpredictable and indirect (Kiely 1998: 91). Caring can feature less routine miscellaneous activities such as house maintenance, repairs and gardening (associated with men) or indeed clothes shopping, banking and the management of household services. This considerable array of tasks and activities suggests that care is a very broad concept indistinct from, or enmeshed with, a wide variety of domestic household practices.

Pointing to the neglect of domestic labour in the social sciences, feminist scholars have conceptualised care and related domestic chores as work (Lynch 1989, 2007; Lynch and McLaughlin 1995: 256). The inspiration to define care as work is derived from a Marxist–humanist conception of human nature although Marx and Marxism often ignored feminist concerns (Hartmann 1979; Bubeck 1995). Marx argued that people realised their basic humanity by reproducing their means of subsistence through non-exploitative labour (Morrison 2006). Care is fundamental to meeting subsistence needs. Marxist, Socialist, and Radical feminists were keen to demonstrate how women were exploited by the fact that care and domestic work were overlooked, undervalued and invisible as work by patriarchy and by capitalism (Delphy and Leonard 1992, 1994). Women's subordinate status in society was said to rest on the fact that women's labour was not recognised in economic and political terms and, therefore, care work was necessarily exploited because the benefits that accrue to capitalism–patriarchy remained unaccounted. Classical economists have not attempted to measure care economically because they believe it is untradeable. However, many forms of care are increasingly commoditised both in formal and informal care labour markets (Folbre and Nelson 2000; Daly and Rake 2003) and to a certain extent professionalised (Bond 1992). The fact that some intimate forms of care cannot be traded does not mean they do not or should not count (Folbre 2001), and indeed the costs of care are well recognised by the state (Simonazzi 2009). To neglect care distorts the true nature of economic activity and negates the significant contribution women give to society as carers (Folbre 2006) creating new social risks (Lewis 2006).

Debates about the nature of care work face many of the conceptual difficulties surrounding the use of the term work, especially what distinguishes work from non-work (Grint 2005), but additionally what distinguishes care work from other forms of domestic labour (Eichler and Albanese 2007; Thomas 1993; Morgan 1996). Some care theorists have resisted defining care as work because they view the application of labour market terminology to the sphere of intimate personal relations demeaning and devaluing the intimate nature of care. A longstanding debate in care theory has addressed the dual nature of care work involving both sets of physical tasks as well as identity and feelings (Graham 1983). Building on Graham's appreciation of this duality of care linking both the elements, taking care of another and of feeling concern for another, Ungerson (1990) made a distinction between 'caring for', as a set of interrelated activities, and 'caring about' as feeling. Broadly, 'caring for' is defined in practical terms as the provision of personal care services, nursing care and other work including domestic services central to the provision of interpersonal needs. 'Caring about' refers to the other-centred disposition or identity that caring work engenders.

Emotional and nurturing labour

So feminists have been keen to explore the interrelation between care, work, and identity and to illuminate the exploitative basis of the care work relation for women. They have pointed out that one of the reasons care has been unrecognised as work is because the emotional work of caring was especially invisible. Caring has been shown to include mental, physical as well as emotional labour (James 1989, 1992; Lynch 1989). One of the reasons that caring work has been unrecognised as work is because emotional labour has been rendered invisible and exploited within capitalism (Hochschild 1983). Emotions have been widely taken to be physiological response mechanisms (Parrott 2001), and undoubtedly there is universal biological basis of emotional responses (Nussbaum 1995; Lyon 1998). However, the sociology of emotion has enabled us to appreciate how emotions are shaped and acquire meaning culturally by the way we recognise them, label them, appraise, manage and express them (Hochschild 1998; Jackson 1993). Hochschild (1998) maintains that people internalise 'feelings rules' about what one should or should not feel in a given context related to the unique emotional dictionaries for different cultures. During interaction with others we employ strategies of emotional management to match our emotional experiences with these 'inner cultural guidelines' or 'feelings rules', and employ an 'emotional armour' to defend against any paradoxes we experience (Hochschild 1998: 11). Emotional work is the social interaction work required to produce positive or negative emotional states in others such as fear, gratitude, happiness, and pleasure. Emotional labour arise in paid work where an employer directs and controls the emotional work of an employee (Hochschild 1983).

Insights about the nature of emotional work or the emotional dimension of work have allowed further exploration of the way emotion is deployed within a wide range of occupations especially those with high service or caring components including the work of flight attendants, librarians, hair dressers and beauty therapists, retail workers, holiday representatives, and among caring professionals such as nurses (Taylor and Tyler 2000; Korczynski 2003; Staden 1998; Williams 2003; Sharma and Black 2001; Guerrier and Adib 2003). Emotional labour is shaped by many factors including religion, nation, race/ethnicity, class, and generation, but foremost in how these 'feelings rules' are organised is in terms of gender (Hochschild 1998). The social formations of emotional work are identifiable but emotional work is nonetheless complex and contradictory for individuals. Emotional work is deployed internally in how we manage the tension between our conflicting desire to experience intimacy and separation with others. It is also deployed externally when we attempt to meet emotional expectations or when expressing emotion is disallowed and what seems like unemotional behaviour such as silence can be intensely emotional; in contrast, talking can be about avoiding feeling emotion (Craib 1998). Amid this complexity doing emotional work can involve both action and inaction because emotion may be expressed verbally or through our behaviour and bodies (Jamieson 2002).

The concept of emotional work and labour has not been sufficient to explain even more hidden aspects of caring work. Though caring involves emotional work, all forms of emotional work are not caring (Lynch and McLaughlin 1995). Emotional labour can be deployed to sell products or services, to instil fear or anxiety, to dissuade and to manipulate, rather than develop bonds of care per se (Hochschild 1983; Pierce 1998). The emotional work of care is distinguishable from other forms of emotional labour because care is nurturing; it is focussed on the well-being of another, and its intention is to produce nurturing outcomes (Lynch 2007). The especially unrecognised nature of emotional care work becomes clearer when it is recognised that some forms of care also involve love: 'the will to nurture one's own and another's spiritual and emotional growth' and 'action and not merely feeling' (hooks 2004: 65). Love is also labour, the care and reproductive labour involved in reproducing self and others and nurturing quality of life physically, emotionally and socially, where the emotional bond is the goal per se (Lynch 2007). Other forms of emotional people-work are not necessarily love labours if the goal is not the relationship itself (Lynch and McLaughlin 1995: 258–9). What distinguishes love and care labour most strongly is how love, as opposed to care work, is fundamentally inalienable and non-commodifiable (Lynch 2007). This intimate zone in life does not respond to the laws of the market; it cannot be marketised or subcontracted because to do love labour demands presence, genuineness, communication and companionship. One cannot, Lynch suggests, pay someone to make love to one's partner, or to hug and love your children, as a substitute to yourself.

Love labour produces outcomes which a number of scholars have analysed as emotional and nurturing capital. Reay (2000) understands emotional capital as other-centred emotional resources passed on through generations which are interrelated in complex ways with the more recognised self-centred economic, social, cultural forms of capital. Allatt (1993) understands emotional capital to be particular forms of social capital (including social networks, sociability, and networking skills) and cultural capital (including institutional credentials and dispositions of dress, mannerisms, self-assurance, and caring values) that are used under particular conditions within affective relations. Allatt includes 'emotionally valued assets and skills of love and affection' and what Bourdieu (1986: 253) refers to as 'an apparently gratuitous expenditure of time, attention, care [and] concern' (cited in Allatt 1993: 143). Lynch and Lyons (2009) define nurturing capital as outcomes of love care and solidarity that give rise to the capacity to nurture others that is available to us personally, socially, and politically and is invested in us historically and individually.

Care work can now be appreciated with this greater level of complexity involving as it does physical, mental, and emotional work that interrelate with feeling and identity. This raises the important question of, what is care in the absence of feeling, especially of love? Can 'caring for' be truly caring in the absence of feeling, 'caring about'? Can love/care be mediated through different forms of work not traditionally considered as care? Should care be confined to those activities related to intimate personal assistance or can other forms of household work be considered care? Controversially, can provisioning, providing, or 'breadwinning' be considered care? These questions are central to many contemporary care debates. Care as work and feeling are complexly enmeshed in practice but our understanding of this duality, at least as an ideal type, helps us to consider when and how 'caring for' and 'caring about' may coalesce or come apart. Pettinger, Parry, Taylor and Glucksman (2005) caution about the trap of searching for a substantive definition of care, given the difficulties posed in clearly defining work from non-work. They argue it is more fruitful to account for work as a temporal and relational concept crossing the boundaries between paid and unpaid work, market and non-market work, and formal and informal work. From this perspective caring work can be then considered as part of the total organisation of household labour which includes not only a variety of household practices but also paid labour that members of the household undertake.

Care and relational identities

Care work and care identities are constructed dynamically in sets of emotional relations based on shared life experiences, mutual assistance, and associated feelings of belonging (Lynch and Lyons 2009; Lynch and McLaughlin 1995: 263; Lynch 1989). Intrinsic to care relations are relative degrees of dependency during infancy, childhood or at times of illness or physical, intellectual, psychological or sensory impairment (Fineman 2008), or as a socially constituted condition of disability (Oliver 1990). To be in receipt of care is often to be in a position of dependency and to be vulnerable, but human life is also lived as relations of interdependency, mutuality, and reciprocity among parents and children, adult partners, and siblings and extended family relatives (Fineman 2008; Lynch 2007; Bowlby, McKie, and Gregory 2009). Care scholars have employed the concept of circles of caring to highlight the differing degrees of interdependence, emotional attachment, and mutuality of care relations, as well as the relative weight of caring obligations (Fisher and Tronto 1990; Lynch 2007; Bubeck 1995). Lynch (1989, 2007) and Lynch and McLaughlin (1995) define three conceptually distinct forms of caring (love, care, and solidarity), related to three concentric sets of care relations (primary, secondary, and tertiary). Primary love relations are characterised by high interdependency and high attachment which accrue intimacy and responsibility over time. They may be chosen relations we develop with friends or partners or they may be inherited obligations we ascribe from our families. Secondary care relations also involve responsibilities and attachments but they have less moral obligation and there is a greater degree of choice and contingency. They are context specific which can and does end when the context changes. Tertiary care relations are relations of solidarity that do not involve intimacy. Tertiary care relations may be voluntary but often they conform to secular or religious norms and statutory codes and principles. Solidarity labour is caring that occurs in a more diffuse sense. Solidarity alerts us to the unity of feelings and actions among individuals with a common interest. It carries a sense of the resistance and strength of united actors with a common mission although it can be viewed as an end in itself. Being wanted, loved, and cared for gives us a basic security and self-confidence without which life would appear alienating and meaningless.

Discussions of meaning within so much sociological thought address the outer cultural spaces of life, linguistic systems, popular and high culture, multi-media, and political and moral belief systems, with little acknowledgement of how much of life's meaning is related to our intimate personal care relations with significant others in our lives. Affective relations, as inherited or contracted relations of dependency and interdependency that involve providing and receiving love, care, and solidarity, are the emotional glue of life giving it meaning and substance (Lynch 2007). Love, care, and solidarity comprise the most basic feature of human life, defining us as human beings and allowing for human potential to flourish in ways that support 'public' life (Lynch, Baker et al. 2009; Nussbaum 1995, 2000; Lynch and McLaughlin 1995).

Caring relations give rise to caring obligations, which although socially, culturally, and historically contingent, are nonetheless systemic (Cheal 2002: 45; Finch 1989; Finch and Mason 1993). Certainly care may be provided as a 'gift', or out of love, but the provision of care is rarely purely altruistic, being subject to numerous pressures and obligations and constraints, including that of 'anticipated reciprocity' (Standing 2001: 25). Within any society care is organised within a complex network of institutionalised structures, roles, and relationships as well as moral obligations and identities that engender particular ways of thinking and feeling on the part of both carers and recipients. Caring obligations are patterned by key social divisions, experiences of inequality and intersectional identities based around age, gender, religion, race/ethnicity, class, disability, sexuality, and marital and family status (Bettio and Platenga 2004; Daly 2001; Ehrenreich and Hochschild 2003; Lynch and Lyons 2009; McKie, Gregory, and Bowlby 2002; Heymann 2007; Chapman 2004: 155). Above all caring is gendered work since women comprise the majority of both paid and unpaid carers in society (Gerstel and Gallagher 2001: 214; Cullen, Delaney, and Duff 2004; Evandrou and Glaser 2003; Strazdins and Broom 2004; Abel and Nelson 1990). Patterns of caring are structured additionally by other social forces including changing demographics, marriage, divorce and fertility rates, longevity and health, economic and social factors as well as the particular historical conditions of welfare states such as the availability of social services and other social supports (Cheal 2002: 93). State welfare policies, for example, influence the meaning and organisation of caring roles, privileging some interests over others especially in terms of defining who should care (Daly and Rake 2003). Cheal (2002: 107) contends that caring is structured by family roles, and the self and social identities, preferences and experiences associated with them, but caring obligations are not simply imposed. The negotiation of roles and identities within families allows for variability and fluidity in caring arrangements. They are nonetheless ideologically constrained by dominant social norms and values and by prevailing social inequalities in paid and unpaid work, resources, status, and power (ibid.).

Despite cultural variations, and the way the family members can feel differentially obligated to care, it is women who most experience a moral imperative to care (Finch and Mason 1993). Women are constituted as carers at the material level through state welfare and labour market policies and at the ideological level through the internalisation of a moral imperative to care (Ungerson 1983). Caring is a choice for men but an obligation for women (Daly 2001: 48; 2003: 68) because gender identity is intensely tied to caring responsibilities:

> the experience of caring is the medium through which women are accepted into and feel they belong into the social world. It is the medium through which they gain admittance into both the private world of the home and the public world of the labour market. It is through caring in an informal capacity – as mothers, wives, daughters, neighbours, friends – and through formal caring – as nurses, secretaries, cleaners, teachers, social workers – that they enter and occupy their place in society. (Graham 1983: 30)

Graham notes however 'caring is not simply something women do for themselves, to achieve their femininity. It is something women do for others, to keep them alive'. It is work hidden by ideologies of female domesticity (ibid.: 25).

Gendered care inequalities

The pinnacle of feminist criticism of women's constitution as carers rests most of all on the fact that caring duties have consequences in how men's avoidance or evasion of caring facilitates the gender inequalities experienced by women in social, political, economic, and affective life (Hochschild 1989; McMahon 1999; Coltrane and Galt 2000: 16; Bubeck 1995; Baker et al. 2004). Caring work gives rise to gender inequalities in resources, respect and recognition, working and learning, representation and love, care and solidarity (Baker et al. 2004).

Power inequalities in caring are found in those who have more say over caring decisions and who are subject to moral obligations to provide care (Lynch, Lyons, and Cantillon 2009). Whether as managers of caring organisations or with private households, men are more likely to make overarching decisions about caring as 'care commanders' whereas women are more likely to make up 'care foot soldiers' doing the everyday work of caring (Lynch and Lyons 2008). Care commanders tend to have no obligations to do everyday work of care except for significant events (Lynch, Lyons, and Cantillon 2009). This itself is an expression of power in private life (Bubeck 1995: 160) showing how 'status in the family, determines both an individual role in the family division of labour and his (or her) share in the family consumption' (Delphy and Leonard 1992: 145–6).

Nevertheless, power and powerlessness are not zero sum; carers have power in caring relations as power is a dynamic relationship constantly subject to conflict and negotiation. Carers can have a high degree of power over care recipients especially where there is a high dependency on the carer, although the power of the carer can coexist with feelings of powerlessness (Bubeck 1995: 149; Rutman 1996). This means that neglect or otherwise poor judgements on the part of carers can have serious consequences for care recipients. At the same time care recipients also exercise power over carers in terms of the moral obligations on carers to provide care (Dominelli and Gollins 1997; Lynch, Lyons, and Cantillon 2009). Power and control can be exercised over the carer in the form of other-directed identities which define caring as a natural (female) moral imperative (Wilkes 1995: 245; Bem 1993; Bubeck 1995: 161; O'Brien 2007). The moral imperative and invisibility of love labour make carers especially vulnerable to exploitation because the nature of their work may go unrecognised even to themselves.

Caring is not solely 'culturally constructed women's work'; it additionally attracts low status, low public policy priority, and is resource deficient (Cullen, Delaney, and Duff 2004: 18; O'Sullivan 2007; Kiely 1998). Caring responsibilities impose direct economic costs on unpaid carers in the form of income opportunities foregone and additionally indirect costs by limiting prospects to accumulate valued cultural capital especially through formal education and through labour market participation (Carmichael and Charles 2003; Van den Berg et al. 2006). Women experience downward mobility because of time taken out of work to care as well as lose out on having higher incomes, pension entitlements, and educational opportunities (Evandrou and Glaser 2003; Cullen, Delaney, and Duff 2004; Galligan 1998; O'Sullivan 2007). A life dedicated to caring is often also a life of economic dependency (especially for women) on men and social welfare (Finch and Groves 1983). Unpaid carers (or indeed carers on inadequate welfare payments) comprise an informal welfare sector who suffer most when the welfare state contracts especially at times of recession (Ungerson 1983). It amounts to a material net burden which restricts opportunities and creates greater dependency on men and the state (Bubeck 1995: 141). Caring work (including domestic, nurturing, and reproductive work) is economically exploited because it is defined as a private family matter obscuring its vital economic contribution to society (Lynch and McLaughlin 1995). Women's unpaid work in the home and women's efficacy as a reserve army of cheap labour is then exploited by political and economic systems (Baker et al. 2004).

Women's care work is also exploited in paid labour markets (Ehrenreich and Hochschild 2003; Jackson 1992) with the emotion work involved in caring occupations especially unrecognised (Duncombe and Marsden 1993; James 1989, 1992; Hochschild 1983). Although there are important differences of status and income between care workers in formal and (semi-) professionalised occupations (including social care workers, home helps, social workers, and early childcare workers) and those within informal economies (including nannies, domestic workers, and *au pairs*), generally, even the most secure and established of caring occupations are low paid and those who undertake them incur an income penalty (England, Budig, and Folbre 2002). Many forms of caring, especially in informal economies, are insecure and non-unionised with low status and unregulated working conditions and often excluded from legal employment protections (Walby 1997; Baker et al. 2004: 127; Daly 2001; Lynch 2007), with migrant women often involved in the most hidden and burdensome caring work (Migrant Rights Centre 2004; Lutz 2008).

Caring obligations can also have serious psycho-social consequences in how it limits one's social horizon and excessive burdens of care can have negative psychological effects. Caring demands significant amounts of commitment and is heavily time dependent (Folbre and Bittman 2004; Jacobs and Gerson 2004). The moral imperative on women to care means women carry a disproportionate burden of guilt when they choose other interests over caring (O'Brien 2007). Women can be perceived to be uncaring when pursuing a career instead of primary caring (Gatrell 2005). Multiple caring obligations often compete for time and space resulting often in less time to provide love labour to others (Lynch, Lyons, and Cantillon 2009). Caring responsibilities can leave the carer feeling powerless, dependent, physically and psychologically exhausted and trapped as a result of having few choices (Bubeck 1995: 140–9). Caring can be repetitive and unrelenting with poor access to respite care (Cullen, Delaney, and Duff 2004), and many carers experience sleep deprivation resulting in long-term health damage (Maume, Sebastian, and Bardo 2010: 746). Some of this is of course compensated by the emotional satisfaction derived from caring, but there are many situations that offer little reciprocal benefits especially when the relationship involves emotional, physical, or age-related disabilities that prevent reciprocity or where there are inequalities of power (Lynch and McLaughlin 1995: 264). For all this women are more likely to neglect themselves as a result of their other-centred orientation (Bubeck 1995). Caring responsibilities also preclude having time to oneself including 'opportunities for social contact, personal satisfaction and self-realization' (Baker et al. 2004: 30). The full-time nature of much caring restricts carers' opportunities to acquire other social goods, fulfil their own needs, participate in social, political, or cultural life and develop social and cultural capital.

Early Marxist and socialist-inspired perspectives have tended to underestimate the emotional–symbolic bonds that tie women to care (Graham 1983: 29) by emphasising the bleak and oppressive nature of caring and household work (Oakley 1974; Barrett and McIntosh 1982). More recent accounts of care have emphasised women's agency as caregivers and illuminated the skilled, reflexive, and reciprocal nature of care and identity (Smart and Neale 1999: 20). They have shown that caring is more than the completion of household work or tasks; it refers to negotiated love relationships with significant others. Chapman (2004: 27) finds that the equation of 'caring for' with emotional labour rather than love tends negatively to equate with lost opportunities for women. This overlooks the emotional and spiritual reward that care advances in terms of opportunities to develop emotional attachments with loved ones and as a consequence endow life with meaning and fulfilment. Love labour is often considered to be inherently emotionally rewarding and self-motivating. Of course this is not always the case but the psychological and emotional benefits of love and caring are especially evident when love is reciprocated (Bubeck 1995). Love work is not entirely altruistic because it holds mutual benefits even when they are disproportionately small for the carer (Lynch 2007). Love labour can offer a feeling of personal fulfilment, intimacy, and interdependence (Lynch, Lyons, and Cantillon 2009). Love and care work can provide a sense of power and control over one's immediate environment and in important relational decisions about one's own and others' lives, and under the right conditions love labour is enormously fulfilling and preferable to other forms of exploitative and alienating work.

Recent scholarship has witnessed a renewed interest in care and inequality (Britzman, Frosh, and Luttrell 2009; Lynch, Baker et al. 2009; Baker et al. 2004). Baker, Lynch, Walsh, and Cantillon (2009) argue that the institutional ways in which society organises care relations – affective systems – are generative sources of inequality. They reason that a holistic conception of equality must include the affective domain:

[I]t is an important issue of equality, and therefore of justice, to ask who has access to, and who is denied, relations of love, care and solidarity, whether these relations are reciprocal or asymmetrical, and whether the ways societies operate help to satisfy or frustrate these human needs. (Baker et al. 2004: 28)

Baker, Lynch et al. (2004: 60) use the term affective inequality to explain two interrelated but conceptually distinct caring inequalities. First, inequalities arise in the way that love and care are accessed with some people having less access to love and care than others. The absence of care, or care without nurture, often as the consequence of neglect and abuse is a deprivation that generates sadness, loneliness, alienation, and despair. Care deprivations impact particularly on marginalised groups such as prisoners and people living in institutional care through processes such as homelessness, imprisonment, and institutionalisation (Baker et al. 2004). Secondly, inequalities arise in the way that love and care are performed with some people undertaking disproportionate burdens of affective work. Affective equality demands fair and equal distribution or compensation for the benefits and burdens to which they give rise (Baker et al. 2004). Affective equality is driven by a concern to equalise access and opportunities, participation, outcomes and conditions associated with the unequal distribution of love, care, and solidarity work. Therefore, the gender division of caring is an injustice in so far as the benefits and burdens of caring relations are unequally distributed between men and women and because of the way that the distribution of this work contributes to other inequalities (Baker et al. 2004; Lynch, Baker et al. 2009).

Conclusion

Caring involves a variety of interrelated forms of work each containing physical, mental, and emotional dimensions that command social time and space and provide us with energy and meaning for life (Lynch 2007). Caring is a complex web of different forms of labour deployed in emotional relationships of varying significance and imbuing a sense of belonging and identity. Caring practices are organised through moral obligations placed on carers and the expectations of recipients. Caring is political in that it involves decision-making power and control as well as economic because, although caring may be based on compulsory altruism and go unpaid, it has direct and opportunity costs for carers and recipients and because of its economic contribution to society. Caring is also a socio-cultural relationship because it attaches particular meanings, values, norms, and patterns of obligation in different societies at different times. Caring is additionally an emotional relationship because it involves intimacy, emotional attachments and interdependency, along with feelings of responsibility, which connect us with our vulnerability and basic humanity. Moreover women comprise the majority of the world's carers. This has consequences for inequalities experienced by women, but it also has implications for men, for the material benefits derived from avoiding it, as well as the emotional rewards related to successfully embracing it.

3
Masculinities and Care

In his insightful book *Family Man, Fatherhood, Housework and Gender Equity*, Scott Coltrane (1996: 152) outlines Human Capital Theory and Socio-Structural Theory as two overriding explanations for why men are less engaged in caring and household work than women. Coltrane notes that both perspectives present actors constrained in their choices by social and economic factors although they differ in so far as the former are accepting of the status quo and the latter are critical. He then outlines relative resources, gender ideology, and time availability as three prominent mid-range theories that further influence the division of household labour. And he finds that 'relative resources, ideology, and time availability are all important to divisions of household labour' (p. 176) and also notes there are other important variables such as how long couples wait to have children. Coltrane's overall conclusion is that as well as taking into account constraining economic conditions he suggests that 'doing household labour is doing gender', that therefore 'gender ideology matters' in how social constructions of gender that 'create narrow definitions of what it means to be a man or a woman' lead to 'differential rewards and limitations' (ibid.: 175).

I agree with Coltrane when he finds that each of the above explanations has explanatory power and that what goes on in families is complex. I agree with Connell (2011: 57) as well who writes that 'no understanding of motherhood and fatherhood is now possible without a reckoning with market forces'. Several factors are related to men's involvement in their children's lives in the contemporary context, including their gender ideology and beliefs in equality, the flexibility of career and labour market strategies, education, income and other class-based resources, care leave and the flexibility of paid work, as well as negotiations of power and meaning with their partners/wives

(Seward et al. 2006). This chapter is concerned with gender ideology and identity as one of the central explanations for why men are less engaged in care than women, and why masculinity and care are antithetical. Care is defined as feminine in terms of affection, tenderness, empathy, intimacy, sensitivity, and intuition (Bem 1993: 127; Coltrane 1994: 45; Prendergast and Forrest 1998), in contrast to masculinity which is defined as unemotional, rational, instrumental, and inexpressive (Hearn 1987: 138–9; Sattel 1998; Rubin 1983; Clare 2000). This chapter considers a number of approaches to the relationship between masculinity and caring within social science that have proven influential in gender studies. The adverse relationship between masculinity and care, and the ways in which care is written out of men's lives, has been explained within the social sciences as biologically essential, functional, political, rational, and irrational, or in various ways a social construction. Regardless of whether considered desirable or not, all of these perspectives highlight the nature of masculinities as an oppositional construct that involves the writing out of femininity from men's lives. The fact that caring is defined as feminine is a major block to how men engage with and identify with the world of care, especially those forms of care most associated with femininity.

The chapter begins by outlining two broad perspectives on men's caring practices in respect of gender equality: one largely optimistic about progressive change, and the other pessimistic about men's will to change. Following this it then considers three broad perspectives on the oppositional relationship between masculinities as care. First, masculinity is defined sociologically as instrumental in contrast to care as expressive. Secondly, masculinity is perceived to be psychologically repressive of care rationality. Finally, masculinity is understood as reflexive in respect of power and emotions leading to contradictory tendencies for both change and resistance in respect of care.

Men's caring practices

The global gender order has undergone considerable transformations in recent decades. Large-scale changes in late-modern capitalism, through processes of labour market casualisation, flexibilisation and globalisation, have facilitated a gradual decline in traditional male breadwinner models of private patriarchy (Young 1990; Peterson 1998; Connell 2002; Holter 2007). Conventional patriarchal masculinity has been undermined by women's increased participation in the labour market, which arguably has contributed to a decline in men's dominance in the public sphere (Giddens 1992: 132), although it has been proposed that these changes have merely marked a transformation from private to public patriarchy (Walby 1997), with gender orders readjusting to contemporary changes (Connell 1998). Crucially, the widespread entry of women into the labour market in Western societies has resulted in men being more involved in caring (Hook 2006) but there has not been an equivalent increase in men's involvement relative to women's overall workload (Daly and Rake 2003: 132). There appears to be a broad consensus in the literature on the gender division of care in Western societies that men have made only limited advances towards equality in caring, with some analyses pointing to optimistic trends while others remaining critical and pessimistic.

Many optimistic perspectives on men's caring practices support the view that women, by and large, continue to shoulder the bulk of caring labour but highlight a variety of positive gradual generational shifts among men. Gender relations are claimed to be more companionate, emotionally involved, individualised, and egalitarian (Giddens 1992). Cross-national studies have shown that men's beliefs and ideals about equality and the negotiation of caring practices are becoming more egalitarian even though the transformation is slow and uneven (O'Sullivan 2004). Men seem more willing to be intensely involved in supportive secondary care roles (Choi and Marks 2006; Kiely 1998: 94; Clarke 2005). For example, the norm that men should now be present at the birth of their children is cited as evidence that men are interested in change (Kimmel 2000), even though gendered power remains a feature of these processes and men can be uncertain about how to be involved (Reed 2005; Johnson 2002).

Optimistic perspectives also tend to emphasise the greater involvement of particular groups of men such as gay male caregivers (Connell 2000: 191; Munro and Edward 2010) and elderly male caregivers (Russell 2007). Men comprise a significant minority of primary carers of adult dependents or children with disabilities with some groups of men doing as much as 50 per cent of family caring in particular circumstances (Kramer 2005). This is especially the case for older men who increase their caring both for their wives and grandchildren, and, while estimates vary, elder male carers are thought to comprise a relatively invisible group of male carers comprising between one-third and a half of elderly carers (Applegate and Kaye 1993; Kramer 2005; Arber and Gilbert 1989). Two dominant patterns of love labour done by older men are when they are caring for their wives, or their mothers where they have lived with them all their lives (Arber and Gilbert 1989).

Higher numbers of elderly male carers reflect increasing demands for elderly men to undertake caring and suggests the decreasing availability of women, particularly wives and daughters, to do it for them. Other factors also intervene in engaging more elderly men in caring including epidemiological, demographic, and political trends that result in greater longevity and extended dependency of the elderly, particularly of women, smaller families, and delayed childbirth. This increases female employment and reduces access to health care in the context of privatisation (Kramer 2005; Pringle 1995; Applegate and Kaye 1993).

Another view affirming men's contribution as carers is that men's caring practices are different than women's and should not be measured using a 'feminist yardstick' (Thompson 2000). Men tend to have more diffuse ideals of caring seeing themselves as having some sort of ongoing commitment and responsibility as a provider (Cheal 2002) in contrast with the way women's tendency to think about the practical aspects of caring for the provision of direct care needs (Fisher and Tronto 1990). Men 'care about' others in the sense of being kind, concerned, tender, and affectionate especially for their partners and children (Cheal 2002: 91; Hayward and Mac án Ghaill 2003).The extent of men's involvement in domestic labour can also be underestimated in how it is defined as care and cleaning. The claim that middle-class men willingly commoditise traditional forms of male domestic labour, such as gardening and domestic repairs, in order to facilitate paid work (McMahon 1999) is also found to be used to facilitate men's greater involvement in nurturing their children. Furthermore domestic 'masculine' gaps are filled often by male migrant workers (Kilkey 2010; Sarti and Scrinzi 2010). The view that men care in different ways is also critiqued. Kimmel (2000: 203) argues that although men may care in different ways than women, these differences are much less than imagined and vary historically and culturally. The nature of men's and women's involvement in nurturing emotional work may differ in terms of their aims, outcomes, and intentions and in their relative contribution but women hold no monopoly on this work (Lynch and Lyons 2009; Lynch 2007; Duncombe and Marsden 1998). Chapman (2004: 205) proposes there is a lot more complexity to men's caring practices, claiming that gendered domestic practices have become much more 'fluid, varied and negotiable' over the past 30 years. He believes that masculine identity is increasingly disaggregated from men's identities based on paid work with men choosing from a range of masculinities. The decline in men's involvement in heavy manufacturing in many industrialised societies has accompanied men's increasing entry into traditionally feminised service sectors (Hayward and Mac án Ghaill 2003: 26) including (semi-) professional caring occupations (Williams 1993; Simpson 2004, 2009; Lupton 2000). Moreover, a new field of research on egalitarian parenting shows how committed dual-care couples can successfully overcome many individual (personality), institutional, and structural barriers to greater equality in caring (Risman 1998; Vachon and Vachon 2010; Mahoney 1995; Deutsch 1999; Gerson 2010).

Pessimistic perspectives would seem to be grounded in a more radical egalitarian critique highlighting evidence of men's continuing power and privilege. Male dominance is said to be shrouded by the myth of the 'new man' (Segal 1997b: 35). Men are presented as reluctant to change their care practices despite much wider changes occurring in the society. Typically these studies convey a gap between the rhetoric and the reality of gender equality among men. Gerstel and Gallagher (2001: 199) claim that men's caring practices 'both within and beyond households, has appeared to be remarkably resistant to a wide range of demographic, social, and economic changes'. Men, they maintain, do not fill the care gap even when their wives are employed or earning as much as their husbands with women substituting for the caring responsibilities that men avoid. Similarly, Coltrane and Galt (2000: 30) note that 'Several decades of research...has shown that most women still perform the bulk of domestic work, remain the child-care experts, and continue to serve as the emotional managers for their families.' Women undertake twice the care and domestic work of men, who have not increased their contribution to unpaid caring in line with women's increased participation in the formal labour market (Drew, Wmerck, and Mahon 1998; Bubeck 1995; Coltrane and Galt 2000; O'Sullivan 2007). Though elderly men are more highly represented as caregivers they tend to work for fewer hours than elderly women caregivers and they also tend to combine care with paid work (Lynch and Lyons 2008; Cullen, Delaney, and Duff 2004). Craig (2006) analyses time-use surveys which demonstrate that fathers spend less time with children (two to three times less), and the time they spend involves less multi-tasking activities, less physical work, less responsibility for managing care, and is more flexible than mothers' even when mothers are often working full time. A notable finding is when men undertake domestic work it is more likely to involve pleasurable, higher status, and enjoyable aspects, such as play, which often involve greater emotional rewards from children along with the benefit of avoiding the more burdensome physical care tasks (Woodward 1997: 267–9; Brandth and Kvande 1998; Gerstel and Gallagher 2001; Craig 2006: 274). Even in co-parent families men's provider status entitles men to longer and more continuous sleep (Maume, Sebastian, and Bardo 2010). Daly and Rake make similar arguments when comparing several Western welfare states:

> Our research identified a robust division of labour between women and men. Responsibility for particular tasks serves to structure and differentiate male and female domains. Overall, though, women not only do the lion's share of unpaid work, but responsibility for such work is integral to women's social roles in a way that it is not for men. These are the most entrenched of gender divisions. In no country has the movement of women into the labour market instigated a proportionate shift in men's involvement in domestic work. Hence, in comparison with men, women approach the labour market with a far greater conditionality and constraint. (Daly and Rake 2003: 153–4)

McMahon (1999) presents a highly critical reading of men's care-free practices, arguing forcefully that the symmetrical family has not become the norm and questioning even modest advances towards equality in caring. Men, he claims, continue to take on the role of head of household in most cultures and tend to have more choice over their degree of involvement with children than women. Men tend to be involved in higher-status leisure activities and consequently they receive a greater emotional pay-off from children and additionally greater praise from partners who evaluate their contribution against the lower caring expectations for men (McMahon 1999: 127). He argues 'the typical husband enjoys a privileged position, with a greater right to leisure and to having his personal needs met by another' (p. 23). This he claims makes men a net drain on family labour-time resources. He also argues that women tend to get more help from other female friends and children than from their husbands. Reductions in care and domestic work are often due to purchasing commodities or co-modifying aspects of the work rather than from husbands taking the slack, but even there it is traditional male domestic work such as gardening and DIY that is more likely to be co-modified (McMahon 1999: 17).

A key argument in these pessimistic analyses is that men will generally only undertake caring when there are no women available to do it for them (Gerstel and Gallagher 2001; Noonan, Estes, and Glass 2007; McMahon 1999: 15; Hook 2006). Noonan, Estes, and Glass (2007) found that men's domestic labour increased when women worked flexible hours hypothesising that this was because women were unavailable at crucial times of the day to take on their usual amount (e.g. mealtimes). Hearn (1987: 110) maintains that men's child caring is generally limited to times of crisis for the mother when she cannot do the caring and is usually confined to the care of the child rather than the mother. What is proposed is that men tend to view their house work as a 'gift' or help rather than as a primary obligation (Risman 1998: 32). Even the idea that men are increasing their support as secondary carers is critiqued on the grounds that it amounts to manipulation or appeasement for their wives' greater workload (Delphy and Leonard 1992). Men frequently take for granted the emotional work that women do for them because they expect it of women, but are more aware of emotional work when they are doing it themselves (Minnotte et al. 2007). Unsurprisingly then from this perspective men overall are more satisfied with marriage because they receive more concrete advantages in terms of the care they receive from their wives (Chapman 2004: 193).

Instrumental masculinities

The ideology and practice of separate spheres, wherein women were defined as carers within the private field of family life, and men defined as breadwinners in the public field of paid work, is a relatively recent phenomenon, emerging in the late 19th and early 20th century in American and European societies (Coltrane 1996). The very notion that motherhood is a full-time career is a product of the industrial revolution which was historically, and continues to be, in many respects economically prohibitive for poorer families, especially in poor world countries where as well as being carers many women are also breadwinners (Risman 1998; Heymann 2007). Just as women were historically engaged in paid labour in the public sphere (especially in proletarian families), men were also involved in household work although tasks were nonetheless gender divided (Lorentzen 2010). Men were involved in domestic labour historically in terms of stereotypical male preserves such as gardening and household maintenance and repairs and also as higher-status domestic workers for those households who could afford it (Kilkey 2010). In some African and Asian societies many men are still involved in paid domestic labour (Bartolomei 2010; Qayum and Ray 2010). The separate spheres ideology has been seldom realised in practice even in Western societies except for their golden age of the 1950s and 60s (Lewis 2001: 63–5).

Lewis (2001) traces male breadwinner ideals to the separation of spheres ideals of Herbert Spencer (1876) who argued that more highly evolved societies contain more specialised gender roles with a competitive and ruthless masculinity best adapted to success within the public sphere, and a nurturing femininity best suited to caring within the private family. It was an ideology that coincided with the 19th-century intensification of industrial capitalism that produced wholesale changes in family practices by, with notable class variations, relegating women to unpaid domestic and care work (Chapman 2004). The notion of separate spheres was modelled on a late-19th-century middle-class protestant-individualist family ideal. Men had previously been more involved in the domestic economy, and though they may have been emotionally distant, they participated in caring as supervisors, teachers, models for morality, and as disciplinarians (Aldous 1998: 7). The 20th century saw the intensification of this instrumental breadwinner masculinity as men's caring roles narrowed to that of economic provider marking a shift from men being visible authorities within the families to part-time family members (ibid.). Men were defined as god's representative within the family whose authority was to be respected; fathers were expected to be rational, objective, and distanced authority figures acting as a civilising force in opposition to the emotional irrationality of feminine nurturing (Seidler 1988).

The ideal of separate spheres was given further legitimacy within American Functionalist sociology by Parsons and Bales (1953) who proposed that complementary *instrumental* (masculine) and *expressive* (feminine) roles were required by the social system in order to deliver social stability and the integration of society as a whole. Gendered social roles were institutionalised in agencies of socialisation such as the family, religion, education, and the workplace. They alleged that specialist gender roles were instilled when, aided by a variety of psychological rewards and punishments to encourage conformity and castigate deviance, men and women conformed to norms prescribing appropriate roles whilst avoiding forbidden ones. Gender in everyday situations is confirmed by labelling processes which provide individuals with codes and cues to filter their actions giving the feeling that one's gender is natural and stable (Kimmel 2000). Over time normative gender roles become internalised when individuals grow to be deeply committed to gender because of how intensely it equates with acceptance, disapproval, and desire. Masculinity becomes effectively an 'internalised social relationship' appearing secure and certain but as Brittan (1989: 20) notes it can also be experienced as uncertain, insecure, and unstable. Early criticisms of functionalist role perspectives within masculinities theory were based on the assertion that the theory lacked the ability to explain dysfunctional, oppressive, or conflicting social roles (Pleck 1976; Pleck and Sawyer 1974). Role Conflict theory came about to explain the dysfunctionality, fragility, and insecurity masculinity within a changing world (Pleck 1981; Ehrenreich 1983). Central to this was the view that the decline of traditional gender norms, along with their deinstitutionalisation particularly within the workplace, meant it had become tenuous for men to identify with traditional male roles as providers (of money, family name, education, morality, authority, and punishment), because these roles had become increasingly shared with women (Kraemer 1995).

Social role perspectives on masculinity have broadly influenced the politics of masculinity and care in two ways. On the one hand they have given rise to a reactionary politics of masculinity that rejects gender equality and rails against the decline in patriarchal and instrumental masculinity, which takes the form of attacking feminism, and liberalism more generally, and seeks to reinstate a conservative and patriarchal culture. This identity crisis that men were said to experience was laid to blame on a wide variety of phenomena believed to undermine traditional gender roles including absent fathers, feminising pampering mothers or feminised schooling, the breakdown of the nuclear family, or gender equality more broadly (Brittan 1989: 25).

Reactionary social role beliefs in separate spheres are extensively criticised as biologically essentialist because, despite their sociological grounding, they ultimately reduce gender differences in caring to innate genetic, biological, or psychological attributes (Connell 1987; Carrigan, Connell, and Lee 1987). Kimmel (1990: 95) argues that both role theory and biological models of gender 'assume a functionalist teleology that suggests that what exists is supposed to exist as a result of biological or cultural evolution' which consequently obscures and naturalises gendered power relations. Role theory inadequately critiques normative masculinity and tends to view alternative roles as deviant and pathological failing to explain the multiplicity, complexity, and conflicting nature of masculinity and how men depart from normative gender roles (Carrigan, Connell, and Lee 1987). Brittan (1989) and Connell (1987: 195) reason that role theory's assumption that gender relations are normal and natural rationalises gender inequality and 'invites' and even 'coerces' male dominance.

Role perspectives have also fed a liberal desire to modernise masculinity because, rather than men being viewed as denied a legitimate role in society, masculinity is perceived to be poorly able to adapt to changing roles (Segal 1997b). Pleck (1976, 1981) proposed that prescriptions on men to fill certain roles are simultaneously vetoes on occupying more fulfilling roles. Part of the existential crisis men encounter from this perspective is created by the unreasonable expectations on men to be competitive, powerful, sexually predatory, and strong (Brittan 1989). The imposition of male roles required men to avoid feminine behaviour and characteristics, acquire success and status through breadwinning, be strong and confident, and be daring, aggressive, and violent (Pease 2002a: 22; Brannon 1976). O'Neill (1981) argued that masculinity was oppressive for men because rigid social roles create a fear of femininity and institutionalise sexism and lead to six patterns of social role conflict and strain: (a) restrictive emotionality, (b) socialised control, power, and competitive issues, (c) homophobia, (d) restrictive sexual and affective behaviour, (e) obsession with achievement and success, and (f) health care problems. A wide range of problematic male behaviours such as homophobia, delinquency, violence, and misogyny were taken as signs that masculinity was emotionally hazardous for men being ill-suited to meeting contemporary expectations for emotional intimacy and expressiveness (Carrigan, Connell, and Lee 1987; Clare 2000; Giddens 1992).

Liberal role perspectives maintain men should be helped to adjust and cope with conflicting expectations and rigidity of character associated with personal troubles arising from an oppressive socialisation. The hope of liberal interpretations is that masculinity can be reformed to enable men to develop more expressive characteristics by changing social expectations, for example, through anti-sexist education programmes. Liberal interpretations have also been criticised because they sometimes assume that men and women are equally oppressed and because they underrate the structural and institutional changes that are required to achieve substantial equality between women and men (Pease 2002a). In highlighting men's pain, suffering, and vulnerability and by presenting men as oppressed they tend to perceive masculinity to be passively socialised, deemphasising men's institutionalised power, material interests, and agency (ibid.), and they fail then to explain why more men do not reject dysfunctional role expectations (Segal 1997b).

Repressive masculinities

Sociological theories underpinning the separate spheres ideology have found close companions in mainstream psychoanalytical theories. Psychoanalytical perspectives explain gender identity as the outcome of unconscious sexual–emotional conflicts fashioned through socialisation processes (Elliott 2000). Social forces, in particular parent–child interactions, regulate and repress what are often taken as natural biological impulses. Unconsciously repressed desires or urges, held in check and managed by the ego, exert a significant and incessant influence over gender identification, for example, as transference – projecting remnants of previous relationships onto new ones. Although identities are to a significant extent governed by these hidden emotional relations, the theory suggests that we have the capacity to develop greater levels of agency when we come to understand repressed emotion. A central theme in psychoanalysis is the process through which boys come to repress femininity they feel within themselves, but as with the role theory, there are differing views on why this occurs, how it manifests, and what the implications are for gender equality.

In making sense of this complex terrain, Stockard and Johnson (1992) distinguish between *phallocentric* and *gynecentric* traditions in terms of their impact on gender studies. Stemming from Freud, *phallocentric* perspectives bestow central importance on sexual drives (libido) and the incest taboo surrounding the 'Oedipal Complex' on the process of gender identification. The Freudian view is that gender identification is instigated by the Oedipal Complex between the ages of 2 and 5 through a process in which they come to identify with their same sexed parent. In normal development the boy puts aside a desire for the mother and identifies with the father. The father models masculinity for the boy, who distinguishes himself from women and femininity. The oedipal narrative explains how boys come to identify with their fathers and to repress the sexual bond they have with their mothers because, encountering the incest taboo, they fear their fathers' anger and disapproval will result in their castration. In this way they come to identify with their fathers, masculinity, and heterosexuality (Weeks 2007). Not having a penis, girls experience penis envy rather than a castration anxiety. They cannot make the transition to identify with men, but instead they retain a close symbiotic relationship with their mothers and the subordination of femininity. Patriarchal domination is for Freud the outcome of the 'successful' resolution of the Oedipal Complex; women accept their subordinate status as a result of not possessing the phallus and, consequently, give up on the possibility of power.

Based on different theoretical basis Jungian psychology has advanced similar essentialist arguments about masculinity. Masculinity is perceived as the outcome of the balance between a conscious masculine persona and an unconscious repressed feminine anima – the products of archetypal collective-unconscious representations of gender

(Kahn 2008; Clatterbaugh 1997). Jungian theorists have proposed that masculinity becomes unbalanced and loses its essential grounding in male values such as honour, valour, and courage, when cultural representations of masculinity become feminised (Bly 1990; Berry 1987; Johnson 1986).

Phallocentric traditions have also been usurped to condemn gender inequality by emphasising cultural and social dimensions of Freudianism in ways that undermine biological essentialism (Mitchell 1974; Fast 1993; Tong 2009). They propose, for example, that masculinity is a flight from the inferiority and social powerlessness that femininity represents within a culture that devalues it (Alder 1928, cited in Connell 1995), or within Jungian psychology by proposing that men are out of touch with their feminine side (Rowan 1989). Lacan's re-conceptualisation of the phallus as the symbol of men's dominance in society has been especially influential in explaining how gender is symbolically configured in relation to difference. (Woman is defined as 'other' to man.) While these cultural representations reassure men's power they also signify the inherent instability of masculinity which is destabilised by what it lacks or leaves out (Connell 1995; Segal 1997b; Frosh 1994: 40; Hall 2005).

Phallocentric perspectives are deeply problematic from the point of view of gender equality because gender relations remain trapped by biological or perhaps equally determining culturalist accounts of patriarchy. Despite the incredulity of Freudianism, for many feminists (Fast 1993: 177) their resilience is a symptom of the inability of other theories to adequately explain how the complex internal mechanisms of emotional and cognitive development internalise and embody social and cultural life. Many gender theorists have been unwilling to let Freud go, either because he has given us a masculinised and patriarchal version of a potentially useful theory, or simply because he was wrong and needs to be unmasked.

Gynecentric perspectives mark a shift away from discourses of paternal authority arising from the 19th century with discourses of maternal love in the 20th by emphasising the importance of the infant's relationship and identification with their mother (Horney 1932; Klein 1928). They have challenged Freud's phallocentricism by focussing on positive aspects of female psychology and revaluing the importance of the mothers, but from an egalitarian point of view key theorists, such as Erikson (1965) and Bowlby (1969), have depicted women primarily as nurturers and thus relegating women to caring roles (Stockard and Johnson 1992; Tong 2009).

'Object Relations' perspectives have been especially influential in this tradition. Object relations perspectives view the libido as object-seeking rather than pleasure-seeking, with anxiety and aggression emanating from the separation from the primary love object (Segal 1997b). Instead of focussing on drives they are interested in how the child attaches emotional and cognitive meanings to internalised representations of lost objects which they then assign with great power (Stockard and Johnson 1992). Within Kleinian traditions the symbiotic mother–infant relationship takes precedence over the cultural and paternal. Frosh (1994: 31) notes how the 'mother and infant are so entangled that the experience of one is incorporated into the experience of the other; this is the prototype for all intense experiences throughout life'. The lost feeling of bodily and psychic narcissism is assigned with great power; psychic life is underpinned by the desire to reunite with 'monad' connectivity with mother (ibid.). Gender identity and personality from this perspective are partly the result of the different ways that boys and girls experience this separation process (Craib 1987: 733–6).

'Feminist Object Relations' theories hold that masculinity is constructed in relation to these early psychic-power conflicts arising from men's separation from their mother's love (Doyle 1995; Rubin 1983; Dinnerstein 1977; Chodorow 1978). As an object relations theorist Chodorow is probably the most influential psychoanalyst in masculinities studies. Chodorow argues that the unequal heteronormative division of caring in families produces different social and psychological outcomes for men and women, and this in turn gives rise to different ways of expressing and experiencing caring and emotion throughout life. In her account of gender identity development the daughter experiences a prolonged symbiosis and a narcissistic over-identification with the mother. The daughter, desiring the symbolism of the father, challenges this symbiotic relationship. However, a transfer of affection in the case of the daughter is never complete and this results in the girl always having stronger emotional connections to women. As a result of the mother's early interactions with her daughter a maternal personality identified around nurturing is reproduced (Chodorow 1994).

In contrast, for boys the mother unconsciously perceives her son as 'Other' because of their sex difference and pushes him away. But the pre-oedipal bond between mother and son is still of crucial importance for a healthy sense of self (masculinity) rather than the oedipal father–son relationship. The way that boys are typically driven to separate from their mothers (psychodynamically and in society at large) is not considered normative or healthy (Segal 1997b; Tong 2009). From this view masculinity is precariously held because the incorporation of the mother is seen as a natural process and separation unnatural. The way that masculinity typically develops from this perspective is not an achievement as in Freudian theory but a loss since boys' pre-oedipal identification is considered feminine derived from their oneness with their mother. Severing this important early emotional connection results in the repression of the anxieties and fears caused by the separation. Men do this by denying their femininity and identifying with the power and prestige of their fathers, the essence of male domination and superiority (Chodorow 1978). What they retain is an unconscious fear and envy of their mothers (unconsciously projected to all women) along with a precariously held masculinity (Stockard and Johnson 1992). Men's fear and dread of women prompts them to focus on achievement, establish separate masculine activities with higher status, and devalue women's roles, but their repressed envy and dread may surface as misogyny (see also Dinnerstein 1977). Men have unresolved and repressed feelings over early psychic separation from their mothers that have resulted in their distancing from the characteristics that femininity represents and identifying with the power and prestige of their fathers (Chodorow 1978). A physically and emotionally distant father can result in boys developing an exaggerated masculinity as a defence against an over-identification with the mother. Men come to define masculinity by internally rejecting attachment and dependency and externally by devaluing the feminine and denying attachment to the feminine world (Stockard and Johnson 1992). This results in an ambiguous unstable identity because unconsciously it creates a tension between the need for mother care and the need for distinction and distance. According to Chodorow (1978) the insecurity and precariousness by which masculine identity is achieved means that it is always questioned. Men must continually deny all things feminine including emotions, connection, and intimacy in order to prove their masculinity to others and to reassure self. In other words, masculinity is defined negatively as the alienation from the experience of oneness and wholeness that mother represents (Frosh 1994). Object relations feminism reveals how masculinity devalues the feminine whilst at the same time expecting the permanent nurture and service of women (Segal 1997b: 47). These psychodynamic emotional patterns are held to explain male domination and patriarchy and the gender division of labour.

Chodorow's theory is critiqued on the grounds that it ignores the significance of patriarchal structures by merely addressing differential socialisation within families (Young 1984) as well as ignoring other social and social psychological pressures on men which hamper nurturing masculinity (Kraemer 1995). It is additionally challenged because it is thought to implicate the role of mothering in shaping masculine subjectivity. The mother understands the child as male long before the child has such awareness itself and relates to the child accordingly (Chodorow 1978). A dynamic is created between sons and mothers that foster developmental opposition to femininity. The gender message to boys is that '[h]e must love her and leave her. But above all, he must show that he is nothing like her' (Edley and Wetherell 1996: 99). The irony is that the object relations privileging of the mother–son bond in the construction of masculinities presents a picture of the mother nurturing an oppositional identity desired by society around definitions of masculinity developed by androcentric norms implying that women are responsible for their affectively pathologised children (Edley and Wetherell 1996).

Nonetheless, feminist object relations theories have been influential because they explain male domination and caring subjectivity as the outcome of inequality in early childcare arrangements and propose that altering them can realise egalitarian gender relations (Chodorow 1978; Young 1984; Craib 1987; Stockard and Johnson 1992: 198). Beneath a fragile sense of masculinity lies the conflicted need for men to identify with feminine values of caring, intimacy, and emotional nurturance as a fundamental aspect of our human nature (Chodorow 1994). Distancing and inexpressive masculine emotional subjectivities are not inevitable for men because their existence is based on the lack of availability of salient male figures of love, affection, and nurturing in opposition to the ever-present maternal mother (ibid.: 45).

Frosh (1994) points out that masculinity in many forms of psychoanalytical theory is constructed in relation to difference rather than as having an essence; masculinity is defined by its distance from, and absence of, femininity, which is equated with weakness, passivity, seductiveness, and unreliability. The symbolic disavowal of femininity involves repressing the maternal infantile bond and all the qualities that it represents (ibid.) even if these qualities vary cross-culturally. Drawing from both Lacanian and Kleinian traditions, Frosh (1994: 24) explains that men find femininity and the unconscious terrifying because they symbolise to them irrationality, being exterior and outside of their control. When masculine identity is threatened or becomes unstable, alternatives are repressed. This results in the suppression of femininity and homosexuality, which is a source of men's hatred, fear, domination, and control of women (ibid.: 89). Since women are the primary nurturers in most societies, writing out femininity tends to mean writing out those characteristics defined as feminine nurturing practices within that culture. This view holds for several different schools of psychoanalysis.

Psychoanalysis has had a significant, if not uncontested, influence on gender studies. Its influence comes from its potential to explain the complexity and depth of emotional conflicts and commitments to sexual–gender identity. Psychoanalysis offers complex explanations for sexual difference, the dynamics of gender, and relations of dominance and subordination. It allows for human agency and recognises the role of emotions and the unconscious in action and subjectivity (Elliott 2000) as emotions such as love and shame merge into a dynamic model of social life (Young 1984). Psychoanalysis adds depth and complexity to sociological explanations and helps to explain the 'intensities' of male misogyny, violence, and gendered insecurities (Segal 1997b). Many psychotherapeutic traditions provide a useful lens by which to understand the intersection between power and emotion in caring relations (Bondi 2008). Nonetheless, despite the contribution of psychoanalysis to gender studies its central thrust is deeply conservative and patriarchal (Segal 1997b; Connell 1987; Zaretsky 1994), and this has divided gender studies about its usefulness (Pease 2002a). Psychoanalytical theory is widely decried for its inferiorisation of women, biological determinism, and phallocentricism (Stockard and Johnson 1992) as well as a methodological individualism that reduce social life to individual psychology (Segal 1997b; Zaretsky 1994). Accordingly it mistakes culturally and historically constructed gender practices for fixed and universal character traits and in so doing supports patriarchy (Connell 2005).

Reflexive masculinities

Though an umbrella term for differing perspectives, microsociological theories typically share a view of the gender as an active – rather than passive – construction, as actors assign meanings to shared symbolic categories (Lorber and Farrell 1991; West and Zimmerman 1991). From this perspective gender is something we do in our everyday interactions, variously construed as a performance, accomplishment, drama, ritual, or a negotiation as actors construct identities from below (Roberts 2006). Gender is not fixed, stable, or secure even if it appears so; it is subject to ongoing construction and interpretation, but gender is not necessarily easy to alter because its construction is constrained by interactional rules, available social discourses, material constraints, and resilient primary identities laid down during early life (Jenkins 2004). Some microsociological theories stand accused of reducing social life to individual calculated actions, or to having an overly instrumental and cognitive bias that overlook the emotional and the unconscious nature of our actions (Roberts 2006). Microsociological theories, however, have challenged the determinist tenets of early gender theory by emphasising the rational, reflexive, and interactional construction of gender through social processes (Ryle 2012). In my view they have more explanatory potential when combined with perspectives that acknowledge the weight of social forces on social actions and, in this respect, they have influenced the two perspectives which I contrast here.

The first approach is manifest in the theories of Giddens and Beck who emphasise the agency side of reflexive-identity choices constructed in the context of individualised self-interested norms of late-modern societies (Beck, Giddens, and Lasch 1994). Giddens (1991) offers a model of reflexivity in which actors continually narrate a self-identity ('project of the self'), founded on the belief that we can discover an authentic or true self, or continually make, remake, or improve it. The focus on self arises from the need to provide life with meaning within the context of a rapidly changing late-modernity where older sources of identity such as class, religion, gender and race are eroding. One of these significant changes is the transformation of intimate relationships, marked by the de-traditionalisation of family, caring and sexual relations, and the concurrent dominance of norms favouring emotional intimacy based on equality of respect (Giddens 1992: 87). In Giddens's (1992: 58–61) model the ideals of romantic love (where falling in love is expected to lead to a life-long relationship) are being supplanted by ideals of the 'pure relationship' (relationships from which we seek mutual emotional satisfaction) and norms of 'confluent love' (love contingent on continual negotiation). This new intimacy we desire requires ongoing emotional communication with others and with self within a context of 'interpersonal equality'. In this model intimate relations are contingent on individualised self-interested negotiations resulting in ongoing re-evaluations and renegotiations as people reflect on their identities and reassess their relational needs in respect of their individual life project. Emotional relations are not then institutionally stabilised or secured, for example, through marriage and this has implications for our sense of 'ontological security'.

Giddens (1992: 117–18) argues that men are subject to new discourses of caring masculinity (especially of fatherhood) as involved, emotionally competent, and nurturing, yet their traditional dependency on women's emotional labour means they resist women's expectation for an ethic of 'confluent love'. Though men are increasingly expected by women to meet these new relational ideals, Giddens (1992: 247, 1994) views the rise of the 'pure relationship' as problematic because men are neither structurally nor psychically prepared for what emotional intimacy requires. Rigid psychological constructions of masculinity, he argues, leave many men with great difficulty in loving others as equals. Giddens notes that men have the capability to love but come to rely on women to do the work of intimacy by generally (although not exclusively) becoming emotionally co-dependent in interpersonal relations. Men are 'able to offer love and care to those inferior in power' such as women and children, or peers but are reluctant to be seen as vulnerable themselves or to disclose emotions in public (Giddens 1992: 131). Giddens (1992: 114) draws on Chodorow to suggest that male language emphasises deprivation as much as it does dominance. On the one hand, post-oedipal masculinity is about the 'defensive repudiation of nurturance' and the identification with the rewards of masculinity, whilst on the other the early sense of oneness with the mother is experienced as a loss and hence a deep insecurity (ibid.: 115–16). Giddens argues that men are challenged to develop a narrative of self-identity that hides the memory of early separation experiences but rather than assuming men are out of touch with their feelings he suggests 'we should say that many men are unable to construct a narrative of self that allows them to come to terms with an increasingly democratisised and reordered sphere of emotional life' (ibid.: 117). Men resist equality in interpersonal relations by avoiding emotional intimacy and reassert their dominance through violence (especially sexual against women) as the sexual–gender order and 'female complicity' breaks down (ibid.: 122).

Giddens acknowledges that people have differential access to life-choices as the ideals of the 'pure relationship' are mediated by class, race, gender, and religion, but the general thrust of his theory emphasises choice and agency. Notwithstanding men's resistances to equality in emotional intimacy, on the whole, Giddens offers us a positive and progressive perspective on masculinities and care because the norms of emotional equality are increasingly ascendant. Intimate emotional relations are also understood to instigate wider social transformations and as Smart and Neale (1999) observe they are a source of agency for women, who by demanding relationships that are more egalitarian and emotionally intimate have paved the way for an emotional revolution (Giddens 1992). Nonetheless, Smart and Neale (1999: 140) argue that Giddens's reflective project of the self is a masculinised project because it is focussed on individualised life goals with little account of other-centred care rationalities, especially for children, although Beck (1992), they point out does. Similar to Giddens, Beck sees modern Western societies characterised by a decline in the importance of collective identities such as social class and a much greater increase in individualisation; they become focussed on self-improvement. The decline in collective forms of solidarity means that individuals are exposed to greater risk and they have to manage the anxieties this generates. For Beck and Beck-Gernsheim love takes on a particular salience as people try to give life a sense of meaning and purpose and a feeling of belonging; love has become the new opiate of the masses that has overtaken traditional collective forms of solidarity in providing meaning to alienated lives (Smart and Neale 1999: 16). Children are expected to fill the void left as collective sources of identity decline resulting in more emotionally intense child–parent relations that place great hope as well as great pressure on them. This is true for men too. Compared to traditional fathers children provide a focus for men's involvement in families (Holter 1995: 127).

Giddens, Beck and Beck-Gernsheim propose that people are real-ising increasing individual freedom and agency and consequently greater equality as norms of emotional intimacy and love prevail. A second approach is provided by Bourdieu and Connell who offer a more constrained picture of masculine reflexivity by placing greater weight on men's power as a domineering force in gender relations. Men are active in acquiring domineering forms of gender that give them power and legitimacy within the gender order and, as I have emphasised, doing masculinity additionally involves the dynamic of writing out and subor-dinating femininity. For Connell (2005), doing gender involves bodily reflexive practices which for men can be a source of pleasure, and it can provide a sense of accomplishment and esteem because of the patriar-chal privileges it realises in terms of access to resources, power, and sexu-ality. However, doing masculinity is also a fraught terrain, containing tensions and uncertainty as men experience pressure to perform socially acceptable masculinity in public. Masculinities are constructed within the context of standards of heteronormativity and as the antithesis of femininity (Brittan 1989). Masculinities are intensively policed by men for signs of femininity and homosexuality because it signifies subor-dination (Connell 1987, 1995; Kimmel 2003; Weeks 1985). Therefore, hegemonic or domineering masculinity suppresses cultures of femi-ninity among men who in turn repress their femininity within. This places men under pressure to perform domineering forms of masculinity characterised by physical control, aggression, conquering, competition, autonomy, independence, hierarchy, and emotional distance (Gilbert and Gilbert 1998; Bem 1993; Kaufman 1994).

Within this context, men's relationships with other men are seen as preoccupied by competition, suspicion and rivalry, and being in control (Buchbinder 1994: 37; hooks 2004: 155; Frosh 1995; Seidler 1989). Power and competition become central forces within exclusive male spaces (Brod 1990: 133; Giddens 1992: 126). Men's friendships are implicated in the reproduction of dominant gender relations whether on the sports field, bar, or business meeting, by excluding women and forming exclusive rites of passage to the cultural and social capital tied up in all male spaces (Remy 1990: 45). Men's anxieties about subordination find expression within all male groups as homophobia and misogyny (Cockburn 1990: 83). Male-dominated spaces are governed by restrictive emotional and behavioural codes (Remy 1990). Within sports these codes allow men to be physically close yet emotionally distanced in relationships (Messner 1998, 2001). The precariousness of masculinity also means that performing masculinity can cause anxiety because it risks failure or being unmasked. The social imperative to demonstrate masculinity in front of other men and women is significant because failure or violation risks being defined as feminine. Men are under pressure to be seen to be strong, virile, commanding and in control, and men feel particularly vulnerable in the context of illness, aging, injury, impotence, or sexual 'deviance' (Fenton and Pitter 2010; Carlson 2008). The performance of masculinity itself is a major investment of emotional energy as men seek to avoid 'giving off' contradictory messages about their masculinity to save face in the presence of others whether through joking, bravado, or avoidance (Connell 2002: 81). Brittan (1989) describes disciplinary processes that embody 'masculinising' social practices in the body and exclude 'feminising' social practices when men are encouraged to deny and repress any feelings and bodily experiences which run counter to dominant masculinity. Boys learn that their status in the world depends on them distancing themselves from femininity and constantly proving that they are men, particularly among other boys and men (Kimmel 2000: 126). The result is 'a masculinity that is always willing to take risks, able to experience pain and not submit to it, driven constantly to accumulate (power, money, sexual partners) ... [yet] ... Masculinity is unresolved – never able to be fully demonstrated, subject to eternal doubt. Masculinity needs constant validation; its pursuit is relentless' (Kimmel 1990: 100).

Conclusion

It is clear in the literature that men are relatively care-free in terms of sharing the burden of care with women and availing of many of its benefits. Although there are aspects of caring that men do that are relatively invisible (Arber and Gilbert 1989), men's lack of caring is also invisible because of the care-free assumption that underpins hegemonic masculinities. Optimistic assessments of what has occurred will argue that gender egalitarianism has modified and modernised gender relations, however, slowly. Pessimistic assessments on the other hand declare that women continue to do at least double the care and domestic work of men, and women's increased participation in the formal labour market has not been matched by men's contribution to unpaid caring resulting effectively in some women doing a 'double-shift' (O'Connor and Dunne 2006; Drew, Wmerck, and Mahon 1998; Bubeck 1995; Hochschild 1989).

The discipline of masculinities studies has extensively addressed the relationship between power and masculinities and a central theme of this discourse is the way this involves writing out femininity from men's lives. What is sometimes implied but less explicitly addressed is how hegemonic masculinities are also care-free. Since hegemonic masculinities (with some exceptions) write out characteristics culturally defined as feminine, feminised nurturing practices tend to symbolise subordination to men. Nurturing practices that are coded feminine signify dependency, passivity, femininity, and vulnerability, the very antithesis of hegemonic masculinities. Feminised nurturing practices and identities are Othered, relegated to lower status, and often vilified as homosexual. In the minds of men they are disassociated with the recognition, respect, power, resources, admiration, and acceptance that men compete for and expect in the public sphere, and opting out of hegemonic masculinity can mean men embrace an illegitimate masculinity.

The affective relations of masculinities have been under-theorised in terms of men's involvement in emotional and caring labour. Emotions can be understood as the bodily reflective resources men deploy when 'doing' gender. Processes of hegemonic masculinities are at work when men suppress nurturing, enact dominant masculinities, and disembody an ethic of loving and caring. Constructing masculinities in these ways gives men the symbolic capital that ensures their legitimation as men – especially by other men – or ensures the subordination of other men. These emotional relations become taken-for-granted and naturalised and deeply embedded in how men relate, and this can extract an affective toll on men's lives. Hegemonic masculinities encourage men to feel shame and inadequate when they cannot live up to dominant goals, and in the process men deny their needs for intimacy and inter-dependence and feelings of vulnerability. My argument that hegemonic masculinities write out caring from men's lives should not imply that caring and dominance cannot coexist. Men can be dominant in some fields of life yet be caring and nurturing in others. An example of this is found in homo-social, homophobic, and misogynist male bonding practices where caring for other men coexists with the denigration of women or gay men (Curry 1991). Sports and other masculinised institutions fulfil men's emotional need for bonding and intimacy and at the same time offer a means to display competitive masculinity (Gilbert and Gilbert 1998; McKay, Messner, and Sabo 2000; Clare 2000). There again, it is possible to display emotional vulnerability and dominance at the same time. Karobov provides an excellent analysis of how men negotiate vulnerability when their female partners refuse to perform emphasised femininities. In this context the more traditional reasser-tion of macho masculinity is replaced with more subtle and socially acceptable emotional strategies:

> Enacting failure became masculine performance art, allowing men to mitigate the vulnerability of sexual rejection by reclaiming the masculine 'virtues' of confidence, detachment, and self-assuredness. Using self-depreciation to perform failure indexes a victim identity that effaces the young men's agency in stories about women's rejec-tion of their sexual desires. Self-depreciation thus creates a victim position that can be playfully tolerated and mocked by young men. Celebrating your own failure is not only self-inoculating but it also immunises other men against the dreaded humour (and masculinity) killer sympathy. Doing self-depreciation is thus the vehicle for male socialization, working as a method of highlighting your own flaws so others would not have to. It frees men to cope vicariously and laugh cathartically at their vulnerabilities from a position of safety and detachment. Rather than challenge oppressive gender relations, doing ordinariness through nonchalance rearticulates power (and thus anchors it) at subtler and more difficult to detect levels of social practice. (Korobov 2011: 69–70)

The use of diverse emotional strategies to assert dominance should not imply that men do not themselves need affective relations as a source of meaning and fulfilment in their lives. Indeed recent masculinities scholarship is beginning to focus on how men resist hegemonic masculinities in daily life (Korobov 2009; Kahn, Brett, and Holmes 2011). Men can remain conflicted about the role of love and care, both in terms of recognising their own emotional needs and meeting them, and in terms of meeting the needs of significant others. But caring relations are dynamic, negotiated and reciprocal; to reap the rewards of love and care one must engage in the work of nurturing others.

4
Masculinities and Emotions

Connell and Bourdieu allege men are collectively and structurally privileged; to be a man is to feel entitled to patriarchal advantages. This gender dualism in masculinities' studies, particularly in Bourdieu, makes an important point about how the gender order is structured to privilege men and disadvantage women. Men receive a patriarchal dividend in terms of higher pay and better working conditions, command more power and have one's (heterosexual) sex politically represented, and men's interests are taken as the cultural and universal standard (Connell 1987; Stutcliff 2001; Fraser 1995; Richardson 1998). A dualistic perspective, however, stands accused of overlooking the extent and nature of differences among men and between men and women and simplifying the complex intersection between gender and power. Seidler (2006) has argued that the understanding of men's lives only in terms of power makes it difficult to theorise men's experiences of powerlessness and vulnerability, nonetheless it is also true that theorising men's vulnerability can make it difficult to theorise men's power. Masculinities studies are apprehensive about theorising power and vulnerability but in truth men's lives are lived out in complex ways expressing both power and vulnerability, and men inhabit multiple relational identities and social locations. We cannot appreciate masculinities without understanding relations of power and dominance, but we cannot understand power and dominance without also appreciating men's emotional lives. Moreover, we cannot deconstruct male power without reconstructing the emotional lives of men.

This chapter kick starts the analysis of care and masculinity by exploring the intersection between power and emotional life in the care conversations with the men. It grapples with the tension expressed above, and found within many other writings about men's lives, that there is an emotional dynamic to dominance, but that this in itself is not the entire picture. How can we make sense of this contradiction between the entrenched problem of gender domination and our basic reciprocal need for love, care, and solidarity? This chapter highlights four important emotional–power dynamics that can be held to account for this.

First, hegemonic masculinity, defined in terms of a hierarchy of power, status and the command of resources is a highly valued social status which men desire. The competitive dynamic which results among men is a driving force in men's lives. Second, the flip side to this is how feeling a failure in that regard can create a sense of inadequacy and status anxiety for many men, emotions which can contribute to the domineering practices of homophobia, misogyny and gender-based-violence as men seek to deflect feelings of shame and project inferiority onto others. Third, the denial of weakness and vulnerability feeds careless performances of masculinity through excessive risk-taking behaviours coupled with the renunciation of caring for self or seeking support. Fourth, men seek to avoid feeling illegitimate as men by evading primary caring, especially when being a carer meets the reproach of others, or makes them feel insignificant and invisible because it precludes them developing legitimate symbolic capital. These latter concerns are especially acute for men who fall outside institutionalised heteronormative structures and social expectations.

Socially valued masculinities

Key to appreciating men's lives is to understand what defines a socially valued masculinity within a given cultural and social context; what forms of capital, embodied dispositions, and social locations are prized by men and how are they evolving or changing? The heterosexual breadwinner and the celibate priest, for example, were two hegemonic ideals for men in modern Ireland (Ferguson 2002), yet to be a priest in contemporary Ireland is arguably a spoiled identity associated with paedophilia (see Ferguson 1995; Keenan 2011; Loseke 2003); the married heterosexual breadwinner is being challenged as a dominant norm. What is common about hegemonic masculinity across cultures is their relation to power, resources and status and, additionally as I will argue throughout, to care.

Legitimate masculinity for the men in the study was in various ways to have power and status associated with particular cultural and economic resources of which paid work was central. Paid work was a major signifier of masculine identity and means of recognition for the men. Not to deny the significance of other interests, or the multiplicity of identities operating in men's lives, including sport, for example (Robinson 2008). It was nonetheless through paid work that men acquired economic and cultural status. Paid work was still perceived as burdensome by some – something they 'got sucked into', 'not the central part of life', 'a means to an end', and a 'struggle' – but it was narrated positively by many – a source of 'security', 'enjoyment', 'satisfaction', 'interest', 'freedom', 'dedication', 'success', and 'fulfilment'.

Paid work was also seen as highly competitive. Fionn, a young (25) married father, stated: 'I do enjoy my working life but I think I'm better than the position I am in as a worker. I think if I was one step up the ladder right now I would be happy but I am still aiming for that. I feel that I am just one-step behind where I want to be at the moment.' Fionn felt that rising the occupational 'ladder' was crucial to 'succeed', 'keep your life on track', and 'to make sure that you don't fail'. Cathal (58) talked about paid work in similar competitive terms. Now retired, he ran his own business, but unlike Fionn he spoke of being a very reluctant participant in competitive masculinity, stating: 'I didn't find it enjoyable. I'm not a competitive person ... I haven't got the killer instinct that it takes to be a good businessman.'

Paid work was important but it was not the only sense in which class status was articulated. Denis was a member of a secret male society comprised of elite men. He noted how the symbolic capital he felt legitimated masculinity and how this related to feeling superior or inferior, commenting: 'if you come from a stately home, then you really don't care too much about how you look or what you drive around in, but if you come from a slightly more humble background, then ... you feel you've got to prove [yourself] to your neighbour that ... you need to be smart and you've got to be well-dressed, and you've got to be driving a nice shiny new Merc or a BMW or something.' Many men might agree that these resources are socially valued by some men, but the capital that takes symbolic form will often vary with racial or class position. Eddie, a community worker with marginalised men, emphasised alternate means by which marginalised men legitimated their masculinity since they had limited access to resources:

[S]ome men would be held in greater esteem than others ... [T]hat can be the lads who are the big [drug] dealers in the town, who would be looked up to by the younger lads. It could be as simple as the lad who is a good pool player [or] ... a good story teller ... [T]here are lads who would be sneered at; you would hear the lads say 'Sure he's only a fucking ejit' ... It's not really economic status but its status in other terms; it varies from the lad who can play pool to the lad who can talk to the Guards [Irish Police]; that kind of thing. (Eddie, community worker)

What Eddie felt symbolically valuable to these men was not so much material success (although it may also be), as 'self-worth, self-esteem a sense of belonging' and the feeling of having 'something to contribute to the people around me! I'm a person of worth! I'm not stupid! I'm not a scumbag! I'm not a wanker! I'm not a waster!' It was a sense of respect and recognition interconnected with feeling accepted, appreciated, and admired. These men, Eddie felt, were totally marginalised and loathed by mainstream society:

Sometimes you hear about men being like a powerful group, a dominant group, an oppressive group. It isn't completely fair because these people don't feel it, or see it, and their lives are not really like that ... Society has been very uncaring for them ... [They're] shat on by the capitalist-patriarchal system. (ibid.)

It made no sense to Eddie, therefore, to conceive of the lives of the men he worked with and gave support to in terms of power and domination. A major problem for them as Eddie saw it was 'you're supposed to be strong with a woman at home, and so the lads are fed all that stuff, but the lads' capability of retaining those goals are completely different. So you're constantly being fed this thing that your success and self-esteem are based on A but if you get as far up as F you'll be doing well'. Eddie understood the problems experienced by the men he worked with to be materially grounded in class and racial oppression, but also reinforced by affective issues. There is a complexity to marginalised masculinities that involves both power and subordination (Cheng 2008), but there is also a caring dimension; they can be despised, feared, unloved and feel uncared for within the society, and their emotional capability to realise competitive expectations for men (and I would argue hegemonic) can be very limited.

Shameful masculinities

A chief dynamic in doing dominance for men is to deny weakness. Men look for legitimacy in the public sphere but in private life there can be a conflict between the need for love and intimacy and maintaining a feeling of superiority. The rationale for power and dominance coexists often with conflicted internal needs for nurturing, caring, and dependence. The measuring of self-worth against acquisitions of power, status, and resources can result in incessant self-comparison with other men (Seidler 1997). Kimmel (2003: 57) points to the shame that men feel when they fall short of hegemonic expectations. Drawing on Goffman he claims that there is only 'one complete, unblushing male' in American society: he is White, Anglo-Saxon, Protestant, Middle-Class, and has a recent record in sports. Regardless of the particular cultural hegemonic characteristics, inability to live up to hegemonic masculinity within a particular cultural context instils a sense of shame in boys and men which becomes an internal shaming voice (Kimmel 2003; hooks 2004). The hegemonic script of masculinities instils an expectation or promise of privilege creating a sense of indignation when unrealised (Seidler 1989; Connell 2005; Kimmel 1990; hooks 2004: 117). Eddie understood the class and racial marginalisation that many of the men he worked with experience, to be also affectively based; these men, he felt, experienced their masculinity as shameful. It is difficult for marginalised men with low status and limited access to resources to feel valued as men (e.g. Cleary et al. 2004), but all men can feel shamed by 'failing' to live up to hegemonic expectations. Elite men, for example, tend to be highly driven and competitive whose focus on maintaining power is caught up with denial of care and emotional distance (Donaldson and Poynting 2007).

Men's reactions to feeling shame and inferiority may take several forms but denial and repression are common responses. Feelings of superiority can be reasserted through misogynistic, racist, or homophobic practices (Seidler 1989: 171; Gilbert and Gilbert 1998; Mac án Ghaill 1994 ; Kaufman 1994). Men's feelings of demoralisation and emasculation in public life are associated especially with displaying power and status within the family (Segal 1997b: 214; Seidler 2003) and several men in the study, including Tom, Peter, Eddie, Fran, Tommy, Geoff, Alex, and Paddy, spoke about intimate care relations becoming a dumping ground for men's feelings of shame in the form of gender-based violence, homophobia, misogyny, and suicide, and there was a sense in which marginalised men who held low status were especially prone to a feeling of failure and inadequacy. Travellers, for example, are one of the most marginalised minorities in Ireland (The Equality Authority 2006). Peter was a community worker and, ethnically, a Traveller, and Eddie and Tom had also worked extensively with Traveller men. Tom felt that marginalised men including Traveller men's experiences of powerlessness and class and ethnic oppression often fed domineering practices:

> [G]uys who realise they are in poor form because of something else and go home and have a row with the wife ... [G]uys who would be on the housing waiting list and would have a meeting with the County Council people, [then] go home in bad form and the wife would be saying 'You promised me we'd be in a house this time last year', and everything blows up ... [I]t's internalised and it's blamed on themselves not being articulate enough and not being able to state their case the same as a country fella, you know in the housing office. (Tom, community worker)

Pressures on men to perform and to compete among men for status can make it difficult for men to establish intimate loving relationships because the enactment of intimate emotions in public threatens men's sense of masculinity (Seidler 1997). Seidler (1989) suggests that by trying to live up to the dominant masculinity, men hide or shut off their feelings, beliefs, and intuitions which do not concur with dominant images.

Men's violence against women is especially notable in intimate relationships where vulnerability is exposed, by exerting power to fend off feeling weak and powerless (hooks 2004: 58–60). Sexual violence reflects men's feelings of insecurity, fear of women, and the lack of traditional means to exert control (Clare 2000; Rachel 2002). Hegemonic heterosexuality rewards men through the cultural promise of sexual gratification, but it is also a significant source of male anxiety. The relentless and compulsive desire it generates leave men feeling threatened, confused, and vulnerable when it cannot be fulfilled (Weeks 1994; hooks 2004; Metcalf and Humphries 1985; Segal 1997b; Brod 1990). Male violence is tied to a fear of intimacy, the rejection of feminine elements of self, and as an assertion of dominant masculinity in the eyes of other men (Frosh 1995; Clare 2000; Buchbinder 1994: 36).

Hegemonic masculinity is also expressed through homophobia and the rejection of effeminacy (Kimmel 2003), serving to repress the 'feminine' in all men and not just for those involved (Segal 1997a). Alex was a support worker for gay men. He alleged that this dominator model operated in how men marked their masculinity through the public rejection and policing of homosexuality:

> Homophobia is used almost on a daily basis to police the boundaries of gender, to police masculinity and to set areas in behaviours and

thoughts and attitudes of what is ok and what is not ok. That is still a very big stick for people to either beat themselves with or for people to get beaten with ... [There are] quite raw experiences of homophobia and marginalisation, ... stigmatisation or isolation which may have come from those experiences. (Alex, support worker for gay men)

As with Tom and Eddie, in Alex's account it was the 'internal wounds in terms of the harm to their own self-esteem, harm to their own self-image' that make men feel 'left behind'. In their personal stories Simon (48), Angus (43), and Pascal (48) all describe struggling to come to terms with their homosexuality in the context of a heterosexist and homophobic society. The pervasiveness of homophobia especially in boys' schools is a key factor in constructing masculinities that deny the feminine and consequently nurturing dimensions of masculinity and has major effects on men's health and well-being (Devine et al. 2006; O'Higgins-Norman 2009, 2008; DHC 2008). Boys' fear of being labelled inferior within the gender hierarchies of schools ironically contributes to the bullying of those perceived as different, disabled, weaker, or gay (Lodge 2005; Minton et al. 2008; O'Higgins-Norman, Goldrick, and Harrison 2010). Seidler (1997: 38) argues men's fear of 'gayness' and 'femininity' is all linked to the suppression of emotion which is 'experienced as a threat to the rule of reason'. Thus to do dominance is to disembody emotion, deny emotional needs, and actively reject signs of 'weakness'. Messner (2001) explains how emotional intimacy between men is intensively policed and managed because they are emotional spaces where ones manliness is exposed and judged by other men. These intimate emotional encounters between men intensify feelings of self-consciousness, shyness, competitiveness, aggression, and bravado. Men often employ misogynist and homophobic humour during these encounters in order to manage the 'schizophrenic' tension between desires for intimacy on the one hand and an imperative to prove masculinity by denying it on the other. Hierarchical relations between men and women and among men are much appreciated within the field of masculinities studies, and the emotional dynamics associated with them are often alluded to. Gender-based violence and homophobic violence within intimate relations are two ways by which men assert dominance over others and defend their sense of power as men. These practices are also the antithesis of care, but they are also powerful. Men's emotional lives, their intimate care relations and feelings are central to how these masculine practices are maintained.

Careless masculinities

Dominant and competitive masculinities can have psychological and physical costs for men (Clare 2000: 81). The gender order, therefore, can also be 'toxic' for men's well-being in the form of high rates of injury, illness, mortality, disproportionate levels of imprisonment and victimisation, and widespread patterns of relational conflict (Connell 2002). Men's attempts to live up to hegemonic standards lead to a wide range of personal problems with which many men struggle, not least their health, education, and emotional well-being. The cultural imposition of hegemonic masculinity leads men to suppress their needs in an attempt to become an impossible masculine product of the mythical 'real' man (Kaufman 1994: 144). As well as providing men with access to power, a domineering mindset may be a contradictory experience that can 'include dehumanisation and brutalisation; omnipotence, sense of importance and arrogance; sense of confidence; restrictions on sexuality and emotional vulnerability; sense of superiority; isolation and personal insecurity' (Moane 1999: 23). Masculine emotional norms can impoverish men's lives by alienating men from loving relations (Kaufman 1994; Messner 2001; Philips 1993). Fran was a Catholic priest. He shared this view reflecting on his experience attending to the spiritual needs of men within his religious community and among his ministry. Denouncing the expectation that men should possess dominating attributes such as physical strength and aggression, Fran commented that men 'come up against difficulties in their lives in terms of relationships, in terms of success and failure, in terms of jobs, in terms of qualifications, in terms of acceptance in peer groups'. Dominant images of masculinity encourage men to be hard on themselves covering up their vulnerability within a competitive male culture where comparison is commonplace and men are driven to prove their masculinity to self and others to sustain a sense of mastery and self-control (Seidler 1997). Within this climate it becomes very difficult for men to accept themselves because they are constantly trying to prove, plan, and achieve and consequently they are living in the future (Seidler 1989: 196).

Managing feelings within the context of competitive masculinities is itself an emotional work. Men who feel insecure in their masculinity are often engaged in intense emotional work to convince themselves and others that they are 'real' men (hooks 2004), and may be likely to define their masculinity inflexibly and perform hyper-masculine behaviour (Kimmel 1990). Men's investment in masculinity is a key risk-factor in men's violence (Whitehead 2005). Risk-taking, bravado, and machismo are typical ways of reassuring masculinity. Inglis (2006), for example, describes the habitus of Irish upper-class youth within a highly competitive gender order that ties male honour to violence, alcohol consumption, and the policing of homosexuality through public shaming. Anger is one of the few socially acceptable ways that some young men can express pain because it is associated with 'strength' and manliness for all men, regardless of class, race, and family circumstances. Young men's investment in being tough and competitive mitigates the feeling of rejection and fear (Blye 1996; Seidler 1989: 45).

Courtenay (2000: 1388) argues that because risk-taking beliefs and strategies are signifiers of masculinity, noting how high-risk health behaviours act as resources or strategies that men use to construct gender which 'contributes both to the defining of one's self as gendered and to the social conventions of gender... In this way, males use health beliefs and behaviours to demonstrate dominant – and hegemonic – masculine ideals that clearly establish them as men'. McEvoy and Richardson (2004: 7) blame men's risk-taking behaviours on men's 'traditional values and attitudes towards gender... Boys and young men continue to be socialised to appear in control, to be strong and to take risks; thus reinforcing their exposure to illness and accidental deaths'. Similarly Segal (1997b: xix) concludes 'it is men themselves, and their attachment to traditional ideas of "manhood", which are very much part of the problem. Many – if not most men – suffer, at least in some ways, as they feel driven to deny their own vulnerabilities, to compete with each other individually, and to dominate more vulnerable groups of men; especially those they constitute as a threat to their own manhood-gay men and ethnic minorities'. Risk-taking is an attempt to present a front of being invulnerable, autonomous, and invincible but gendered risk-taking is highly correlated with poor sexual, emotional, and physical health outcomes (Broom and Tovey 2009). Compared to women men have higher mortality rates at all ages (especially lower-class men) for all leading causes of death (especially road traffic accidents and suicide) and are also more likely than women to leave their conditions until they have deteriorated (Mc Evoy and Richardson 2004; DHC 2008). Significant health disparities are evident not only between men and women but also among men (Directorate-General for Health and Consumers 2011). Masculinity is associated with poor lifestyle choices (Gough and Conner 2006) and avoiding medical or other care unless that care is perceived to be vital in restoring a sense of masculinity (O'Brien, Hunt, and Hart 2005; Hale, Grogan, and Willott 2010). Risk-taking performances and strategies among men are mediated by class, 'race', and age and vary depending on the resources available to them and their negative effects are disproportionately spread among different groups depending on their location in the gender order (Connell 2000: 182–4). Low-status men tend to be higher risk-takers because their masculinity is constantly tested and undermined (Courtenay 2000) and because they hold more rigid and inflexible definitions of masculinity that denies vulnerability (Springer and Mouzon 2011). In general white, middle-class, heterosexual, and able-bodied men are better protected against affective deprivations (Baker et al. 2004: 8–9). But risk-taking practices are also socially acceptable evidenced by the fact, for example, of how difficult it is to get men's health concerns taken seriously politically (Richardson and Carroll 2009).

Clare (2000) argues that although femininity has been historically associated with weakness and illness, increasingly masculinity is associated with pathology. He suggests men are like a bursting dam of unmet needs and consequently are often depressed and angry. A common way for men to deal with these unmet emotional needs is through denial and repression. Depression exists in men because of the demand for perfection that is denied to most men (hooks 2004: 158). Masculinities' denial of hurt and vulnerability make it difficult for many men to acknowledge and process grief and sadness, often grieving in isolation without rituals of mourning (hooks 2004: 161). In the care conversations male suicide was raised by several men as an issue that had affected them personally (Fran, Alex, Geoff, Tom, Eddie, Paul, Tommy, Paddy, and Greg). Clare (2000: 83) interprets the growth in male suicide as a consequence of men's 'emotional control, reticence, stoicism, independence and vulnerability'. He argues that whilst women tend to 'cry out' men are more likely to 'lash out'. Male suicide, he argues, is a demonstration of the ultimate keeping of control combined with the impact of changing social and biological factors that intensifies suicidal propensity. Male suicide is particularly resilient because men are unable or unwilling to access emotional support and social networks as men are less likely than women to seek help and support for physical, emotional, and relational difficulties or even to recognise that they need support (ibid.). The way in which hegemonic masculinity denies vulnerability and prohibits the expression of emotion fuels suicidal behaviour amongst vulnerable men (Cleary 2012). High rates of male suicide, especially for young men, cannot be explained by 'notions of a generalised crisis' among men because they fail to account for differentials in power and economic status showing that it is particular groups of men that find change challenging whereas others embrace and benefit from it (Cleary and Brannick 2007).

One of the core themes in the literature on men's caring centres on men's reticence to acknowledge the need for support because they are conditioned to feel independent, invulnerable, and self-reliant, and they have not learned to communicate emotionally and talk about intimate personal problems (Cleary 2005; Clare 2000; Brod 1990; Mahalik, Good, and Englar-Carlson 2003; Möller-Leimkühler 2002; Jakupcak, Tull, and Roemer 2005; Hoyt 2009; Broom and Cavenagh 2010). Male primary carers are not necessarily an exception to this. In fact Seidler argues (1989) men can care for others easier than recognising their own needs and caring adequately for self because it exposes their vulnerability and dependence which is at odds with their vision of self. Male caregivers can find it difficult to seek support because it means admitting vulnerability and they can also have less extensive friendships and care networks to draw from than women. They also feel it is their responsibility to manage the home situation alone (Weinland 2009; Applegate and Kaye 1993; Fraser and Warr 2009). Dave (34) saw this emotional stoicism affect his father's caring for his wife:

> [My Dad] is very stoical... He will come and ask me if he needs me to help out or my mum will sometimes ask me, 'Oh I think your dad wants to do this but I don't want to ask him because he has to look after me',... my dad is aware of not putting upon me... I think my father has dealt with it in a very physical way rather than an emotional way... he would say 'oh I'm fine, I'm fine but it's very hard on your mum'. So he wouldn't necessarily talk about the way he feels about it... but never really about where he is right now... I think he concerns himself a great deal with her needs rather than how he perceives himself as a carer. (Dave, 34)

It is a problem for men to admit need or vulnerability in caring because they have inherited a strong sense of autonomy. They do not want to admit needing help:

> I prefer outside help [than asking extended family]. I am not good at accepting help actually; I am not good at asking for help. I can accept home help because they are getting paid for it... I am not good at somebody offering, if an aunt say offered to you know 'why don't you call me for an hour?' I generally wouldn't take her up on the offer. That is to do with a problem I think I have with accepting help. (Angus, 43)

Based on his experiences as older men's support worker Paddy similarly argued that older men were reluctant to admit the need for care and support because it contradicted their sense of self-reliance so intrinsic to their sense of masculinity:

> Country people are very proud. Pride is an awful problem especially with single men or bachelor men like you know they would be too proud. I know people who would be living in very poor circum-stances...Housing accommodation is available to them but they won't accept it because they wouldn't accept a hand out as they call it so it really is a problem with some people...It is something that happens in the generation of men and it probably goes back to the fact that a lot older men were children back when Ireland was a very, very poor place and life was very hard at the time during the Second World War and like a penny was a lot of money to a lot of people. (Paddy, older men's support worker)

Ultimately Paddy perceived these emotional and practical care dynamics as detrimental to men's well-being because it led to their dependency on women's physical and emotional care work by undermining their capacity to care for themselves even in basic practical ways:

> A lot of men when they lose their partner, like they have never made a cup of tea in their life-time, and when they lose their partner they have to be cooking for themselves. They don't cook what they should be cooking or eat what they should be eating and definitely it causes a problem...[T]hey live on tea or bread as much as they can or boiled eggs and things. They don't get cooked vegetables or potatoes or cereal or anything like that. (ibid.)

Men's performance of invulnerability and assertion of careless mascu-linities are also men's denial of care to self. Public health policies and practitioners are acutely aware that reducing men's risk-taking practices and altering the scrip of masculinity so that men can feel comfortable seeking help when physical, social, and psychological difficulties arise in their lives is key to men's health and well-being and is key also to whole-some relations with other men, women, and children in men's lives.

Illegitimate masculinities

Masculinity is deeply tied to men's public personas and the fact that men achieve legitimacy through socially valued practices in the public sphere means that doing primary caring is for many men enacting a feminised identity; a situation unfathomable to most men. Cathal (58) spoke about losing respect as a carer:

> People would think much more of me for running my own business than minding my children. You get a few people like the odd single mother who says 'God I don't know how you manage it's difficult being a women it must be more difficult being a man'. But it's a general rule if I was a very successful business man I would get far more respect for it in society. (Cathal, 58)

Cathal felt that even though men can receive increased recognition from women when they do caring, their caring is often perplexing and unappreciated by other men:

> Women would always think, 'God aren't you wonderful' I suppose and men would probably be fairly indifferent. I can't even think of a man's reaction ... women would say how did you get custody ... men ... they wouldn't be that interested, whereas the women would be more interested. I suppose I would get more respect from women being a single parent than a man ... a lot of men I would know casually it would be beyond their grasp being able to consider being a single parent ... the younger men I work with now they think in terms of drink, sport maybe fast cars, maybe girls somewhere down the list it would be completely beyond their realms of what they could think about being a single parent as a man it would be outside of their range completely so it wouldn't come up. (ibid.)

The interests and identities of men, in general, are constructed in ways that make becoming a primary carer incomprehensible to men. Why would men want to undertake work that is typically unpaid, undervalued, and defined as unproductive women's work (O'Connor and Dunne 2006; Lynch and Lyons 2009; Badgett and Folbre 1999)? Being a primary carer means living a life of economic vulnerability which is counter to hegemonic masculinity (Lynch, Lyons, and Cantillon 2009). The invisibility experienced by primary carers like Angus and Cathal was understood also by men who had not done primary caring, such as Dave:

> I certainly couldn't see my male friends as being understanding of this at all ... 'Why did you give up your job?' ... The pressure brought to bear is great, it's unspoken, it's unchallenged it's everywhere ... it is very hard for men to think of themselves as full time carers of

children or older people...it's just not part of their world you know...It would be changing their own identity...I don't see that happening any time soon. (Dave, 34)

More than invisibility, men can experience rejection from other men when letting go of dominant masculinity (Connell 2005; Buchbinder 1994). As Holter (1995: 101) puts it, 'men cannot easily be "in" their gender and "in" families at the same time. They break the default rules one way or the other, since if they participate in feminine tasks, their masculinity comes into doubt, whereas if they stick to traditional masculinity, their domestic participation remains a question mark'. This can be especially acute for men who already hold low status. Peter worked as community workers for Travellers and as a Traveller himself he talked about the 'external pressures and feeling that you are being laughed at and you're being called a woman' makes caring virtually taboo among Traveller men in public. Although he could understand the pressures on Traveller men he described it as 'macho bullshit and peer pressure coming to bear on you so you find other ways of contributing, other ways of supporting... [You] don't do it in public but you do it in the home, ... you wouldn't take a child out to the shop...but you just might mind the child for an hour at home so it's not done in public view'. According to Eddie and Tom, and supported by other research on marginalised men in Ireland (Goodwin 2002), the difference between men who can show caring in public and those who feel too ashamed to is that the former have additional means beyond breadwinning to define themselves as men. Eddie and Tom pointed out how many men they encounter in their community work that are involved in practical ways in caring to the extent that they had decided to set up a parenting group for men. They noted that sometimes the men are primary carers for children during the day while their children's more-employable mothers attend paid work. Working-class men can be more egalitarian in practice because they can have a greater day-to-day involvement in care (Shows and Gerstel 2009). By contrast middle-class professional men are often less involved in caring because they tend to invest more time in their work. This is because of the higher value they place on their careers and their profession (Shows and Gerstel 2009). Shows and Gerstel (2009) found that middle-class fathers did not experience being involved in 'public fatherhood' as shaming because, they speculated, they felt that their masculinity was reassured through their careers. They identified working-class fathers to be more engaged in 'private fatherhood', in the day-to-day care of children. The status of high-income fathers allows these men to cross the border to caring with less shame/suspicion (Doucet 2006: 203).

Being a primary carer is a contradictory position because men are expected to be dominant yet to be a carer is subordinated and feminised (Dominelli and Gollins 1997). Men who face dealing with the loss of status and identity associated with paid work often emphasise 'masculine qualities' of caring and distance themselves from feminine mothering (Doucet 2006: 195). Research about men working in diverse non-traditional (feminised) occupations similarly highlights the status anxiety men feel because caring is perceived to be feminine. For example, despite the varying reasons men choose to enter non-traditional occupations, including the desire to receive greater intrinsic satisfaction from their jobs and changes in labour market opportunities (Bagilhole and Cross 2006), many studies have revealed the 'role strain' men experience because their masculinity and their motivations are questioned when doing this work (Simpson 2005; Evans and Frank 2003). Facing this challenge men typically strategise to reassure their masculine status. Sometimes this involves avoiding or disengaging from the work altogether especially where there are few ways of shoring up one's masculinity while doing so (Nixon 2009). Another option for men in female-dominated occupations is to avail of the hidden advantages of the 'glass escalator' by climbing the occupation ladder into more senior masculine positions (Williams 1992, 1993, 1995; Evans 1997; Isaacs and Poole 1996). Not all men 'choose' to engage in feminine occupation, especially true for economic migrants and lower-class men. In some situations male domestic workers can feel like 'failed patriarchs' because they have not been able to earn like their fathers, yet the irony for poor men is also that paid domestic labour offer opportunities to define oneself as a provider (Qayum and Ray 2010; Bartolomei 2010). Within this status-diminishing context, men develop strategies that shore up traditional masculinity in distinction from female workers, or by reconstructing a non-traditional masculinity that also reassures dominance (Cross and Bagilhole 2002; Christie 2006; Lupton 2000; Simpson 2004). The contradiction of men's caring work in terms of gender equality is that it can both reconfigure and re-establish gender hierarchies (Agadjanian 2002; Robinson, Hall, and Hockey 2011).

Heteronormative masculinities

Men look for legitimacy in public spaces and public pursuits as well as within the private spaces of family life. Historically men's caring legitimacy was achieved through men's traditional role as breadwinners in intact heterosexual families. Men without this traditional status face numerous symbolic, emotional, and institutional barriers to being more involved in caring. Separated/lone parents experience many challenges as carers. Single/separated/non-resident fathers in Ireland encounter specific problems related to social stigma and suspicion, poor education, unemployment and housing and access to gender appropriate support services (NESF 2001; Corcoran 2005; Ferguson and Hogan 2004). In Irish law unmarried women are automatically awarded custody of their children and, therefore, it is through (heterosexual) marriage that men automatically acquire father status. Institutionally and historically the courts have found it difficult to consider men as primary carers (Coulter 2007). Some of the men felt a strong sense of illegitimacy when they could not construct themselves in patriarchal roles in families and this was especially true for Paul who was a fathers' rights activist. He had experienced divorce and argued vehemently that men can no longer feel proud of their traditional roles as fathers because he believed post-separation/divorce arrangements advantage women and disadvantage men:

> If the guy gets separated and the mother gets the house and he gets thrown out, where does he live? How does he have an environment whereby he can provide for his children the sense of, the ambiance of a home that can give him legitimacy and self-esteem within his relationship with his children? ... I'm looking after my children on an equally shared basis and I want the respect for doing that. I am denied that! ... It's cost me money, it's cost me a career. (Paul, fathers' rights activist)

Paul felt denied the legitimate status of traditional fatherhood in terms of respect, self-esteem, money, household and career, and he laid the blame for this squarely on feminism. He did this to the extent that he argued along the lines of Sheppard and Cleary (2007) that women are motivated maliciously to fabricate abuse. He proposed that women's decreased dependency on men's earnings has fed a malicious tendency for women to accuse men of domestic violence as a means of getting men out of the house. For him 'domestic violence is a toxically incentivised industry with safety orders, protection orders, ... vehicles for getting control of the family problem. I mean whoever gets the house, gets the car, gets the kids, gets the pension; that's what is up for grabs!' Though men have no monopoly on violence (Irwin and Chesney-Lind 2008), the overwhelming evidence is that disproportionately men are perpetrators of domestic violence and women are victims (Kimmel 2001; Dobash and Dobash 2004) and fathers' rights claims like this represents a backlash often particularly against vulnerable women (Dragiewicz 2011).

Research has exposed the 'contemporaneous residual conservativism' by Irish males towards lone mothers compared to women's attitudes which tend to be more favourable (Rush and Richardson 2007: 96) with farmers holding especially conservative attitudes (Rush, Richardson, and Kiely 2006). However, blaming lone mothers for social ills is not solely the preserve of conservative ideologies. Discourses of lone mothers in liberal societies tend to define lone mothers both as a needy group and as a social problem rather than lone parents being victims or lone parenting being a choice (Cheal 2002). Irish men's attitudes are no doubt related to contemporary liberal discourses as well as more traditional Catholic conservativism, but both of these world views occur in the context of neo-liberal market ideologies hostile to welfare dependency (Rush and Richardson 2007: 99). Although Ireland is a weak Anglo-Saxon welfare state that values greater social protection than the United States, the Irish Developmental Welfare State faces 'an international neo-liberal consensus which views social protection from labour market participation not only as illogical but also as immoral' (Rush, Richardson, and Kiely 2006: 145). Individualist tendencies in contemporary Irish society mean that people are judged on the basis of success or failure in terms of their economic productivity. Within this logic, those excluded from economic 'independence', such as single parents, are deemed a burden, and blamed for structural problems, as Hillard (2007: 98) argues the imperative of 'productivity' is at odds with affective family life.

Giddens (1992) claims that women's flight from financial dependency on men is coupled with women's flight from the emotional and care dependencies of men on women. Similarly Paul believed women's financial independence meant that men often feel less needed (and less desired) by women. Paul clearly felt robbed of his masculinity by the changes in family life that have provided women with greater freedom and less dependency on men. Paul argued the decline of male breadwinning has been devastating for men on the grounds that feminism and a feminised state has robbed men of breadwinning masculinity. He lamented the decline in 'patriarchy' which he felt has 'destroyed the self-esteem of men'. In this context he maintained it is 'much more sustainable for [women] to go to the more reliable father which is the state, which is the substitute father who can pay you housing allowance, children's allowance, childcare, crèche care, training if you want it, medical, than some guy who may or may not and you have to negotiate with him'. Paul declared that the state has undermined fathers' roles as breadwinners by supporting women financially to care for their children and in so doing he laments the decline of women's financial dependence on men. He admitted frankly that patriarchy was a male entitlement that had been robbed from men. Paul's solution to the situation that separated fathers' experience in court disputes is to argue that the patriarchal family should be reinstated.

The renewed emphasis on fatherhood and fathers' rights in recent decades occur against the background of men losing power, authority, and control within families over children and women (Segal 1997b; Smart 1989). Patriarchal identity has become more insecure for men where they fall outside of traditional families (Castelain-Meunier 2002; Drakich and Bertoia 1998), because it can leave men who hold traditional definitions of manhood with fewer ways to affirm masculinity (Seidler 2006: 14). As Gerson notes:

> The decline of primary breadwinning, along with the rise of new alternatives for men, poses a threat to those who have maintained an allegiance to the good-provider ethic. The erosion of support for their choices leaves them feeling nostalgic for the past, embattled in the present, and worried about the future. (Gerson 1993: 277)

The sense of superiority expected by patriarchal masculinity is also threatened within a climate of greater gender equality that has seen the legitimacy of male violence weakened, the self-confidence and assertiveness of women increased, and the decline of the patriarchal nuclear family (Clare 2000). The power and respect that men have received from traditional patriarchal relations have declined leaving traditional patriarchal masculinity feeling less assured, threatened, and in crisis (hooks 2004: 32). Calls to reclaim traditional fatherhood often represent a resistance to gender equality and a backlash against women (Coltrane and Galt 2000). The reaffirmation of traditional gendered relationships is a way of blaming women for problems of the economy and capitalist relations (hooks 2004). Paul presented the problems that separated fathers faced in accessing care relations in Ireland as an assault by women on a traditional and proper gender order. Ironically, lamenting the decline of the traditional family based on stable heteronormative marriages ignores the fact that this narrow conceptualisation of family life gives little space for single/separated fathers to be involved in nurturing. Legislation that defines men as economic providers exclusive of defining men as nurturers is based on the concept of economic rational man (Smart and Neale 1999: 178). Certainly evidence suggests that liberal values have increased in relation to work and family life in Ireland but traditional values are supported by substantial minorities (Fahey, Hayes, and Sinnott 2005: 152). International Social Survey Programme data show that women in Ireland are less convinced that 'married people are happier' than men and are more likely to agree that 'one parent can raise children as well as two parents' (Rush, Richardson, and Kiely 2006: 150). These attitudes surface against a background in Ireland where patriarchal structures supported by church and state are declining and women have greater freedom to reject men who cannot live up to contemporary emotional expectations (Leane and Kiely 1997; Kennedy 2001). Since, as Paul argued, fathers have become dispensable as breadwinners, their relationship with their children is also precarious. On this basis he maintained that if men are provided with equal rights and resources they will gladly take on primary caring responsibility for their children. He professed that if you give fathers 'a nice house and a car; the sort of resources you are prepared to give single mothers and then sell that. Sure everybody would want to do it! There wouldn't be a woman left in the country with a child. You'd have every fella saying, "I want one of them."'

Paul emphasised men's exclusion from caring because of the decline of traditional breadwinning roles. However, his argument raises problems not just from the point of view of gender equality for women; it also reinforces discrimination on the grounds of family status because unmarried fathers are defined outside the heteronormative family (Walsh and Ryan 2006). Geoff and Alex were support workers for gay men. They claimed homosexual men are often excluded from fathering roles precisely because these roles are defined heteronormatively. They pointed out the diversity of situations in which gay men become fathers, which includes previous heterosexual relationships and having children with lesbian women. They emphasise institutional discrimination and social stigma as particular problems. Fathers (including donors and unmarried fathers including gay fathers) who fall outside the heteronormative marital regime may have to resort to the courts to secure legal guardianship, a situation, as Ryan-Flood (2005: 191) notes, that essentialises motherhood and provides fodder for anti-feminist men's groups to claim oppression. The ambiguity of the State towards fathers who fall outside heterosexual marriage is evident in how gay men in Ireland are actively sought as foster carers by health authorities yet denied adoptive rights, marriage, or parental rights as 'Civil Partners' in homosexual relationships. Until recently homosexual partnerships had no formal legal recognition in Irish society with no rights to adoption, guardianship, or the right to marry to confer these rights (Kee and Ronayne 2002), but newly recognised civil partnership legislation continues to ignore gay fathering (Government of Ireland 2010). Globally gay parents face a precarious, irregular, and often hostile relationship with the state (Rimmerman and Wilcox 2007). Societies such as Sweden, where gender equality and men's involvement is highly valued even where family forms are irregular, fair better at including men than societies where there is a 'largely unsupportive social context' for alternative family forms (Ryan-Flood 2005: 201).

Geoff highlighted how gay men have to defend their rights to be fathers because of their sexuality noting how 'Society's homophobia again can have a big impact [with] gay and bisexual men feeling afraid, in terms of bringing up kids, from society's homophobia because they shouldn't or they are bad parents or they can't be parents. But also then in terms of society's homophobic impact on the children themselves, in terms of the bullying that happens in school.' Alex also talked of the silence surrounding gay fathering among gay men themselves that, 'It tends to be a bit of an unspoken on the gay scene, I know a number of men who have had children in previous relationships, some of them still have contact and play an active role and some of them don't. But I know a number of those men who are fairly open about it on the social scene but it is not something that is really talked about.'

Geoff claimed the pernicious association of homosexuality with paedophilia often made parenting a 'no go area'. This included the fear that their sexuality could be exploited as in family court disputes: 'There can be fears that can be used as an issue in court around custody...Or there may be still a lot of anger from their partner directed towards them over them being seen as that the relationship broke down because they came out, so their sexuality can be identified in that broken relationship as a reason why the relationship failed.' Simon (48) had personal experience of this. As a separated gay father and shared carer for his children, Simon describes his sexuality as being a 'family secret', and he was particularly concerned that his children (boys) would be exposed as having a gay father and its associated risk of homophobic bullying.

Rather than feeling proud of their contribution to the care of their children, gay men and their families face fear, shame, and hostility. The problems that many gay men face developing a positive self-concept as a result of their subordinated and stigmatised status (Edley and Wetherell 1997) are compounded by families who collectively hide a father's sexuality as a family secret.

Power and vulnerability

This chapter has explored the relationship between hegemonic masculinity and emotional life in relation to themes arising from the personal and political care conversations. Competing perspectives on this relationship can be found within men and masculinities studies, ranging from Goldberg's (1976) depiction of men as oppressed to that of Bourdieu (2001: 60), who compares masculinity to the status and psychological disposition of nobility, and to Hearn (1987) or Stoltenberg (1989), who tend to perceive of men as a privileged sex class (Ashe 2007). Connell's (2005) masculinities theory was ground breaking in thinking of men inhabiting disaggregated classes whilst retaining a structural designation as dominant. This allowed us to consider male dominance whilst simultaneously acknowledging that not all men are similarly privileged as well as the idea that dominance can have costs for men.

This view of masculinities continues to pervade the field overall but it is challenged, for example, by Seidler (2006, 2007) who argues that masculinity is also oppressive. Connell places greater emphasis on the power that men exercise over women (and other men) collectively through systems designed to favour men and individually by recreating relations of superordination and subordination in daily life. Seidler challenges the central position of power in the construction of masculinities, emphasising that while power is important in understanding men's relationships, it is also a cover for men's vulnerability. Seidler (1997) argues that dominant notions of masculinity are intimately caught up with both power and an emotional dynamic of superiority and inferiority between men and women. Although he is clear that men's power must be acknowledged, he distinguishes the cultural power of masculinity that creates the identities of individual men and the experience of power of individual men. He proposes that 'we can still keep an open mind about the nature of "difference" as long as we are aware of how relations of power and subordination have traditionally formed them' (Seidler 1997: 99). Seidler (2006) argues that masculinities must be understood in relation to their specific culturally inherited, emotional constructions rather than what he sees as the dominance of a power perspective on masculinities. Seidler (2006: 24) critiques Connell's framework of hegemonic masculinity as a universal framework for conceptualising masculinities because, he suggests, it holds a disdain for emotions in men's lives. He claims Connell is uncritical of rationalist traditions and argues that '[d]ifferences of culture, religion and nation become invisible as relations between diverse masculinities are theorised exclusively as relations of power' (ibid.: 27).

Seidler (2006) maintains that Connell dismisses men's emotional suffering and does not fully acknowledge the personal as political. Just because men are in more powerful positions, he argues, does not mean that they cannot suffer and that we need to recognise the violence that men do to themselves in their denial of their vulnerability, fear, and intimacy (Seidler 2006: 57–8). Seidler maintains that when masculinities are understood solely as power and political constructs, men are cut off from exploring their emotions and the ambivalent masculinity that they have inherited, historically and culturally. Seidler's (2006) proposal is to engage with how masculinities are constructed (and deconstructed) emotionally as a way also to grasp the complexity of power. Relationships are constructed to meet needs which are not just about power over others; for example, men and boys learn that in order to survive in competitive societies they need to be strong. Seidler (2006: 71) claims that 'by grasping how power works to undermine self-worth and reduce people to mere matter...that we show how power works through emotions, bodies and institutions'.

Connell has, however, acknowledged the centrality of emotions and sexuality in gender relations and in personal transformation although she has not given emotions the attention she has given to large-scale macro aspects of gender relations (Connell 2000). In fact, Connell's theorising of emotions and sexuality is also generally confined to the macro level of analysis. Whereas Seidler emphasises historical, religious, and cultural constructions of masculine rationality, Connell places more emphasis on global–economic relations of capitalism. She claims masculinity is closely tied to a technical rationality because of men's position in relations of power and production. She (2005: 178–9) shows how the logic and practice of rationality create emotional crises in men's lives. She contends that pure economic rationality is actually incompatible with men's 'categorical authority' opening contradictions between equality of opportunity and men's relations of dominance over women, and creating tensions within hegemonic masculinity. These increasing tensions within technical–rational work relations mean that men seek solace and emotional support within the nuclear family.

Whereas Seidler (1997) rejects the idea that all men are always powerful, Connell (2005) proposes that it is because of male power and privilege that men experience 'toxicity' or affective disadvantages. For Connell (2005) it is the identities and relations of dominance which sustain the non-affective relations of men. Connell (2005: 249) outlines a statistical balance sheet of gender justice and equality. She notes that the disadvantages are 'broadly speaking, the conditions of the advantages'. By assuming the power available to men they enter into an oppressive realm; a realm that has emotional costs attached. By benefiting from domestic labour and women's emotional work, men lose intimate connections. Yet the gains and costs are spread unevenly among men and it does not work out that those most privileged economically, politically, and culturally are the most disadvantaged affectively.

I see in these perspectives differences in emphasis rather than in kind, which, if anything, expose the complex interrelationship between power and affective life, an intersection that illuminates important tensions and contradictions in masculinities. On the one hand men's collective and individual power are often obscure within the context of a male-dominated society that expects white, middle-class, heterosexual men to uphold dominant positions in society (Kimmel 2000). However, on the other hand, men can inhabit contradictory power locations based on 'racial' or class distinctions (Kaufman 1994), and a presentation of men as 'always and only powerful', as blindly obedient to patriarchy and always privileged obscures how many men victimise because they are victimised (hooks 2004: 26–7 and 139). Men have a conflicting interest in change because the gender order oppresses as well as privileges men and this gives men some interest emancipator change (New 2001). Power in personal life operates through complex relational dynamics rather than fixed and static structures (Mac án Ghaill and Hayward 2007) and vulnerability as well as power feature in these relations (Seidler 2007). Understanding how men engage in social practices at the intersection of complex and dynamic multiple identities and material social locations is key to perceiving the operation of power in practice. The intimacies of care relations can expose men's vulnerability in contradiction with men's identity as powerful and invulnerable and sometimes intimate relations become the dumping ground for men's frustrations and feelings of inadequacy.

Recent theorising on equality provides a useful framework with which to explore the interrelationships between masculinities and equality (Baker et al. 2004; Lynch, Baker et al. 2009). By proposing that inequalities have multiple dimensions (representation, respect and recognition, working and learning, resources, and love, care, and solidarity) they allow us to consider not just how men and women can be charted along different dimensions but, additionally, how different groups of men related to them. Social class in Ireland is markedly correlated with social inequality (Munck 2007) which intersects with gender, disability, sexuality, as well as minority ethnic and other statuses in how inequalities are formed and reproduced (Bradley 1997). Men's experiences are shaped not only by their position within class and racial hierarchies but also in how these locations intersect with generation, sexuality, family status, disability, and so forth. Gender discrimination intersects with other experiences and these sometimes contradictory experiences of power have particular affective components (Baker et al. 2004; Russell et al. 2008). From this perspective certain inequalities are also generated by the affective sphere, but masculinities studies have not sufficiently considered affective relations as generative sources of inequality in themselves. Although Connell (1987, 2002) defines emotional relations as a major pillar of the gender order, she has not expanded on this as much as she has on political, economic, and cultural relations. She also defines emotional relations more in terms of sexuality and relations of desire rather than in terms of caring. Yet men's bodies and emotions are important in theorising male domination for Connell ([1995] 2005) who emphasises the importance of bodily reflective practices in constructing male domination and hegemonic masculinities. Similarly, Bourdieu's (2001) theory of habitus helps to explain how, through an active process of capital accumulation, cultural and social processes literally embed in bodies and become taken for granted. He shows how a central feature of male domination is the way that masculinity writes-out the feminine from men's lives in a process of constructing a sense of masculine superiority.

Many masculinities writers, however, resist the exploration of men's emotions and emotional life, fearing, I suggest, that it negates men's power. There are well-grounded reasons for these fears because one of the key insights of masculinities writers is that men's power and privilege are often invisible to men because of their privileged social location (Kimmel 1993; Hanmer 1990). The fact that the invisibility of privilege exists as an obstacle to perceiving domination does not alter, however, the importance of exploring emotional relations as an important aspect of how dominant masculinities are constructed. Victor Seidler (1997, 2007) is one of the few writers who is attempting to open up discussion on emotional dimensions of men's power (as well as aspects of men's emotional lives that do not centrally involve power). He claims that by understanding more about men's fear of vulnerability we can understand more about men's resistances to change.

Conclusion

The conversations with the men demonstrated how dominant definitions of masculinity are defined in terms of acquisitions of power, resources, and status and these competitive and hierarchical relations remove caring from men's lives. Men can experience and respond to hegemonic expectations in a variety of ways, and affective relations appear to be central in how different kinds of masculinities are denied or nurtured. Masculinities have important affective as well as political, cultural, social, and economic dimensions. Access to love and care is interconnected with power, status, and resources and the decline of traditional patriarchal relationships and institutions has shaken men's affective security when they hold traditional identities and when they fall outside traditional relations. However, feeling good about being male is intimately tied to how one feels and is perceived in relation to other men as it is in relation to women. Although advantaged in terms of resources, status, power, and income, men often receive less care by defining themselves as not needing it (Lynch, Baker et al. 2009). To fully understand men and gender relations we need to understand how men feel about their lives with all its hidden privileges, expectations, contradictions, and inequalities.

Hegemonic masculinity is not all about power and control in the public sphere but it is also about affective relations both in the private and public sphere, especially where men deny responsibility for care and yet expect to be cared for. Contemporary egalitarian theory that explores inequalities of love, care, and solidarity allows more space to consider inequalities in more complex, multidimensional, and contradictory ways. Thinking about how men provide and access love, care, and solidarity as conceptually separate from inequalities in social, political, cultural, and economic life is important. It allows room to theorise both the affective inequalities that men experience and how men contribute to affective inequality by avoiding caring or by constructing harmful masculinities. It also helps us to consider how these inequalities interface, reinforce, or reduce inequalities in other areas. The concept of affective equality has the potential to unite men and women around affective concerns (Baker et al. 2004: 209). It also has the potential for critical studies of men and masculinity to begin to theorise men's pain (Seidler 2006) without losing site of men's power and oppression (Segal 1995; Hearn 1999). Men's affective relations are all too often ignored by egalitarians (until recently) and profeminists; the space left empty by critical voices is too easily occupied by reactionary ones.

5
Nurturing Femininities

How do men define care? What do they understand by it? How do the meanings they assign to care relate to their identities as men? What sorts of negotiations about the meaning of care are occurring among men (and women)? Many of the men in the study endorsed feminist assertions about the involvedness of caring, and how caring engages an ethical mode of being defined as other-centred and selfless. Rather than accounting for the work of care in a flippant fashion, indifferent to the effort, skill, and complexity involved, care was defined as physically and emotionally demanding. They proposed that caring requires expert and specialist attributes, and they inferred that caring values are morally superior to the self-interested rationality widely prevailing in society. What we find here is the way the men consider identity to be expressly tied to caring and nurturing deeply tied to femininity. The idea of nurturing femininity amounts to a pervasive discourse which is used to construct an ideal type of caring. Whilst this can imply essentialist notions of femininity as the biological antithesis of masculinity, it need not; what the men depict here is the antagonistic social construction of masculinity. By imaging themselves to be inadequate, incompetent, or uninterested nurturers, men easily distance themselves from feeling obliged to care. Aided by an individualist ideology of free choice the unequal division of love and care labour can be rationalised on the basis that carers have chosen care work because it fits their psychological makeup, social interests, and self-identity.

Nurturing capabilities

Upon initial reflection care was invariably defined and spoken about negatively by association with a diverse range of activities designed to satisfy a wide assortment of different care needs characterised in the first instance by physical dependency. To be a recipient of care was to be incapable of feeding, washing, or fending for oneself and therefore to be deemed 'in need', 'disabled', 'helpless' 'powerless', 'invalid', 'ill', 'handicapped', 'looked after', 'incapacitated', 'in care', and 'cared for'. While descriptions of what caring involves ranged from 'doing your best for people' and 'friendship' to relatively complex activities, the primary meaning of caring was said to be the provision of physical and practical assistance including 'washing', 'cleaning', 'helping', 'bodily assistance', 'cooking' and 'feeding', 'supplying' 'providing', 'financial assistance', 'helping people get around' (e.g. to church or hospital), 'sharing interests' and 'supporting education' through 'teaching' and 'advising'. Angus (43) was a home carer for his elderly parents. He spoke about 'the physical aspects, the emptying of commodes for both parents, the cleaning as much as possible ... bringing to the toilet ... of not sometimes making it to the toilet and cleaning it up and changing'.

Studies have identified men's high regard for caring work (Masciadrelli, Pleck, and Stueve 2006), and it was very notable in this study how the men appreciated the deep emotional and moral nature of caring. Some descriptions of emotional caring work were rather bland (e.g. 'looking after another'), but many of the men outlined more elaborate understandings:

> To mind somebody or take care of somebody ... to be there to support that person, help that person, get through something or achieve something, ... maybe comfort as well, ... helping them grow, you are bringing them up ... it could be being there, having a shoulder for them, or you could give them advice ... [or] literally helping them do all the basics, the necessities of life. So there are lots of different types of care I can see. (Fionn, 25)

There again a few men including Pascal, a single gay man, age 48, broadened the definition of care to include solidarity:

> Immediately when you said the word care I saw a baby's face ... But also caring is being concerned for rather than having to physically care for someone ... I care about lots of things ... I care about the environment, I care about poverty, I care about people, ... or whatever. (Pascal, 48)

The emotional dimensions of care were appreciated by most of the men. Providing emotional care meant giving 'support', 'companionship', 'nurturing', promoting 'happiness', and 'quality of life'. Jamal, a married

Muslim father, age 32, suggested that care was about being there to help and support either physically or emotionally: Care could be 'hands-on care to either the elderly, the disabled and so on... it is about help, it is about being there for someone who needs you. It is not only about physical care... you have got emotional care... emotional support is an aspect of care itself'.

More specifically it was less the emotional work of care than the attributes of carers which revealed the way that these men appreciated the challenges that constitute care work. There was no question that the men regarded care as emotionally demanding and highly skilled, and because caring was defined as having a high emotional content, in the men's eyes it was necessary for carers to be, above all, emotionally accomplished, much in keeping with conventional understandings that effective caring requires sentient and expressive communication abilities and emotional intelligence (Goleman 1996; Richard 1990; Egan 2009). Carers were believed to need an emotional disposition that embodied 'selflessness', 'tolerance', 'patience', 'empathy', 'devotion', 'love', 'self-awareness', 'compassion', 'spirituality', and 'understanding'. And they were expected to be 'good listeners', 'easy going', 'non-aggressive', 'non-judgmental', 'in tune with their feelings of vulnerability', and 'knowledgeable about peoples needs', as well as possessing a 'good personality', 'a sense of humour', 'a practical sense of the world' and an ability to make 'informed decisions' without being 'overwhelmed'. Contrasting the view that men are poor at recognising emotions, that they are emotionally illiterate, or that emotional work is invisible to them, the stories show how these men were aware of and appreciated the emotional side of caring. Several conversations, for example, raised the importance of attentiveness, intuitive listening, and empathy in caring, and this meant prioritising the needs of dependents over self:

> Being able to listen and hear what the person wants rather than you thinking you have the answers... Allowing them to refuse what you have on offer... [not] taking away that person's autonomy... caring needs to wherever possible be set by the person being cared for [even if]... it might take them a long time to realise they need more care than they think they do.... I think the person being cared for should be at the centre of care in the decision making. (Pascal, single gay man, age 48)

Just as feminists have highlighted the time-intensities of caring (Jacobs and Gerson 2004), caring was understood as involving a great dedication and commitment of one's time. As a full-time home carer Angus (home carer, age 43) was acutely aware of 'Time not being your own … being dedicated to somebody else's needs almost constantly'. Dermot, age 35, was unemployed and a secondary carer for his young step-daughter. He talked about care being emotionally relentless with few opportunities to avail of 'down-time' in comparison with paid labour:

> [Carers] have to have a lot of time for people and put people before themselves and I know that can be emotionally draining … It takes a lot of time and energy … Working in an office you can switch off but you can't really do that if you are a caregiver … It takes patience and time and energy and stamina. (Dermot, 35)

Dermot understood the nature of caring as a dynamic and inter-dependent relationship involving mutuality and reciprocity:

> [Care] for your partner … meaning you will sacrifice your nights out and stuff like that if they are sick or if they are not feeling well or depressed you give them a lift you encourage them to do things if they are feeling down or a bit useless you pick up on their good points … that's kind of care, you build their self confidence and they build your self confidence, you work towards building each other's self confidence that's kind of care to me. (ibid.)

Moreover there was also an awareness that emotions are communicated physically through our actions as well as verbally (Craib 1998). Charlie was a retail worker, age 28, and in a relationship but he had no children or care responsibilities. He considered a good carer to be

> someone who is not afraid to show their love and can show it … some people can't physically show someone care you know … If there's someone there that changes the bedclothes or change their clothing … I suppose that's a way of showing love … some people can't say the words. (Charlie, 28)

The men's descriptions of caring in highly emotional terms demonstrated their respect and positive evaluation of care in social life, as well as their admiration for carers, as well as how challenging they understood caring to be.

Nurturing labour

The men's appreciation of care as intricate and taxing revealed their anxieties and reticence about doing this work. Infused throughout the care conversations were the men's reflections on how burdensome many aspects of caring are, and many of the men defined the emotional dimensions of caring as especially challenging and unrewarding. Upon repeated readings of the transcripts it became obvious to me that the way men constructed care within the context of the gender-care conversations was not only a reflection of how they perceived caring, but also a means of rationalising their relationship with care; the men's constructions of care as especially emotionally skilled was a way of distancing themselves from feminine aspects of care. This offered men with a way to express feelings that they should not have to do caring, at least in ways stereotypically defined as feminine. Thus, their masculinity was implicitly defined in ways at odds with what was expected from a good carer.

One manifestation of this was the way some men spoke about how unrewarding care could be. Research has addressed in a limited way the difficulties that men experience engaging in emotional care work, but less in terms of reciprocity; the rewards that they may or may not take from doing care work. Douglas was a farmer, age 48, and married with children. He felt care might 'not always be as rewarding as it is meant to be'. He recognised the emotional burden of the carer suggesting having to 'talk through' difficult issues 'you could end up being the person wanting care'. Nor could Liam, an accountant, age 36, single with no care responsibilities. He could not imagine how caring could be rewarding:

The [caring] responsibilities of a parent to their children [is] something I have tried to understand... [I have] never really been happy with my conclusions that I have understood how people cope and deal with that responsibility. I consider more... someone's duty and effort rather than the rewards and the benefits and the feelings of pride that parents are supposed to have. (Liam, 36)

Caring occupied a contradictory social space for some of the men. On the one hand care was an integral feature of daily life that demanded that it be valued and that everyone be involved in caring in some respects. On the other hand, the emotional demand of caring was seen to require emotionally specialist skills and attributes:

Anybody over a certain age who has had a little bit of training [can become a carer]... (pausing and reflecting). I'd like to say anybody could be able to do that but some people can't. They have to have some patience you know especially if it's elderly or disabled person... you just can't be going in there getting annoyed with them. I mean in an ideal world I would love it to be everyone but I don't think everybody can do that job or be a carer. You have to be warm as well...you have either got it or you haven't...Emotionally you have to be in touch with yourself...I only looked after my Nan for a couple of months and it was very draining it's hard work and not everyone can do it. (Charlie, 28)

In this passage Charlie moves from a position of inclusivity (that anyone can be a carer once they are 'over a certain age' and have 'a little bit of training') to exclusivity (that 'it's hard work and not everyone can do it' that 'you have either got it or you haven't'); from a position where anyone can potentially learn caring emotionality to one where these attributes are inborn.

Surrounding the issue of emotional labour is the presumption that caring capabilities are inherent. The idea that caring requires special skills or training occurs within the social context wherein people receive little or no formal training for caring. Carers are expected to learn to care 'on the job' or as a result of gendered familial socialisation. The lack of education for caring is based on the presupposition that caring comes naturally. The skills, capabilities, and knowledge required for caring are presumed innate in women/girls, yet ironically women/girls are also more likely to be exposed to informal and formal caring education. In contrast, men/boys are assumed to be naturally uncaring and are therefore not generally targeted with caring education. Boys and young men need to be prepared for sexual responsibility, pregnancy, and fathering (Ferguson and Hogan 2007; Nixon et al. 2010; NESF 2001); they should be helped to develop skills to resist dominant masculinity and harmful ways of being men (Hyde et al. 2005; Hyde et al. 2008; Mac an Ghaill, Hanafin, and Conway 2004; Featherstone, Rivett, and Scourfield 2007), and homophobic bullying. New fathers require education and information to support their involvement with their children (Deave and Johnson 2008). However there continues to be a silence surrounding issues of homosexuality and intimacy in schools (O'Higgins-Norman 2008), and this is even more pronounced in respect of care. Despite wide support among parents (McCormack and Gleeson 2010), attempts to teach boys reflective emotional–relational skills that question dominance and help boys value different ways of being men can be often staunchly resisted by conservative reactionary forces within and without schools on the basis that this knowledge is feminising men (Mac an Ghaill, Hanafin, and Conway 2004; Gleeson, Conboy, and Walsh 2003). Whereas education for sexual relations is debated within educational circles, there has been a particular silence around the issue of care in education especially for boys. While it is imperative that all citizens are educated for care (Lynch, Lyons, and Cantillon 2007), the fact that boys are socialised in accordance with the assumption that they are incapable of caring can make caring education more important in order to counter those assumptions (Hearn 1999). Gendered imperatives for girls to have a caring orientation and for boys and men to be dominant negatively affect men socially and academically (Lynch and Feeley 2009; Kahn, Brett, and Holmes 2011). Education for care and caring citizenship must be placed on the political agenda (Lynch, Lyons, and Cantillon 2007). The silence surrounding educating citizens for love, care, and solidarity is based on the liberal belief that the model citizen is rational, autonomous, and care-free and consequently education prepares citizens for economic, cultural, and political life rather than for relational caring obligations (Lynch, Lyons, and Cantillon 2007; McClave 2005).

Selfless identity

The contradiction between feeling capable or incapable, interested or uninterested, and willing or unwilling was a noteworthy theme in the conversations. Many of the men struggled to locate themselves as caring men within the context of care defined stereotypically as feminine nurturing, yet at the same time there was an awareness of their own care needs and desires. The men's understanding of caring as emotionally specialist work revealed the different ways that they positioned themselves in relation to that work. Some of the men distanced themselves from feeling obligated to care by defining themselves as emotionally unskilled, whereas for some men (admittedly fewer), it allowed them to position themselves as caring. Rory was a manager aged 55. He saw himself as caring and emotionally competent but, nonetheless, argued that not feeling emotionally equipped was a legitimate reason to choose not to engage in caring work. He felt it 'important that people can see where they are at, what they can offer, [and] what they can't offer. If they wish to care ... it's knowing what you can do and people know what they can offer and know their limitations'.

Here we see another central narrative running throughout the men's stories; they tended to define their caring obligations through this prism of choice. Some of the men's apprehension about emotional aspects of caring leads them to conclude that, although in an 'ideal' world anyone can do caring, it should be undertaken by choice. Thus feeling emotionally ill-equipped for emotional caring work provides a rationale for the men to avoid it. However, being self-aware of one's caring limitations and choosing caring as a 'free choice' is a privilege unavailable to those compelled to care. Women in Irish society are subject to much greater moral obligations to do caring work and women's 'choices' are based on having more limited care options (Rush, Richardson, and Kiely 2006; Lynch and Lyons 2008; Hayes and Bradley 2006; O'Brien 2007). The narrative of choice is in many ways morally safe, in the sense that it locates the source or action upon free-acting individuals unencumbered by structural constraints. From this perspective those who choose to care do so freely, perhaps because they feel caring a calling in life and are good at it, and those who avoid it because they would not be doing anyone service by choosing otherwise. Men's choices are then constructed within the context of not being socialised into the requisite skills, implying that carers have chosen to care based on feeling emotionally capable. Care 'choices' are facilitated by a gender regime that legitimates what is desirable cultural and emotional capital for men and women, which itself is the product of nurturing work we have inherited. For many of the men not doing primary caring was an easy choice because they were not expected to do so. What these stories contain is the ideology of choice; a discourse that allows for the rationalising of one's involvement in care.

Exceptions are found in how particular men feel an obligation to care, arising from a sense of duty, especially for older men, for their wives or for sons to care for parents when no one else is available. This was so for Angus, a full-time home carer, age 43. He explained becoming a primary carer to his elderly parents because he felt responsible and no one else was available to do it. As a single gay man with no other care responsibilities he was available to take care of his parents. Angus nonetheless drew on a narrative of 'choice' to help him cope with the burdens that being a full-time unpaid carer presented:

> If you think of it as a job and something you are good at. So sometimes when I am particularly tired I think, 'Well my job at the moment is caring, and it is my job', and that removes me slightly from the situation so that I can look at it for a little while as 'I am getting paid to do this, I am good at it, it is my job'... If you are beating yourself up all the time or if you are self pitying or if you are blaming your siblings or blaming somebody else for not helping enough and you are not allowing them to help... I think self awareness is a huge issue, I mean to do it in a proper frame of mind. (Angus, 43)

Male carers often adapt to caring work by drawing on a professional model that defines caring as an occupation, allowing men to emphasise traditional practical, instrumental, and managerial skills (Thompson 2005; Russell 2007; Clarke 2005). Similarly, Angus argues effectively that when faced with caring responsibilities we can choose a caring identity and therefore choose to embody the attributes of good carers; by changing our definition of the situation we can thus change our reality.

The conversations highlight the different ways that men feel about their own capability and potential ways that these feelings are constructed in respect of their interests. It demonstrates a tension between the valuing of caring on the one hand and men's resistance to doing emotional caring work on the other. This relates to how masculinities and femininities are defined in relation to caring as well as how gender identities are experienced physically and emotionally. By characterising caring in terms of an opposing 'feminine' emotionality, although overlooking the multiple activities and forms of labour involved in caring, the men implicitly understand how central emotion and emotional labour is to love and caring work. Emotion may be demonstrated through actions (Craib 1998), but emotional caring depends on sensitivity, intimacy, understanding, and touch, and love labour especially depends on an emotional and inalienable relational bond (Lynch et al. 2009). By defining caring as highly specialised emotional work, the men rationalise their own incapability and avoidance (McMahon 1999).

Closely related to a narrative of other-centred emotionality was the attendant theme of selfless love. An idealised carer was constructed by the men to embody a selfless, sacrificial, duty-bound, and dedicated disposition orientated to family and community. Liam's depiction of compassion epitomises this understanding:

> What I feel the person needs is compassion in the literal sense. Compassion meaning the taking on of someone else's sufferings, the understanding of someone else's sufferings, the willingness to put aside the self; to understand that it can be fulfilling to forget your own problems, your own difficulties, and to make someone else the focus of your attention. (Liam, 36)

The ideal of selflessness, in contrast to the instrumental rationality which was held to define the public sphere, was perceived to be motivated by an ethic of care within the private sphere. The men recognised the compelling nature of other-centred care rationalities which grow more intense depending on whether they related to primary, secondary, or tertiary care relations (Lynch 2007). Dermot (35) proclaimed how 'Caring for your family, that's blood you know ... [for example] if they want to move house you get off your arse [and help] ... If your friends need a hand you would always put your family before [friends]'. Angus (43) too claimed to 'believe in a sense of duty, which is kind of old fashioned, so I believe that families should look after each other, parents should be responsible and look after their children. Children should look after their parents.' Families were presented as the space that held society together, as an emotional haven from an isolated and uncaring world. This was true even for men with relatively unconventional family forms like Simon, a middle-class academic, age 48, a gay father with primary caring responsibilities for his children:

> I just think that the way our society is organized at the moment is a disaster you know. The post-nuclear family is an isolated thing ... [The family is] ... us versus them ... the bulwark against anything bad going on ... and that is falling apart in some ways ... There is too much potential for that isolation and not enough connectiveness within families and that is getting worse. (Simon, 48)

Although many of the men avoided explicitly mentioning gender despite the gendered context of the interviews, the ideal of selflessness was gendered feminine because it was based on an ideal of motherhood socialised into an ethic of care and deeply dedicated to family. The selflessness with which they referred was implicitly and sometimes explicitly modelled on an image of maternal devotion. Jamal (social care worker, age 32) considered that 'parents are doing a great job at home but once the child is outside, say in a crèche [child care] or pre-school, I have a problem with that ... I believe that a child should be looked after in his or her early stage of development at home by the parents'. Conor, age 57, a married farmer with children, was more explicit by claiming 'When I hear the word "care" I suppose I think about the care and attention that [my wife] gave to the children here and that she has been giving to my brother as well, you know ... She does everything, and she'd do anything for any of them I'd say.'

The idealisation of motherhood is nothing new (Pheonix, Wollett, and Lloyd 1991), but what Conor alludes to here is an iconic ideal of Irish womanhood associated with Catholic theology and a conservative Irish State. The intrinsic connection between patriarchal Catholic social thought and men's power and domination (Schneiders 2004) is enshrined in the image of maternal duty, and devotion was embedded within the 1937 Irish Constitution (Government of Ireland 1937: Articles 40.1, 41.2.1 and 41.2.2). Here it defines women as primary carers within the marital heterosexual family (although a constitutional referendum has been recently proposed with a view to gender-neutral wording). Women are quite explicitly defined as care workers, whose role was the socialisation and moralisation of disciplinary workers required by church and state (Inglis 1998).

Care for Conor is imagined in terms of a gift of female altruism and identity, but this view fails to recognise is the exploitative basis of the contract; women's unpaid labour in the home. The characterisation of the ideal carer by some of the men as saintly with carers sacrificing personal, social, economic, and emotional concerns for the person cared for (and doing so willingly) gives rise to the belief that caring is debased when it is motivated by self-interest. The care that some of the men want is based on a warm, secure, and trustworthy femininity; an identity less preoccupied with power and public pursuits as Bubeck (1995: 148) observes '[W]omen's self respect and feelings of self-worth do not necessarily depend so much on any of the public indicators of power such as success, powerful positions, or control of material resources, but often on their being needed, by and being able to help others'. Consequently the way that masculinity is defined becomes incompatible with caring (ibid.: 160).

This ideal of caring femininity was not uncritically endorsed. Rory advanced the argument that apparent female caring altruism can sometimes be self-serving, driven by hidden motives related to fulfilling co-dependent needs; the need to be seen as caring and to fulfil a caring role:

> People who are anxious to help are anxious, primarily anxious. I suppose I'm wary of people who need to help. I think it's important that people know what they are doing what needs need to be met...I think that is important that people know their own needs and their own motivations and they recognise the purity of them and impurity of them and how motivations are...So that kind of self-awareness is very important...It's also important I think not to develop dependency that you don't set yourself up for life you know. (Rory, 55)

While Rory presents an understanding of the reciprocal nature of care, altruism in this context tends to be defined in negative terms. As with the other men, care here is seen to be corrupted when involving self-interest.

Feminine care ethics

What we find overall in the stories is an ideal type of caring defined primarily in terms of dependency work focussed on the physical and practical needs of care recipients. However, the ideal-type carer is one who is especially emotionally and cognitively skilled at doing caring work, and their identity is constructed as sacrificially other-centred based on a strong sense of family duty. The ideal-type carer represents a love labourer who embodies a gendered nurturing capital which is highly trustworthy and devotional and is modelled on a stereotyped feminine and maternal role. Such a model of caring conflicts with many of the ideals of masculinity in several respects; in terms of dedicating time to public goals, holding an instrumental orientation to the world, and being competitively career focussed.

The men's idealisation of the carer is aligned to the belief that men and women have different moral and care rationalities. Feminist psychoanalysts have argued that gender differences in moral reasoning and caring are socialised in early childhood. Based on a critique of the gender-blind nature of Kohlberg's moral development theory, Gilligan (1982) distinguished between a rationalistic ethic of justice and emotional–relational based ethic of care. Within Cartesian and Kantian morality of universalistic autonomous, individuated and rationalistic actors, masculinity is associated with reason, abstract thought, and rules and principles in contrast with feminine ethics associated with intuition, feeling, receptivity to others, and contextualised thought (Bubeck 1995). Rather than defining women as inadequate moral actors as Freud implied, gendered socialisation is said to give rise to a superior *ethic of care* in contrast to the masculinised and instrumental *ethic of justice*, which is understood to be crucial in developing social caring based on a relational, interdependent, and vulnerable concepts of self (Larrabee 1993; Kittay and Feder 2002; Fineman 2008). Women's morality, power, and identities derive from having responsibility for caring relationships whereas the justice morality associated with men is said to derive from concepts of justice, fairness, rights, rules, and identities associated with the public sphere (Sevenhuijsen 1998). Men are self-orientated, thinking in terms of 'I', and women are other-orientated, thinking in terms of 'we' (Giddens 1992). However, from this perspective women's 'compulsory altruism' or caring imperative (Lynch and McLaughlin 1995; Bubeck 1995; O'Brien 2007) can be claimed as either a superior source of moral reasoning that needs to be reclaimed and re-valued, or a source of symbolic domination because it naturalises 'vocational dispositions'

(Bourdieu 2001: 57). Feminine ethics are often critiqued on the grounds that emotional judgements are irrational, but emotions are rational in so far as they enable us to discern which attachments are important for our well-being and to make moral judgements (Nussbaum 1995a, 1995b). Furthermore, feminine care ethics and feminist care ethics are, however, not identical (Lynch, Lyons, and Cantillon 2007). A feminine ethic of care can be critiqued on the grounds it represents servility, passivity and, in practice, construct femininities that support normative masculinity (Bowden 2000). An ethic of caring femininity might be considered a form of *emphasised femininity* because it is constructed to support and legitimate men's roles in political, economic, and cultural life (Korobov 2011; Connell 1987; Schippers 2007). It therefore facilitates the construction of masculinities which are care-free. The projecting of emotional care onto women in the private sphere allows for the construction of masculinities that are care-free in the public sphere and care is written out of public citizenship.

The stories highlight the significance that the men place on the embodiment of a caring habitus that embodies a feminine ethic of care. The high value placed on caring in the private sphere can often have a high cost for carers (Lynch and Lyons 2009a). The assumptions that the men bring to caring identity and practices are highly idealised since there is no choice not to do caring for many carers. Except for a small minority of male carers like Angus (43), men are unwilling to assume this subordinated identity as a carer. The selfless and sacrificial standard by which many of the men define caring seems very high considering there is an acknowledgement that caring work is very difficult and contains few rewards. Liam (36) provides an example of this contradiction by suggesting, on the one hand, that the carer should be selfless and 'understand that it can be fulfilling to forget your own problems', but at the same time finds it difficult to understand 'how people cope and deal with that responsibility'.

Nurturing capital

Caring as the embodiment of selfless and other-centred emotionality was a central theme within the narratives. However, the stories portray anxieties and a sense of moral panic about the decline of caring values in society and about the inadequacy of caring services to fulfil love-labouring roles. The emphasis the men placed on these traits revealed a more general anxiety among the men about the decline of nurturing capital along with its associated feminine caring habitus. This can be connected to a wider apprehension within the Irish society arising from the care gap that has resulted primarily from women's entry into the paid labour force over the past twenty years (Fanning and Rush 2006; Lynch and Lyons 2008) within the context of minimal state intervention to support caring and reliance on private for-profit sector to fill the void (Daly 2001b).

The sense of moral panic is demonstrated by several sub-themes related to the ascendency of the dual-breadwinner family, the decline of vocationalism, the marketisation and profitisation of care services, and the incompetence of the State and state regulation. For some of the men the decline of care capital represented a general threat to the social order. This was especially acute for Cian, a 49-year-old-disabled man, who was heavily reliant on the care of others. Cian said, 'I dread to think where we are going to be in ten or twelve year's time, it really is getting to an awful state. You know where you have kids growing up now and they have no more respect for dog, man or beast.'

Standing (2001: 21) maintains the provision of care heightens numerous anxieties for recipients and providers related to competence, expertise, quality, trust, reliability, cost, and reciprocity. Graham (1983: 29) suggests the reluctance of many to trust the state to provide care is because care services are perceived to 'lack the very qualities of commitment and affection which transform caring-work into a life-work, a job into a duty'. This was true for the majority of the men who were highly distrustful about the quality of care services (including childcare, disability, and elderly care), which were typically viewed as incompetent and inefficient. Dave, a 34-year-old social researcher, maintained:

> the State is approaching care at the moment...it's just so neglected...and completely neglectful of the person...I just wouldn't be trustful of the State at all. I'm very wary of that despite my left wing principles I very much see the State or communities taking more of a role but...I wouldn't have confidence. I wouldn't put my trust in those systems as they are configured now. (Dave, 34)

Rory, a manager, age 55, believed state institutions are simply incapable of providing emotional care:

> I think...in institutions there is a language of ideas and a language of action, there is no room for a language of emotion...you cannot care without emotion but...there is no space for emotion...it's not

that the whole care dimension is gone because they need to set up systems...but it's like setting it up on two legs of a three legged stool...The people in the system consistently work to include it, good people, but it's like they are going against the grain of the system...because then it would be less standardised, less predictable, less projectable, and less accountable. (Rory, 55)

Aside from debates about how quality of care can be provided in caring services, these men were aware that social services cannot provide love (Lynch 2007). Part of their anxieties is based on fears that as familial care obligations decline, and as the structures of paid work make it difficult to meet these obligations, the sanctity of love–labour relations are undermined. There was additionally a great deal of apprehension about families being increasingly trapped by the demands of paid work to the detriment of love labour:

Niall: You have mentioned that you would be worried or a little bit untrusting of some of the other childcare arrangements like the crèches and that kind of thing. Would you see family care as the ideal kind?

Conor: Yes, I would, but you see it is not easy to manage it. That would be the perfect scenario but it doesn't work because everyone is working. Like even the grandparents...sure they are probably working as well and so then where do you go, you have to go for professional care then, you have to go to the crèche or hire someone in, a nanny or something. So it is a kind of a vicious circle; what do you do? It is a sign of the times. Like this affluent society now, and we can pay for what we want...I often wonder how much better off are you by the time everything is paid for.

The love–labour relations of family life are defined as a haven from the distrustful and dangerous instrumental rationality of the public world. Love labour is described as a familial obligation that is vital not only to safeguard one's immediate family but also for the health of the wider society. Not only do the stories contain a great scepticism about the ability of the Irish State to provide or regulate care adequately, but there is considerable apprehension arising from the marketisation of care and the profit motive in care. Simon (48) argued what 'we have created is a society that ultimately doesn't care. The politics is based on a presumption that the market forces dictate everything and so that therefore leaves those who are vulnerable right! At all ages in all respects! That means anybody who is outside of the mainstream and that includes old people and young people, disadvantaged young people in particular.' Cian (49) declared that social care services were 'dangerously close to disaster, particularly elderly...Like when you set up elderly homes and you put it into the private sector...you are asking for trouble'. He expressed 'serious doubt over the care element' 'because remember, that client in bed A, he is there as a profit, right, so number one, that person has to be making money for you to be successful...make a profit out of vulnerable people...dangerous'. For Cathal (58) this translated also to the motivations of carers who sought a wage for caring because he had found it so demanding:

> I think it's a huge problem who cares for the children... It's not so much that I disapprove of crèches [but]...caring for your own children is so hard that you are never going to want to care for someone else's...I mean money wouldn't pay me to mind someone else's child. So I would be automatically suspicious of someone who was going to do it for 10 euros an hour. I would have to say they can't be doing it right you know that's the way I would look at it. (Cathal, 58)

Receiving pay for care was felt by several of the men to be corrupting the care relationship. Conor (57) lamented the decline in women's vocationalism and therefore unpaid or low-paid labour in the public sphere, proposing we should ' maybe bring back the nuns'. This 'bring back the nuns' mentality contrasts self-serving instrumental rewards with caring; it laments the decline of a vocational ethic among women and its associated servile identity. Men's anxiety about care and love labour is not only about the decline of traditional family structures and the mistrust of public caring services, it also portrays apprehension about men's access to loving and caring labour and the identity on which this labour is founded.

Although the moral obligations of love labour are often discussed in gender neutral terms, they are implicitly and sometimes explicitly coded as a female moral imperative. The encoding of love labour as an idealised maternal femininity is demonstrated in the first instance by the fact that many caring anxieties were averted when women were available to undertake them. Greg's (51) experience was 'Once my son came along [my wife] gave up work and she didn't want to be putting the young fellow into a crèche, she wanted to look after him.' Facing a lack of trust in public care meant confronting choices between love labour and paid work. However, when the choice meant that 'one of us would have given up work' it is generally a moral–emotional 'choice' borne by women. Women face a greater moral imperative to care because their choosing paid work over care is more often construed as neglectful.

Although these anxieties transverse the different groups of men, men who relied on caring services because women are unwilling or unavailable to do the caring were more positively disposed towards them, as Graham (26) believed: 'I think when they are run properly and they have trusty staff I think they are great. I had [my daughter] in one, it was only two days a week, it was more a pre-school rather than a crèche... I know they are expensive... but [it's ok] if both parents are in full time jobs and they can afford to pay it.' Even for these men, however, their anxieties about the quality of public care were mitigated when care services were able to replicate a feminine caring environment. Fionn (25) saw that 'All those people [who work in the crèche] are really like... it is filled with females, I haven't come across any males in that environment, I wouldn't say there couldn't be but... [the females] can all be very motherly to all the little girls and boys and care for them if they are upset.'

Love labour was seen to be uncorrupted by the self-centred rationality of public or for-profit care services. The status attributed to the nuclear family as a haven from an uncaring world and the duty of care this places on family members, particularly women, intensifies anxieties about caring when familial caring obligations are perceived to be declining. The perceived decline of care capital raised the daunting and dreading prospect of one's own physical dependency particularly during times of illness, senility, infirmity, and disability and the dependence of one's children:

> Like you would have done enough and cared for your own children that they would have that much respect for you and they might keep you at home as long as they could... I'd say it will lead to a situation in a few years time where the younger people that are growing up now, the nursing home will become a convenience for them to put the old people in... There are people who go into nursing homes... out of convenience... they could be cared for at home. They want to be at home... the family doesn't care enough. (Conor, 57)

Conor articulated clear tensions and anxieties around the consequences of non-family care with some of the men feeling trapped in a 'vicious circle' because the family 'doesn't care enough' because 'it's not always possible in today's society'.

Conclusion

Gender identity is central to how caring is defined and constructed. Caring and love labour construct a strong sense of identity because of the deeply moral and affectional nature of the work focussed on the needs of the other person and on the mutuality involved in affective relationships. Caring work places a moral imperative on some people to undertake caring and naturalises this obligation by socialising the requisite cognitive and emotional skills and knowledge in the carer. Thus, caring is feminised in how it constructs a feminine gender identity. Identity is integral to understanding caring relations including its 'depth, complexity and multidimensionality' and 'gendered character' (Lynch, Baker et al. 2009: 8). If love labour is central to personal identities and if caring is primarily a female imperative, then what does this imply for masculinities and the way they are constructed? Although it is possible to have a feminine gender identity and not have a caring identity, it is currently not possible to have a caring identity that is not associated with femininity and therefore, feminised.

The discourse of *nurturing femininity* is a master narrative, or an ideal type, that operates in the men's care stories as a relational necessity for the construction of oppositional instrumental masculinities. But to say that these relational constructs are entirely and always oppositional is inaccurate since not only can they contain contradictions in practice, but particular men will relate to them in different ways depending on several factors. These include the caring obligations they have, their age, and their position in the labour market. The men's stories also evidence an internal dialogue about the meaning of care and their role in caring as they reflect on the shifting gender landscape. Their position location within the labour market and the obligations that places on them in respect of care and the care gap they encounter appears to be crucial in nudging this dialogue in a direction that suits their material location.

6
Breadwinner Masculinities

Chapter 4 highlighted the importance of paid work in men's lives showing how central it was to realising a socially valued masculinity. In keeping with this men understood that their principal role in caring was as breadwinner (earner). In one sense this is unsurprising given how in modern Ireland throughout the 20th century to be a primary breadwinner within the marital heterosexual family was the dominant expectation for men (Kennedy 2001; Rush 2004). Ferguson (2002: 124) argues that being the good provider within the heterosexual family, exclusive of a broader concept of masculinity as nurturing, was the traditional way Irish men constructed hegemonic masculinity. In another sense the prominence of breadwinning in the lives of these men is a little surprising considering first the widespread entry of women into the labour market (O'Sullivan 2007), secondly popular discourses depicting men as involved nurturers (Henwood and Procter 2003), and finally the increasingly complex combination of earner–carer relationships in European societies (Daly and Rake 2003: 73). Still studies rank Ireland and Britain amongst the strongest breadwinner models in Europe with France an example of a moderate one and Sweden a weak one (Lewis 1992). Even today, despite women's radically altered participation in the labour market and the undermining of male breadwinner ideology, male breadwinning practices remain resilient in many European societies (Holter 2007: 431) and especially in Ireland where they comprise a significant minority of household arrangements (Nic Ghiolla Phádraig and Hillard 2007; McGinnity and Russell 2008).

Breadwinner imperatives

Paid work was very important for the men in the study because it enabled them to define themselves earners as well as carers. They understood that if men are able to meet the valued expectations as earner–breadwinners they achieve a sense of masculine caring respectability, as well as the status of fathering and the emotional satisfactions of a secure family life much in keeping with Ferguson's claim about the traditional dominance of married heterosexual breadwinning (2002: 124). This held true for the men from different age, class, and cultural backgrounds, but individual men assigned varying meanings to breadwinner masculinity; for all men it did not exclude nurturing, nor the sharing of breadwinning and caring.

Denis was a wealthy member of a secret male society. He presented a very privileged image of what being a breadwinner involved commenting it is 'nice that the woman is at home having the dinner on the table and looking after the kids and having them all washed', and he talked about his breadwinning role as 'a different aspect [of caring], it's a different sort of pressure'. Peter, a Traveller activist, emphasised the practical caring nature of breadwinning that involved 'making sure the family is maintained, ... supported in every aspect, ... financially, that there is heat, a roof over one's head, children are being supported in attending school and their growth and development outside of school' and practically by 'going to the shop, lighting the fire, making sure the house was warm'.

Male breadwinner family relations traditionally promised men an authoritative role within families in the context of a subordinated role in work (Hayward and Mac án Ghaill 2003: 43), work which can drain men's energies for love and emotional labour (hooks 2004: 94). Similarly several men spoke about the emotional intimacies of family life being a reward for the demands that paid work made of them. Many of these men felt they had little choice but to be breadwinners and talked about feeling drained by the toil of paid labour and providing obligations. Paul, the fathers' rights activist, for example, said 'where guys are at work and they are not getting a lot of fulfilment from their jobs and they are not rated at work and you go home and your kids think you are great. Like you can't fix anything at work but when you go home you can't get anything wrong'. Declan was a union representative for working-class men. He felt that 'the man is out doing his best to make enough money as he can to raise the family, pay the mortgage' and considered breadwinner responsibilities as the 'daily drudge having to slog in to the office or the factory' which consequently meant that many men 'just do the 9 to 5 and get the hell out of it again and try and get home or get to the pub'. Similarly, Conor, a farmer in his late

50s, perceived breadwinning to be a practical economic imperative, as a 'struggle' to 'get by' and realise a basic 'quality of life':

> We had five children by the time we were 33 ... [it was] nothing only a struggle, I suppose, financially, like we were married at 24, we built a house and five children within nine or ten years so it was heavy going but we were happy and everyone was healthy and that was all that mattered I suppose. (Conor, 57)

Many of these men explained the time drain that paid work involved and commented how this restricted their ability to do other things including participating in other caring roles. The fact that men's work and breadwinning were defined as an imposition, sacrifice, and burden by some men, contributed to the feeling that these roles were under-appreciated as caring. For example, Douglas, a farmer in his late 40s, felt men's breadwinner roles were under-appreciated, commenting: 'I would have done those buildings, I suppose I would have liked for [my wife] to be able to come out and see it as something we all achieved ... Everything is taken for granted. Massive things that I would have done.' Therefore, paid work was not only defined in instrumental terms, but it was also framed by a number of the men as a means to express a caring masculinity in the public sphere. In fact practically all of the men in the study perceived themselves as caring through their work, and while a few of the men were employed in caring or community work settings, even men like Liam, a 36-year-old accountant, felt they expressed caring through their work. In fact Rory defined his caring in his workplace to be particularly masculine. Rory was 55 and worked in a managerial role that frequently involved facilitating groups and managing conflict. He said:

> I'm a middle aged man and there's something about mentoring or having a certain amount of experience or something perhaps maybe you see things or experience things and it's not about telling people things but maybe it's about being able to understand especially in this work and some of the struggles that people have. (Rory, 55)

Thus for many men caring is not always synonymous with doing intimate personal care work, and they did not perceive themselves as uncaring by not doing it. There was also a sense that many men emotionally engage in their work in ways that provide them with emotional rewards which compete with the reciprocity we are led to expect from having a greater involvement in caring. That men's work can be emotionally fulfilling and offers a means for men to express caring has been under-explored in the literature. In the social sciences, men's work is analysed primarily in terms of power, status, income, and identity but rarely in terms of caring, either as a means to express and demonstrate care or to feel cared about (especially as an earner/provider). In the care conversations there was also, however, some regret that one's commitment to paid work out of a sense of caring limited one's involvement in family life. Douglas spoke about his generosity and charity to others through his work as a farmer:

> My values have changed an awful lot. I would have been far more sensitive towards other people and I would have seen it as not very rewarding; they kind of see it as being a soft touch ... If you are considerate and helpful and you are not a bully ... always helping people out ... I wonder is there any reward for putting those people first? ... I wonder should I have spent those couple of hours with my children? (Douglas, 48)

The breadwinner imperative, and its association with men's caring, additionally had a flip side; not being able to construct oneself as a breadwinner was seen as an obstacle to defining oneself as caring. Dermot (35) talked about not being able to demonstrate his care for his daughter as an earner because he was unemployed:

> [After a long period of unemployment] ... I went down and got myself a job ... which made me feel a bit more mature ... I kind of feel a bit responsible for her now that she calls me her step-dad which to me is you know motivation for me to care for her and give her the things that she wants and later on in life when she grows up send her through college. I can't have my partner pay for the whole lot. If [my step-daughter] is ever stuck anywhere after a disco or anything like that or if she wants a lift to or from Dublin ... I think that is motivation for me to care for her to look out for her. (Dermot, 35)

Working-class men like Dermot can feel their masculinity under threat when they are unable to define masculinity through breadwinning (Gerson 1993). Goodwin's (2002: 164) study of men in Dublin exposed how men 'feel down, worthless, lazy, emotional, incapable, inactive, negative, lacking self-respect, weak and "not a real man"', as a result of being unemployed and because they could not define themselves as breadwinners, although men may use various discursive resources to defend their masculinity in the face of unemployment (Willott and Griffin 1997). But it is not just working-class men who experience this sense of emasculation. Ni Laoire's (2005, 2002) research on Irish farmers shows a similar pattern. Irish farming masculinities, traditionally based on 'breadwinning', 'independence', 'hard work', and 'pride', are experiencing crisis tendencies because farmers are struggling to stay on the land. Consequently farmers' chances of reproducing traditional patriarchal structures are limited because of diverging gender roles and expectations and are, therefore, finding it difficult to live up to hegemonic farming breadwinner masculinities. Breadwinner expectations can be especially poignant in particular cultural contexts especially cultures which value traditional gender roles including Irish Travellers and other Gyspy communities (Cemlyn et al. 2009). As a Traveller himself, Peter noted '[T]he Traveller man perceives himself as the breadwinner full stop... [I]f he feels that he is not contributing in a tangible way to the support and the maintenance of his family; he feels a failure in some way. You know he feels he has let his family down.' Older men also can experience a feeling of emasculation upon retirement, not least because ageing in Western culture is associated with declining and losing masculinity (Spector-Mersel 2006). Paddy was a voluntary older men's support worker. He explained how older men can often feel emasculated by doing caring work because it reminds them that they are no longer 'productively' employed. This perspective was reflected in the conversations with Dessie (46) and Dave (34) who described how their fathers had to struggle to reconstruct their masculinity as caring on retirement.

Defining men's caring as breadwinning, and defining men as caring by doing paid work, reduces the expectation that men should share equally in hand-on-caring work. The equation of breadwinning with care can mean that men's sacrifice of caring to paid work is not as much of an emotional trade off as it might be; in fact, not being in a breadwinner role means some men feel they are not caring. In contrast, women have more to lose emotionally by sacrificing caring to paid work because they are judged to have a greater moral obligation to care. In short, women feel judged when not caring and men feel judged when not earning (Doucet 2006: 209).

Nurturing proscriptions

Ferguson's (2002) observation that breadwinner roles historically wrote out nurturing from men's lives was supported by several men in their conversations. Now retired from his business, Cathal (58) explained how he had 'spent so much of my life trying to fulfil all of those [providing] needs...it is only in the last number of years I have stopped to think well there is a whole other life and I don't have to kill myself working harder to provide things for other people'. He complained that institutionalised breadwinner expectations offered him little opportunity to consider nurturing aspects of care:

> I just don't think I had all that much time to spare to be paying attention to the caring. They would have had care and attention...but it just wasn't something you could stop and contemplate...and what form it took it's hard to say...I wouldn't have thought about it very deeply at the time...It just would have been a very low priority. (Cathal, 58)

The exclusion of care roles from men's lives was all the more evident for Cathal because he ran a business as well as being the primary carer to his four children after his marriage broke up. Cathal fought a custody dispute with his wife over the care of his children and successfully became their sole custodian. Yet he felt trapped by breadwinner expectations because all the while the courts considered the primacy of his breadwinning role and found it difficult to consider him a primary carer. The system, he felt, could not conceive of men as primary carers, and when they were called on to undertake this role they were not only shrouded with suspicion but were still expected to be primary breadwinners:

> I had always felt I would leave because it never occurred to me there would be any other outcome. One of my friends said to me...'Well look she's the problem why should you leave?'...it ended up me getting a barring order against her and getting custody of the children...It was very, very difficult and very, very long drawn out and very expensive...If our genders had been reversed and she got a barring order against me I would simply be told to go away whereas in order to get a barring order against her I had to provide her with the means, an apartment on her own...I have always had to work quite hard because when I got married the woman stopped working [Up until 1973 a Marriage Bar applied to many women in white-collar occupations in Ireland requiring them to cease their employment upon marriage (Fahey 2003).] and you had to support the family from a very early age. Then when my marriage broke up and I took custody of the children. I still had to work very hard because I not

only had to pay maintenance but I had to maintain the children and everything as well. (Cathal, 58)

Greg (51) recounted a similar story. He spoke about the surprise on the part of social services at his wanting to take on a primary caring role for his children when his wife was unable to after she became ill. Greg came across the ambiguity of the State about men's role in caring. The social services, he claimed, were on the one hand 'basically saying are you going to stick around with the children or will we put the children into care?' Greg felt surprised and shocked that social services would consider he might want to leave his children in care because he was a man: 'And my reaction was that the children were mine and they were not going into care, if I had to go on the dole [unemployment welfare payment], we'll get through this, my children are staying with me.' On the other hand, Greg noted how supportive social services were when they realised he was a caring father:

[When social services] saw I was more hands-on [they] were very good...there was a bit of a surprise that I didn't just up and leave...Some people actually said to me 'Fair dues to you for sticking around, any other fellow would be off'...mostly from women...they assumed that if something goes wrong that the man just shags off...there was support...there was a lot of surprise which kind of irked me. (Greg, 51)

The way that men in Ireland were traditionally defined by the state as being care-free is reflected in various ways that men interface with the state as carers. Men's rights groups argue the courts discriminate against men and favour women, and historically the courts have assumed caring to be women's responsibility although there is evidence to suggest this has changed (Coulter 2007). Nonetheless, the relationship between masculinity and care services is highly problematic. According to Ferguson (1998: 33) 'men present to the helping services in two ways: as a problem; and as men who have problems'. Especially in respect of childcare, men are commonly perceived as dangerous and their involvement is shrouded in suspicion (Cameron 2001). More particularly men are defined as sexually dangerous and violent. For example, institutional abuse and neglect scandals in Ireland have involved mainly (though not exclusively) men in recent decades (O'Sullivan and Rafferty 1999; Ryan 2009; Ferguson 1995; Keenan 2011). Studies show how social services can act in contradictory ways in respect of men's caring, sometimes allocating more care resources to support male carers because they are perceived to be less competent and, therefore, have greater need (Cullen, Delaney, and Duff 2004; Bubeck 1995: 164), although sometimes allocating fewer and gender insensitive services because men are overlooked as potential carers or perceived as dangerous (Ferguson and Hogan 2004; Pringle 1995). Child-protection discourses can marginalise men from caring and hinder gender equality by depicting men as essentially dangerous (Connell 2000: 192). Fathers can be excluded from nurturing roles by the practices of social services when men are uncritically and often inappropriately defined in this way (Ferguson and Hogan 2004). Brown et al. (2009: 25) argue that child-welfare discourses view fathers as 'deviant, dangerous, irresponsible and irrelevant' and suggest further that men's absence in child welfare is 'inextricably linked to blaming mothers' which 'ignores potential risks and assets for both mothers and fathers'. Involved fathering has many benefits for children and should be actively supported in ways that do not compromise gender equality or negatively affect the well-being of women (Featherstone 2009).

The imperative that men should be earners exclusive of a role in nurturing confines men to a one-dimensional role in their families. For this group of men at least, male breadwinner norms were resilient because not only did they facilitate the legitimation of masculinity through paid work and other publicly orientated pursuits, additionally they satisfied the expectation that men care as earners. In other words, the strong association between paid work and breadwinning meant that men's work was defined as love labour by many men, both because their earnings practically contribute to family well-being ('care for'), and because their intentions, or feelings, are caring ('caring about'). Many of the older men especially defined their breadwinning as a determined role that was heavily socialised, internalised, and institutionalised, yet the deinstitutionalisation of male breadwinning has undermined men's feeling of contributing to their family when men's involvement as carers is equated solely with providing. Breadwinning is the traditional way that men have achieved respect and recognition. They feel proud, accepted, and loved as fathers because their resources as providers are highly valued and women were dependent on them. The discourses and practices that regulate breadwinner masculinity, whilst potentially drawing men into limited amounts of caring, and not discounting the contribution they may make to their families or that they feel care ('care about'), also restrict the amount and types of nurturing that men practice. Those men who continue to hold rigid breadwinning definitions confront a social climate that increasingly values dual-earner-carer roles and expects men to possess a more nurturing masculinity.

The career imperative

Paid work and participation in the public sphere remains central to how masculinity is defined, and heteronormative breadwinning operates as a master discourse that regulates men's caring. Coinciding with ideological shifts favouring men's greater involvement in nurturing (Henwood and Procter 2003), the dominant male breadwinner model of the 20th century has given way in Western societies to a variety of dual-earner-carer models which see both men and women juggling and negotiating caring responsibilities in families in more complex ways. The shift from a male breadwinner model to dual-earner-carer models has not seen an even or progressive path to gender equality. Change has been patchy and uneven even amongst the Western societies (Kremer 2007). Men remain principally defined as primary breadwinners and secondary carers and women are principally defined as primary carers and secondary breadwinners (Lewis 2001b). According to Daly and Rake (2003: 169–70) people in the Western societies continue to have too much of the traditional male breadwinner model and too few opportunities to achieve the model they most desire, 'the one and a half earner arrangement'. Risman maintains these 'cognitive images of parenthood' are incredibly resilient:

> Mothers, employed or not, are still expected to nurture their children emotionally and physically. Fathers are still expected to earn a family wage, even when that is not possible. Fathers are also expected to help mothers with nurturing, but they are not judged incompetent if they do not help very much as long as they continue to earn a good living. (Risman 1998: 47)

Though male breadwinner households remain strong in Ireland in comparison to many other European societies, they have been surpassed by dual-earner-carer households as the dominant model (McGinnity and Russell 2008). Dual-carer relationships raise the prospect of men benefiting from a fuller involvement in nurturing work, and men's active participation as fathers can allow women greater freedom from restrictive moral obligations to care (Doucet 2006: 243). The reality has been somewhat different with the full sharing of care workloads a stalled revolution (Hochschild 1989; Gerson 2010). This stalled revolution is explainable, in part at least, by the fact that men attach such a high value to their identity in the public sphere especially through paid work and because male breadwinning continues to operate as a principal narrative for how men define themselves both as workers and carers. Nonetheless, as women's participation in the labour market in Ireland has dramatically increased, it is a narrative in tension with an institutional context favouring dual-breadwinner practices (Creighton 1999; Meyer 1998; Hilliard and Nic Ghiolla Phádraig 2007). In contrast to many of the older men's depiction of breadwinning as an imperative, men who were under the age of 40 considered dual-breadwinner roles now institutionalised, and this they believed reduced the possibility for any parent to become a primary carer. Dermot's (35) attitude was typical in this respect. He suggested 'the financial pressure nowadays is too much ... you would need a second mortgage with childcare fees and the two parents would have to work end of story'.

The tension between men's investment in the symbolic capital that paid labour provides and their investment in love labour is especially notable for young fathers who spoke about the pressure of having to manage paid work and caring. Fionn was a 25-year-old financial services employee married with a young child. He was eager to build his career, but he was also a committed family man who maintained he was an equal participant in caring with his wife. He explained there was 'no easy ride ... none of this snooze lark ... straight out of bed, shower and get yourself ready'. He commented: 'I have to get up at 6:00 in the morning, get myself ready and then between 6:30 and 7:30 get myself and my daughter ready for crèche, drop her to crèche and then get to work myself .' Nonetheless, Fionn talked about being highly committed to building his career and was very conscious of his occupation status. For him it was imperative to maintain his place on the 'ladder':

> If I lost my job tomorrow it would be a big problem. So work is always a priority that I have to work and the study that comes with work because I do exams as well to further my development in my job ... If I want to achieve what I want to achieve then I have to put a lot of importance into this ... If I want to maintain this job and improve on it I have to treat it with respect and that is why it is a priority. (Fionn, 25)

Hooks (2004) proposes that men's commitment to paid work can mean that they experience a sense of panic when they face spending time with self or family in 'non-productive' ways. Similarly Seidler (2003: 218–19) talks about 'slowing down' and spending time with small children can be difficult in a culture that values 'speeding up', and when they do it can bring up unresolved feelings for men because the means of performing a valued identity is removed. Men, he believes, often sacrifice the emotional bond with their children because they think that they can develop it later when they have more time, only to find this more challenging than they had imagined (Seidler 2003: 222). Men's failure to realise the value of doing caring for their happiness and well-being is a problem for men (Clare 2000; Seidler 1989; Jump and Haas 1987). A chief obstacle to this is that men are unwilling to lose the command of resources, status, power, and identity that public masculinity offers (May 1998; Pease 2002b; Palkovitz, Copes, and Woolfolk 2001). Aldous (1998: 16) notes that 'Being active fathers goes against the definition of traditional masculinity. Giving up authority to wives, taking on dirty, demanding and unpleasant chores of child care and losing leisure time are aspects of current prescriptions of fatherhood that make it hard for most men to conform.' For these reasons primary caring men often try to remain connected to traditional sources of masculinity including paid work (Doucet 2007).

The significance of paid work for masculinity is especially pronounced when men feel the pressure to be more involved in caring, such as when men become fathers for the first time. Many men increase their investment in paid work when they become fathers (Percheski and Wildeman 2008). Women's housework tends to increase after significant life-course transitions such as upon marriage or cohabitation or after the birth of a child whereas men's tends to remain stable (Baxter, Hewitt, and Haynes 2008). Many studies have shown how men only marginally increase their caring and domestic work when women are employed, feel less compelled by guilt to increase their time with their children, and often increase their involvement in paid work when they transition to parenting even when they hold egalitarian beliefs (McMahon 1999; Fox 1997; Thomas 1990). Similarly, Fionn (25) described the increasing significance of paid work in his life since becoming a father:

[My career] has grown in importance since I have become a father because there is the classic tradition where you provide for your family but yet in this day and age both parents provide for their family... Work is always a priority as well. I would never just miss a day of work for any reason other than it is a big reason to miss a day of work. ... The only day I have called in sick this year was because my daughter was sick that day and no one else could take her so I had to you know. (Fionn, 25)

Like Fionn, Graham (26) acknowledged his 'helping' and talked about wanting to be more involved in caring:

> Oh I'd avail of [parental leave], yes, absolutely, if needs be ... when [my daughter] was born ... well I got three days paternal leave ... I think that is a bit unfair because you need to be there ... while your partner or wife is getting back on their feet. I mean for a first child they keep you in maybe two days in the hospital, so that is two days off, the birth and the day after, and then when she comes back home you are back at work the day after ... And that is when she needs you ... around the house doing things and helping a bit. (Graham, 26)

However, being in a less secure working-class occupation as a maintenance technician Graham believed there would be little sympathy for his need to avail of greater care time. He felt it wouldn't be such a problem if it was a 'special case' like if his daughter was 'very sick' but 'if it was a case of me going in and saying "Look I want to work part time because I want to spend more time with my kid". "I think that might be" they would say "So does everybody, but you can't do it"'. The contradiction is clear for men in the study like Fionn and Graham; though the emerging norms governing men's involvement in caring expect men to be both breadwinners and nurturers (Henwood and Procter 2003; Borchgrevink and Holter 1995), and intimate partners (Giddens 1992), paid work and participation in the public sphere remain central to how masculinity is defined and to renege on paid work is to fail to legitimate their masculinity.

Care-free workers

Opportunities for men like Fionn and Graham, and several other men in the study, to become more involved as fathers are restricted by the limited care leave entitlements that accrue to men in conjunction with normative gender expectations. However, among other factors, occupational status seems to offer crucial leverage in negotiating care time. Many professional dual-career couples are successfully using their educational and occupational cultural capital as leverage to negotiate more egalitarian care relations (Risman 1998: 154). Negotiating care time can be easier for professional workers with established careers if individual managers are sympathetic to care responsibilities (Lynch and Lyons 2009). As a middle-class academic, Simon (48) was in a strong position to negotiate flexible working arrangements when, as a separated father, he took on shared primary care responsibilities for his two teenaged children with his wife:

> I completely changed everything; how I lived and how I worked. I got the arrangement from the job to work from home and I was looking after the kids... I did manage to get a reasonable balance with the work inside and the work outside and I did manage to manipulate the situation... I started a bit of a rebellion... they eventually bought me off... since then I haven't had a job as such... the organisation... was actually quite far thinking in the flexibility they could give me at the time and I did push it. (Simon, 48)

The flexibility associated with self-employment was a great advantage to Cathal (58), who managed to run a business and provide care to his four children as a single father because he had the freedom and resources to be able to do so:

> I ran my own business... I then brought the business home... it gave me a great deal of flexibility as I could work in the evening or whenever, but of course if I had had an ordinary job where I went out no I couldn't have done it. It wouldn't have been possible... I had to look for ways of making my career flexible... to pay the mortgage pay the ex-wife, pay the children's school fees and at the same time spend a significant amount of time with the kids. (Cathal, 58)

Greg (51) was not a professional worker but his female employers were sympathetic to his situation when he became a primary carer for his children permitting him considerable flexibility in work. Greg was lucky in this respect because other men with working-class occupations including Fionn (25), Graham (26), and Tommy (49) spoke of more restrictive experiences. Tommy felt himself lucky that his employer and work colleagues permitted him certain flexibilities when he took on a primary caring role for his children, but it was on the understanding that this was borrowed time. He found his colleagues to be 'very supportive' in that they 'understood the predicament that I was in... the nature of the work that I do, I could be given time off... it was an unwritten rule that if you did get time off you were going to do it some other way anyway and it worked out like that and balanced itself out anyway'. This meant that negotiating care time placed you 'under pressure to do your work and people want results in your work and if you are not providing the results then you are underperforming and you have to carry out the tasks of your work and if you can't do that then, you know, goodbye.' This feeling that you could be underperforming was also experienced by Dessie, a 46-year-old farmer in partnership with his brother. Dessie was adamant that he wished to be more involved in caring for his two children, one of whom had an intellectual disability. However, as a self-employed farmer, he did not feel entitled to take time off to care and he talked of feeling inadequate because he believed he was not giving enough to paid work as a result of care obligations.

> I actually felt very, very inadequate... I was also in partnership with my brother and, you know, if you are in partnership with someone you are expected to carry the role but no one understood... I was so torn... I felt I wasn't giving to my work... I felt very, very stretched... I was actually close to having a nervous breakdown at one stage over this and I could see that [my wife] was wilting as well and it was very, very difficult. It was a very black moment in my life and there was nowhere to turn. (Dessie, 46)

Dessie spoke about feeling 'pulled in both directions' because he wanted to be more involved in caring for his family:

> I am extremely aware... that particularly in the earlier years and when I was maybe under the umbrella of my parents I found it extremely difficult to actually get them to understand and therefore I was pulled in both directions; needed at home in my place and needed in the farm. And in many cases it was the farm that took over and not my family situation, and I actually regret in many ways that I didn't have the strength to help out in the earlier years more. (ibid.)

Cultural and organisational pressures on new fathers to continue to be loyal and committed care-free workers result in some men who reject these standards being placed on a 'daddy track' in terms of being overlooked for promotion and career advancement (Gerson 2003). While the institutional obstacles to involved nurturing may be frustrating for some men as they can be for women, women tend to develop strategies which continue to promote their autonomy, whereas men tend to revert to 'neo-traditionalism' (Gerson 2010). Motherhood, or the expectation that one will become a mother, is a disadvantage for women who do not conform to the ideal unencumbered worker (Carney 2009), but fatherhood is not necessarily a disadvantage or equally disadvantageous for different kinds of men. In fact for some men becoming a father helps men realise a patriarchal dividend. Fathers with characteristics associated with hegemonic masculinity, stereotypically white-middle-class professionals, who have traditional gender divisions of labour at home, often receive a 'daddy bonus' irrespective of whether they work longer hours since becoming fathers, as Hodges and Budig (2010: 742) note 'becoming a father is a source of privilege for privileged men'.

Some dual-breadwinner models can advance gender equality when supported by progressive welfare systems (Rush and Richardson 2007) but many continue to write out care from economic and social life relying on women as the default carers (Lewis 2001a). Though the majority of welfare states are transitioning from male breadwinner models of care provision, they often replace them with models that retain gender inequalities (Daly and Rake 2003). The result is a dominant family system where women are primary carers and only secondary earners and men are primary earners and only secondary carers, or as Holter (1995: 101) astutely remarks, men effectively amount to a 'reserve army of domestic labour'. The European Union, for example, as Walby (2004) argues, resists addressing the women's burden of care on the grounds that the principle of subsidiary makes any intervention a matter for individual Member States and because it is founded as a neo-liberal project that considers the needs of citizens as workers rather than carers, and also because it is committed to fiscal conservativism. However, she also notes how within the EU there has been some movement in terms of considering the needs of the parent–carer, and the regulation of non-standard forms of work which promotes gender equality. There again, different Member States deal with care responsibilities in different ways with some states having much more radical ambitions and better outcomes. Progressive change is far from straightforward or even across different European societies (Lewis et al. 2008). For example, far in contrast to the 'use it or lose it' or Daddy's month policies of progressive welfare societies, such as Sweden, Norway, and Iceland, which reserve part of care leave for fathers in order to reinforce men's roles as carers in families (Daly and Rake 2003; Lewis 2001b), there is no statutory paternity leave entitlement for men in Ireland which, along with the UK, is also unique in Europe in not having paid parental leave (Daly 2001b: 41). Parental leave does encourage men to be more involved with their children (Tanaka and Waldfogel 2007; Nepomnyaschy and Waldfogel 2007) and social policy interventions can alter the legal and moral framework that underpin care-free masculinities (Gregory and Milner 2011: 14). Men can, however, be slow to take up on parental leave because of other factors such as the lack of available and affordable child care, because of apprehension about the effect of child care on children, because they don't feel acknowledged as carers as men, and because they fear it will affect their careers and earnings (Holter, Egeland, and Svare 2009; Gaertner, Puchert, and Hoeyng 2005). In practice then, although they do better, even societies with progressive policies on gender equality struggle to realise gender equality in care work (Bjornberg 2002; Seward et al. 2006).

Though more progressive societies emphasise gender equality goals as well as labour market objectives, the care policies in Western societies generally view care as a barrier to work rather than work itself (Standing 2001). This means that rights in respect of care are justified primarily in respect of the right to paid work (Daly and Rake 2003). When caring is considered by welfare states, interventions are primarily geared to support women's caring in the home or increase women's participation in the labour market rather than redistribute caring between men and women (Government of Ireland 2007; Daly and Rake 2003; Stratigaki 2004). Daly and Rake (2003: 161 and 170; Daly 2001b) note the inconsistencies of many welfare state policy goals and outcomes in terms of care and gender equality. The involvement of states in supporting women's labour market supply through 'family friendly' policies often leaves the negotiation of who does the care to the private sphere. In this way, State interventions function more to prop up the gender order or at best to mitigate the worst effects of gender inequality rather than tackle structural inequalities. Ireland is a good example of this. Caring is primarily defined as private concerns with individuals and families expected to organise their relations in whatever way they can, and preferably by buying individual solutions on the for-profit market (Hayes and Bradley 2006; Rush 2006; Daly and Clavero 2002). Entitlements that exist are geared to retain workers (especially women) rather than to promote equality and men's caring. Both Fionn and Graham were employed in multinational corporations, which again tend to individualise care as a private concern for workers (Zimmerman, Litt, and Bose 2006), set against the background of minimal state intervention to regulate care leave entitlements (Cullen, Delaney, and Duff 2004). Similar care-free gender regimes are found in the legal profession (Bacik and Drew 2003, 2006), in higher education (Grummell, Devine, and Lynch 2009; O'Connor 2008), in small businesses (Drew and Humbert 2010), and among entrepreneurs (Drew and Humbert 2011).

Approaches to equality as sameness are generally modelled on male care-free norms. On this basis women, and men with care responsibilities, will only benefit if they are in a position to act the same way as men or women with no care responsibilities. Care leave available to different men in different cultural and legal contexts affects men's opportunities to be more involved in caring for children or other dependents and undoubtedly equal care leave entitlements for men would be a significant advance for gender equality in caring. However, these constraining factors can also be overplayed. Fionn and Graham also felt the competitive pressure to achieve in work overriding considerations to sacrifice work-time to care time. Graham said 'I hate to make it sound like I have a problem minding my child, ... I don't, but it would be impacting on my career and my future and I'd have to sacrifice college and I don't think in my job I am in a position where I can ask for half time, it's pretty much all or nothing.'

The relatively care-free status of Graham and Fionn exists within a highly competitive organisational and cultural climate where men (and perhaps increasingly women) are expected to be care-free, and the management of care responsibilities is expected to be a private affair. Negotiating masculinity and caring depends on women's informal care work because the gender order especially institutionalises caring as an individual responsibility for men. Countless studies now show how men's investment in their careers is enabled by the willingness of women to undertake the caring. Men like Fionn and Graham ultimately manage to invest in paid work because the care gaps they encounter are filled by women. Fionn commented 'We have my daughter in crèche three days a week and then [my wife's] mum or my mum takes her the other days' and Graham mentioned 'if it ever did come to [missing work] my mother would gladly help out...I am lucky in that, I am blessed that I have such a good support structure at home...If I can't be there, my mother would be there'. It is this invisibility of women's care labour which 'supports an economic system that continues to operate as if workers are disembodied people with no family responsibilities' (Risman 1998: 42). The implicit assumption of the prevailing model for caring relations is that men can delegate the bulk of their love–labour obligations to their wives, mothers (or sisters and daughters) and that their involvement in love labour can be reduced to quality time. Men are excused from doing much of the emotional caring work, judged less harshly than women for being less involved, and praised more when they do nurturing work (McMahon 1999).

Neo-liberal masculinities

Contemporary gendered care obligations emerge within the socio-economic climate of rapid capitalist expansion and globalisation allied to the neo-liberal pursuit of a purely market-regulated society (Harvey 2005). This neo-liberal order has given rise to shifting gender practices globally and locally (Connell 2005; Segal 2007), although within neo-liberalism 'patriarchal gender relations are re-shaped but not transcended' (Connell 2011: 55). Though globalised production produces localised forms of masculinities, there is a global configuration around the logic of neo-liberalism in the form of 'Transnational Business Masculinity' [TBM] (Connell 2000: 52; 2005). Neo-classical economics define people as purely rational actors in pursuit of economic and social ends (Craib 1992), whose primary concern is personalised human capital acquisition (Lynch, Cantillon et al. 2009). The ideal neo-liberal worker is defined as an independent, rational actor who is perceived as mobile, flexible, highly productive, and unattached and this sets the agenda for men's relations to privilege self-reliance and intense competitiveness (Hearn and Pringle 2006a; Knights and Tullberg 2011). The neo-liberal worker is, therefore, a masculinised worker who is expected to be care-free, independent, rational, and self-sufficient with an instrumental orientation to the world (Lewis 2001b).

The 'Rational Economic Actor' (REA) represents an 'anti-care' 'model of the citizen' that is increasingly institutionalised as an entrepreneurial machismo within an intensely masculinised public sphere (Lynch, Baker et al. 2009: 17). These codes of high-status global masculinities are self-centred rather than other-centred because the traits of aggression, independence, flexibility, and competition are highly prized by global capitalism. Androcentric working practices institutionalise and construct the citizen–worker in relation to these masculine norms (Rantalaiho and Heiskanen 1997; Gaertner, Puchert, and Hoeyng 2005). Caring occupations, for example, are increasingly organised around male institutional norms of managerialism and professionalism which clash with caring norms including vocational moral imperatives (e.g. see Allen 2001). The REA is ever more institutionalised in educational and political codes that dictate the need for instrumental and performance-driven managerial practices in employment creating hierarchies that subordinate women and non-hegemonic masculinities (Grummell, Devine, and Lynch 2009). The individualised adult-worker model fails to recognise care as fundamental to human existence. Masculinities premised on need to succeed, achieve, and compete mean men have little interest or investment in care or love labour unless it entails an instrumental gain (Seidler 1989: 26); emotional ties become sacrificed to performance and productivity (Connell 2002: 101; 2005: 257).

This neo-liberal ideology of advanced capitalism has dominated the Irish political and economic landscape throughout the 'Celtic Tiger' years (O'Sullivan 2007; Coulter and Coleman 2003). Ferguson (2002) maintains that TBM has replaced the heterosexual breadwinner and the celibate priest as the most hegemonic form of masculinity in Ireland. He argues that men are spending less time with children and rather than witnessing more men involved in care generally, the care of children in families, childcare services, and schools is increasingly done by women. Although men may ideologically embrace a new discourse of nurturing, in practice the feminisation of care is increasing. Ferguson (2002) claims there is a sense that men in Ireland are slowly adjusting to changing caring expectations, whilst others are resisting reforming gender relations and are struggling with conflicting demands. While there is a willingness for men to change, dominant definitions of masculinity as a competitive–worker–producer pursued by neo-liberal capitalism has increasingly privatised, individualised, and, by default, feminised caring. Although women carry the care burden, it is masculinity and masculine norms – to which women are also subjected – that embody the prototypical neo-liberal worker. The fact that men are expected to be care-free marginalises men who would like to do more caring; it legitimates male domination in the public sphere and it subordinates men who become full-time carers.

Men are rarely willing to embrace identities that delegitimise them as men, but they don't want to write caring entirely out of their lives. The intensive, other-centred realities of caring contrast markedly with contemporary norms of individualised self-identity (interest) and the reflective life project, and neo-liberal discourses of masculinity based on competitive individualism. So how do men deal with the contradictory expectations on the one hand to be involved nurturers and on the other to be competitive care-free workers? The career imperative and lack of care leave opportunities that Graham (26) talked about constraining his involvement in caring were integrated into a breadwinner care narrative that allowed him to engage competitively in paid work whilst at the same time realise caring goals. Becoming a father, he explained, 'has made me want to do better... I am very focused on my career and everything I do now I kind of do with her [his daughter] in mind... Sometimes financially it can be a bit of a strain, especially since she started school... It's just I suppose it made me want to do better for myself ... So the better I can do I can provide for her'. Just like Fionn (25), being a good father meant being a good earner/provider.

Thébaud (2010) claims the negotiation of caring practices is not simply a matter of power exchanges, it is also a matter of gender ideology. The 'hegemonic gender expectation that men should be breadwinners' (p. 349) affects the negotiation of household practices and Thébaud's cross-national analysis suggests differences are discernable in cultural contexts with stronger male breadwinner norms. 'Doing masculinity' in more conservative cultural contexts is more pronounced, restricting the scope for men to engage in caring, but even in more egalitarian contexts men feel the pressure to live up to gender expectations. Accordingly, Thébaud claims that breadwinning is optional for women but not for men. The ideology that me should be breadwinners, therefore, continues to shape men's practices, though in varying ways in different societies.

Nonetheless, the degree to which different men feel excused from nurturing and other forms of caring varies, with only a minority of the men defining themselves exclusively as breadwinners. Even when breadwinning is understood as a medium for love labour there is an acknowledgement that it sacrifices nurturing and other forms of caring to earning. Therefore, men make trade offs between their investment in masculinity through paid work and their investment in love labour within primary care relations. Sacrificing one's investment in paid work for caring means reducing one's investment in hegemonic masculinity and the competitiveness of work means for many men it is like an 'all or nothing' choice. When caring and occupational imperatives clash, and when women are unwilling or unavailable to fill the care gap, work-based masculinity is rigorously tested. The way that men are affected by and respond to these challenges depend not only on the extent to which they accept stereotypical associations between masculinity and paid work and femininity and unpaid caring, but also on how they perceive their masculinity legitimated in public life.

At least for these men, their allegiance to breadwinner discourse is resilient because not only does it provide a means to satisfy instrumental goals associated with having a dominant masculinity, but it also has affective dimensions as it enables men to see themselves caring by providing material security for those they love or care for. For them caring entails a sense of 'caring about' and some men are involved in 'caring for', if not for all on an equal basis with women. The meaning of breadwinning for these men is that it involves having both instrumental and caring goals and, therefore, it allows men to balance their investment in affective and instrumental aspects of their identity within the contest of what is expected of them. Several factors are important when men do confront care choices within the prevailing gender order (Gregory and Milner 2009: 5). These include the rigidity of the gender difference ideology they hold and the extent to which they define caring as unmanly. The degree to which their masculinity is defined through paid work also impacts on how much men have to lose by reneging on a care-free masculinity. And the cost varies with social class position. For low-status ethnic minority men, as Peter highlighted, the cost was measured in terms of the immediate censure that displays of public care would elicit from his peers.

Conclusion

Men's interests in paid work in the public sphere clashes with love labouring when caring expectations impinge on the amount of time, energy, and effort men assign to their work. In some cases this means that men feel caught between caring obligations and careers. However, love labour and paid work can be less in conflict than might be presumed. First, men are rarely called on to make a choice between investing in their identities through paid work by taking on primary caring responsibilities. Secondly, men can feel they are contributing equally to caring either by believing they have an equal and complementary workload, or by sharing certain aspects of caring. Thirdly, (dual) breadwinning continues to operate as a master narrative for how men define their caring and so they feel they are caring when contributing as earners. Fourthly, as well as offering a means to acquire instrumental symbolic capital, paid work can also offer men a means to express care; to feel they are 'caring for' and 'caring about' others, and therefore, to also feel appreciated and admired by others for their caring in public. Thus the contradictory meanings assigned to the caring rationale for men's investments in paid work helps in explaining the resilience of gender practices. An important finding therefore is that despite increasing expectations on men to be involved in nurturing in various ways, men do not necessarily compromise a sense of themselves as caring by investing time and energy in paid labour; for some it can, but for others investing more in paid work equates with greater caring.

Men can find the benefits of love labour difficult to grasp since doing primary caring contradicts masculine identity constructed in the public sphere. The public sphere where masculine identity is achieved and preformed is not only important for men because of the status, resources, and power that it provides men, but, moreover, for its affective rewards in terms of feeling desired, loved, appreciated, and affirmed. Embracing a feminised caring masculinity exposes contradictions between definitions of love labour as sacrificial and selfless and definitions of masculinity as care-free, irresponsible, adventurous, independent, and committed to the public sphere. This is evident in how men can find it difficult to realise the responsibility of caring or find it rewarding. Cathal (58) compares his life to the care-free life his brother has enjoyed; he concludes that, on balance, the caring rewards are not worth the economic and social sacrifice he has made. Similarly Liam (36) finds caring so burdensome that he cannot comprehend how anyone would want to do paid care work because of its paltry economic rewards.

Masculinity is not only about power, status, and resources but it is also about the bodily emotional and moral aspects. The emotional relations of the gender order include the emotional attachments and commitment men have to the public sphere as well as their primary care relations. Going against the affective social expectations and the norms of desire for men risks being defined as unmanly and being denied the love, care, and solidarity of other men (and often, of women). To be a primary carer is to lose hegemonic masculinity and this is interpreted by many men as a moral judgement of their inferiority.

7
Nurturing Masculinities

The conversations overall demonstrated a considerable degree of uncertainty among men about their role in nurturing care. Many men continue to be subject to inexpressive norms, although this is stronger for some men. Nonetheless, there was considerable ambiguity among the men about their involvement in nurturing because dominant definitions of caring equate it with femininity. For these men at least, their experiences suggest that dominant definitions of masculinity are the antithesis of dominant definitions of caring because dominant masculinities are defined in opposition to femininity. Being 'soft', intimate, and sensitive is said to go against dominant norms, conventions, identities, or innate dispositions for men. Some men claim that men have different ways of dealing with emotions, whereas others define these emotional differences as a problem for men. Though emotionally expressive care norms have exerted a strong influence on contemporary Irish masculinities they are not so ascendant among men to permit them to easily embrace primary caring. Many men are greatly apprehensive about how to be men in an expressive way, but different men react to these norms and negotiate masculinities in different ways. The fact that masculinity is stereotypically defined to be emotionally inexpressive has implications for men's involvement in nurturing care, and the topic of men's emotionality was a major theme in the conversations.

Men and nurturing

Most of the men in the study had an interest in having a care-free life and only a minority 'chose' otherwise. Nonetheless, the men's personal accounts of their involvement in nurturing care work were reasonably diverse with many of the men talking about having caring obligations to their partners, parents, kin or friends, and for fathers, especially for their children. Fionn (25), Graham (26), Jamal (32), Dermot (35), Dessie (46), John (47), Simon (48), Tommy (49), Greg (51), and Cathal (58) in varying amounts all claimed to have been involved in hands-on care work with their children. Conor (57), Douglas (48), Adam (73), and Nevan (74) claimed more traditional and less hands-on roles with their children. Having no children, Cian (49), Pascal (48), Liam (36), and Charlie (28) also had very little care responsibilities although Charlie for a short time claimed to have cared for his mother and grandmother when they were ill. Angus (43) was a full-time primary carer for his elderly parents; Dave (34), Rory (55), John (47), and Douglas (48) claimed to be secondary carers for elderly parents; and Conor (57) also facilitated the care of his brother who had an intellectual disability.

The men spoke about their care relations being important to them, but there was considerable variation in how they accounted for the level and type of involvement in nurturing care work. Although many of them claimed to be involved in various aspects of care beyond bread-winning, several men stated having little input into nurturing aspects of care. Being emotionally distant and practically uninvolved were more typical for older men like Adam (73). As a wealthy, retired business man Adam defined his caring role throughout his life to his wife and three children in terms of preparing them for the external world; for life in the public sphere:

> I must say I should feel guilty because it was my wife who looked after all of those things you know...I must say I was occupied with busi-ness...So I wasn't a good parent in that sense...My business requires me to be away a lot...I wasn't that settled father you see but I took care of them...We sent them to give them an education and we took care that they had a good home...Any opportunity I had...I would bring them to see the world and on occasion we would discuss what was a good next step or what wasn't good you know. (Adam, 73)

Therefore, based on the 'opportunity' that arose Adam took care of his children by providing education, a home, and by introducing them to public masculine-defined spaces. This was also the case for Conor (57) who, while perceiving himself in a caring role for his children and his disabled brother, acknowledged that 'My wife...she looks after [my brother]...you know, feeds, and washes his clothes and looks after him the very same as one of her own.' Again, this was similar for Douglas, a

48-year-old farmer with six children. Douglas had inherited the family farm because he was the eldest son, and therefore he was responsible for providing care for his elderly mother. His inheriting the farm had led to considerable acrimony with his three sisters, a not uncommon event (see Pitts et al. 2009), and incidentally a situation that constructs women farmers and farmers' wives as helpers (Price 2010). Douglas explained the quid pro quo as the expectation that he provide care for his mother. While defining his care in breadwinner terms, he additionally claimed to be involved in caring in a supportive capacity:

> Whether you inherit a farm or just a house, the person who stays at home tends to have the responsibilities ... I'd make sure my mother would get her breakfast ... I'd still make sure that there is somebody there to bring her here, bring her there, make sure she is ok ... I don't tend to get recognised for that; that is a responsibility. I have no problem with that responsibility ... but [my sisters] don't tend to recognise it or they never said thanks for doing that. (Douglas, 48)

Lynch, Lyons and Cantillon (2009b) describe men's typical involvement in caring as 'care commanding'; whilst not totally absent from care, men tend to be involved in more formal events, such as birthdays, religious ceremonies, family outings, and various supportive care roles. Like Douglas they wish to be involved to some extent in managing the primary caring ('care footsoldiering'), or the everyday work of care or others.

In contrast to men like Adam, most of the men claimed to have a greater involvement in primary caring at 'all levels' including 'feeding' 'cooking', 'cleaning', 'school runs', 'school meetings', 'health appointments', 'ironing', 'shopping', 'administrative arrangements', 'reading stories', 'changing nappies [diapers]', 'preparing bottles', 'brushing hair', 'cleaning clothes', 'preparing lunch', and 'emotional work'. Declan reflected on his experience working with men in his capacity as a trade union official. He alleged that the men he worked with were increasingly sharing caring:

> [A] lot of the men who come in here are asking for help from us for their children's clubs ... they are becoming much more involved with their kids. That wouldn't have been the traditional image ... Their wives are working in many cases ... They are anxious to get time off to share the responsibility of looking after the family. That's changed tremendously! (Declan, union representative)

And in doing so, he maintained, men are constructing more nurturing masculinities:

> The people I look after would never have been categorised in the category of changing kids' nappies [diapers] or minding children. That's changed a lot now and there's a lot of hurt and pride and all the rest, but they are coming round beginning to learn that's the way of the world now, and that's what it takes for families to survive and some are liking it... Circumstances change people tremendously... They are forced to dig down deeply into their emotions and find that they have what it takes to share with people and to bond with people and to help people around them. (ibid.)

Declan's insight is that men are being forced to change because of material circumstances, and this process of change calls on men to make deeper emotional changes; a contradictory process that entails both benefits and burdens for men. The conversations with many of the men in the study matched Declan's observation that men were increasingly willing to be actively involved in caring. Jamal also pronounced his commitment to equality in caring. Jamal was 32 years old, a married and practicing Muslim with a young child, who also worked as a care worker with adults who had intellectual disabilities. He spoke about being a willing carer should the need arise:

> Sometimes it comes to my mind that my mother is getting old and if needs be that I'll have to look after her... I'd definitely do it... I would be willing to look after my mother – even my brother or even my sister, if it happens that I have to, I'd have no problem with that, it is my duty. (Jamal, 32)

However, it was also typical for men to claim to be less engaged in infant caring. John (47), for example, maintained to be very involved in sharing the care of his three young children with his wife, but expected women to be more engaged in the care of infants than men. He said:

> The kids it's a sharing responsibility... [and my wife]... takes them to school in the morning, I come home early pick them up get dinner for them... we take turns putting them to bed, we try and divide it up as much as we can so that neither one of us is seen as the main care provider but with small children it is always the mother, it always is. It's until they grow up that the father feels more a role for them. (John, 47)

Fionn (25) was more assertive about the equality in his relationship. He claimed his caring for his two-year-old daughter was 'very much 100% equal' although he acknowledged:

> there would be times where I need time to do things and no problem, she will do it ... I play football on a Wednesday evening and she will put [our daughter] down ... and she will run her bath and read her stories and put her to sleep. And then the next day she say 'I want to go and go out for a walk with my girlfriends' and I will provide the same assistance there. (Fionn, 25)

The research did not quantify or validate the reality of men's involvement in practice. While there is an affinity between men's beliefs about being involved in caring and their practices, there can also be significant contradictions. For many men there can be a gulf between men's rhetoric of egalitarianism and their practices (Thomas 1990). While holding egalitarian beliefs is associated with having a greater involvement with children (Seward et al. 2006), there is no automatic link (Gerstel and Gallagher 2001: 213). Egalitarianism can be endorsed by men as a way of resisting the anachronistic imaging of traditional masculinities (McMahon 1999: 89; Finn and Henwood 2009), and conservative men, despite their ideology, can be involved in nurturing in practice (Bartkowski and Xu 2000). Nonetheless, the men's accounts of their involvement in caring lend support to many other studies, both quantitative and qualitative, that demonstrate persistent gender divisions of care and domestic work in Irish families (CSO 2010; McGinnity and Russell 2007, 2008; McGinnity, Russell, and Smyth 2007; McGinnity et al. 2005; Lynch and Lyons 2008; Leonard 2004; Cullen, Delaney, and Duff 2004). A time-use study on the division of both paid and unpaid labour within Irish households by McGinnity and Russell (2008: x–xii) usefully illustrates and mirrors similar findings from many other studies cross-nationally. Remarking on women's increasing participation in the labour market they found that:

> the typical reduction in average time spent in unpaid work is not sufficient to compensate women for increases in paid work ... Women generally reduce their time spent in household work when they have a paid job. However, this is far less than a one-for-one reduction, so even when they spend a similar amount of time on paid work as men, women are still found to do more domestic work, particularly at weekends ... [therefore] women's total workload is higher than

men's. Based on our estimates, women work on average around 40 minutes longer per day than men, including both paid and unpaid labour and travel time. (McGinnity and Russell, 2008)

This highlights the fact that while within the traditional male-breadwinner households there was a negligible difference in the overall time committed between men and women, within dual-earner households they found

women do more paid work (and less unpaid work) than women in male breadwinner couples, and men do less paid work (and more unpaid work) than men in male-breadwinner couples. Dual-earner couples also spend less time on unpaid work per average day than male breadwinner couples. Nevertheless, there are still gender differences in the allocation of time to employment and unpaid tasks in dual earner couples, with women having on average a higher workload than men...Having young children leads to a much greater increase in women's unpaid workload than in men's, regardless of the woman's hours of paid work. This holds for both weekdays and weekends. Thus, the female share of unpaid work is greater among parents than in couples without children. At the same time, in couples with children, men do more paid work on weekdays. As is found in other countries, parenthood brings a reallocation of time for both men and women, resulting in a more traditional division of labour. (ibid.)

Studies highlight that 'radical changes' have occurred in Irish families especially in terms of women's greater participation in the labour market, yet 'there is a stubborn lack of change in the gender division of unpaid labour in the home' (Rush, Richardson, and Kiely 2006: 143). What these studies find is the actuality of men's involvement lags behind their professed attitudes which have modernised particularly in terms of their involvement in childcare (Hillard 2007).

Reciprocity and mutuality

Appreciating the actuality of men's caring practices is crucial in understanding the nature of gender inequality but this study took a particular interest in the meanings of care in men's lives. Central to this are the feelings of love and belonging that caring engenders. In the conversations caring obligations for one's children or parents were noted to provide life with meaning and purpose by giving life a clear focus and a feeling of solidarity. Caring was believed to offer common rewards, including feeling loved and respected for doing it, experiencing emotional intimacy, and feelings of self-esteem, respect, and competence. Doing caring made the men feel 'responsible', 'competent', 'proud', 'challenged', 'joy', 'fantastic', 'happy', 'brilliant', and wanted, especially – although not exclusively – in respect of the care of children. Many men spoke enthusiastically about being fathers and about family life, especially relatively new fathers, such as Graham (26) who 'just couldn't see it any other way now... [my daughter] is just the best thing that ever happened to me... I can't really put it in words'. Jamal (32) felt the same: 'I have a nephew... I love him and still love him... I thought he was like my son before I had my daughter born. But once my daughter was born my nephew just went second class now... I mean my daughter is just like a marvellous experience that I cannot compare to anything else'. After becoming a father Greg (51) felt 'made up' explaining that 'the kids were the makings of us to an extent... If we didn't have children would we have gone our separate ways... It solidified... it kind of made us a unit and even to this day everything you plan for is around your children'. Likewise Dave (34) talked about his care obligations for his mother as a source of family unity, strength, and solidarity. He said 'My mum's illness... it has brought to bear certain issues about our own emotional state as a family and has made us think, made us re-evaluate ourselves as a family as part of a unit rather than as separate individuals.' So it was evident how love relations rewarded men with reciprocal benefits; they were not all about self-sacrifice. They also felt good about themselves for doing care even if this was sometimes couched in negative terms as relief from feeling guilty about being care-free or care-less. Charlie (28), for example, spoke both about the joys of caring for his mother and grandmother and about it offering relief from feeling guilt for not doing it:

> Just sitting in hospital with [my grandmother], talking to her... helping her eat. I quite enjoyed it... I just felt happy that I was spending time with her. And caring for my mum I enjoyed, I felt wanted, I felt like I was paying back a little bit... I felt good in myself because... I was actually doing it and I could do it... it was easing my conscience as well... I was doing it for myself as well. (Charlie, 28)

Charlie was relieved that in a small way at least he could pay back the care debt he felt he owed.

As noted in Chapter 4 men can receive a negative reaction from other men when doing primary caring, be it censure, or by being ignored, or treated with incredulity. Sometimes, however, male caregivei s can receive a 'hero like' status as a result of their caring (Lynch and Lyons 2009b). Angus (43) could relate to this experience:

> I think any man that I have talked to that has been in a caring role for his own parents...they realise...you get a different kind of recognition from fellow carers, even if they have only done it for a few months...In my situation I think you get a lot more, not pity, but thanks...as if a man isn't expected to care for his parents...I get people constantly saying 'Oh, aren't you great, aren't you wonderful...oh look, he's made the tea' it is almost a sense of amazement that I can keep house and look after my mother and bring her to the toilet and stay up all night. So I think women are probably taken more for granted in the caring role than men are. (Angus, 43)

Reciprocal emotional benefits were highlighted by the men as motivation to care, but there was no question that they also defined caring to be appreciably burdensome in several respects. A significant theme related to the amount of time that caring took. Fionn (25) felt his commitment to caring for his young daughter was in competition with his personal interests:

> It was a big learning curve, the first four months, so that was very tough. And completing my degree and having a child at the same time and working, all that was a big, big challenge because you never had a moment really just to sit down and flick on the TV and take it easy for an hour. That just didn't exist...I just wanted to achieve and make time for your partner and try and make time for the other parts of your life,...just playing a game of soccer or going for a job...these things keep ticking...Because I find that if I go through a week without either going to the gym or playing soccer, I am unhappy, to be honest. I need them in my life to keep me happy. (Fionn, 25)

Cathal (58) felt that his caring responsibilities had deprived him of time to enjoy life, and he believed that the emotional rewards of caring were exaggerated. When asked whether this investment of time and energy as a single parent had now paid off as his children were now adults he commented frankly:

> Now I have my children but I can certainly give you lots of good reasons for not having them [not said jokingly]. I don't think there would be a huge hole in my life if I didn't have them...It's such an

enormous thing... In the last few years I have become aware I can do what I like now and go where I want and do as I please but that's the first time, I mean I'm nearly 60, so I'm only learning that by default. (Cathal, 58)

Despite Cathal's reflections on the burdens of care, he nonetheless saw becoming a carer to be a relatively easy transition because he considered he possessed a caring personality. He said having a caring responsibility 'wasn't so hard... because I had always considered somebody else... it's only the last few years I have realised what having your own freedom is like. So I have mainly as far as I can remember have had a caring position'. John (47) was married with three young children. He felt the strain of trying to balance multiple care obligations to wife, children, and his elderly mother. He said:

I would always see [my elderly mother] at weekends and bring her over here that sort of thing and get her out of the house for a while and I would call over once or twice in the week but often that is quite difficult when you come home in the evenings get the dinner, feed the kids get them to bed and it's half nine... mother would be getting ready for bed anyway. (John, 47)

As a result of these demands caring held negative connotations for John; it represented losing freedom, money, and time for self ('free-time' and 'me-time'):

[Care]... It's a word that sends a shiver down my spine, ... it's responsibility, it's demanding it's time and a lot of effort..., my day has been divided in blocks of hours. My life was never like that; it was come as you please, do what you want... Even as a teenager I came and went as I pleased... that was how I lived my life and all of a sudden your life is divided, ... sleep, ... get the kids up, breakfast, get them ready for school, work, go to my mother on the way home see how she is, come home get dinner, put the kids to bed after a while your 24 hours are suddenly divided into sections all dedicated to everybody else and nothing to yourself. So the word has a connotation that sends the goose bumps down my back you know. (ibid.)

The time constraints of full-time work make attractive the idea of quality time for hard-pressed parents. Both men and women can experience time pressures to be involved but women can be especially constrained because of dual roles as carers and paid workers (Warren,

Pascall, and Fox 2010). Men and women can also interpret the meaning of quality time differently in relation to their different caring roles (Snyder 2007) and though spending time is important, engaging in routine care tasks features less for men than it commonly does for women (Milkie et al. 2010). McMahon (1999) claims men are more likely to advocate quality over quantity time because of how much time commitment caring involves. Similarly a few of the men held that care could be condensed into quality time. Pascal (48) suggested 'you can be the kind of really busy person ... [and] ... might not have the time to have quality time with somebody, and you can be the kind of person who has all day for someone. I think both are equally valid for different forms of caring'. Douglas (48) supposed: 'My career wouldn't have allowed me to have been as well involved [with my children] as some others. But I would have given them quality time of a different sort. I would have taken them around to see particular things and given them quality time that way, and they tend to recognise that I suppose.' Lynch, Lyons, and Cantillon (2009b) proclaim the myth of quality time which supposes that care can be infinitely condensed to allow for increased productivity and time to pursue other life goals.

But John said 'More than time it is worry. There is always that thing at the back of your head about if my mother falls; if she gets sick ... it's an emotional drain rather than a physical. It does your head in'. Care was something that John accepted as a duty but not something to be relished:

> Looking after my mother the past couple of years I have found a conflict goes on in yourself between wanting to go and do this and I can't because my mother is in a home or she's not well or whatever it might be you know. You have to knuckle under and this won't last forever she's 82 years of age and I know she's not going to last that long. But I really just have to just get on with it, that type of thing. (John, 47)

John feared care because he had experienced how demanding it can be. Likewise, Dermot (35), who spoke at length about having to under-take lots of care and domestic chores as a child for his younger siblings, emphasised the monotony of doing caring full time:

> I don't know if I would be able to give up work to look after my step child ... I wouldn't like to be stuck in a house 24 hours a day, 7 days a week. I'd like to get out and about and do my own thing ... looking

after a child 24/7 it would probably get to me after a while...get on my nerves...it would drive me mad. The monotony of going round cleaning a house and cleaning kids bedrooms and making dinner; it's a monotonous job...it does get to you after a while. (Dermot, 35)

As well as deriving emotional benefits from primary caring, men also found caring to be burdensome. Dominant definitions of masculinity defined as independent, care-free, adventurous, reckless, and irresponsible contradict caring defined by obligations, availability, commitment, dependency, sensitivity, and responsiveness. Nurturing masculinity is also challenged by the devaluation and invisibility men experience when doing nurturing, the 'worry' of emotional work, and because of some of the demands of emotional intimacy. Nonetheless, the sense that caring responsibility is a burden is lessened when caring is undertaken by 'choice' and when men take a professional and task-oriented approach to love labour.

Negotiating nurturing

Men's involvement in caring has been traditionally sanctioned through gendered practices not only as breadwinners, but as disciplinarians, educators, instrumental socialisers, masculine role models, and protectors. The men in the interviews also spoke about their involvement in caring in gendered ways. Disciplinary practices for children were one such area. Although child disciplinary practices are not uniquely gendered, they can, however, take on particular gendered qualities in the form of a disciplinary paternal protectiveness with fathers perceived as principal disciplinary and authoritarian figures. Many of the men emphasised their role in the provision of education and moral guidance to 'equip for life', 'teach right from wrong' instil values, and 'keep them out of trouble'. Dermot (35) identified with the disciplinary practices of his working class background which he contrasted to his partner's suggesting his daughter 'knows how far she can push me and I won't go over that. I've said to her...I'm the adult you're the child you do what I say until you are 18 years of age and then you can do whatever you want...[My partner] just gives in and gives her whatever she wants because she just wants peace and quiet'. Simon (48) was a separated father whose heterosexual marriage broke up when he revealed he was gay. He subsequently shared primary caring responsibility with his ex-wife for his two teenaged children. He also identified with feeling disciplinary and protective towards his children ' I have to be the law here I have to say no ... this is an instinctive thing in me ... the care that I have to provide that it's difficult and it's ambiguous and I'm also drawn in to areas that I don't know the answers to either but I have to know the answers ... it's the caring part of it as well. Me needing to protect them in a way.' However, Simon felt very comfortable doing emotional care work and uncomfortably compelled to take on stereotypical disciplinary roles.

> Well the emotional work has always been present for me in that I tell my kids all the time that I love them ... I hug them. If they have something wrong with them ... we talk about it. I think my wife partly plays the good cop, bad cop where she doesn't tell me she's doing the good cop. And so I end up being the bad cop but I think that's just a male identification ... I often find myself being like the judge the authority and I don't necessarily like the idea of that. (Simon, 48)

Men can find it difficult to develop nurturing practices with the context of pressures to be disciplinarians. Dessie (46) felt a similar pressure but emanating from wider family influences. Dessie supported his wife's primary care role with his two children, one of whom has Autism. He didn't want to be perceived as a traditional or 'square father', wanting to be emotional, intimate, and compassionate with his children, but he described this a 'challenge' because of the pressure he felt to be punitive emanating especially from his more traditionally minded father. Dessie provided the anecdote of when his son (who has Autism) was exhibiting very challenging behaviour. When Dessie's father suggested 'Would you not slap him for that?', Dessie said he 'looked at him and I got very, very angry, and then I got very hurt and I didn't say anything, well I just said, "Well this is just such an ignorant statement from someone who doesn't understand" and I thought well no one seems to understand.' So Dessie did not feel he filled the stereotypical mould and experienced the pressure to be a traditional father to be overbearing. Dessie eventually found support in a local men's group and this helped him to understand more about Autism as well as how he could work with his wife to provide better care.

Shared emotional care in families is not without jealousies arising from the triadic separation and attachment relations between parents and children even in families which are intact and where parents have a strong commitment to equality in caring (Risman 1998: 124; Balbus 1998). The sense of uncertainty about how to be involved in caring is particularly intense for separated/lone fathers. Separate/lone parents often encounter complex legal, practical, and emotional struggles in separation, custody/guardianship and residency disputes (Manning, Stewart, and Smock 2003; Kiernan 2004; Corcoran 2005; Smart 1989). The growth of fathers' rights movements has highlighted shifting expectations about men's post-divorce caring. Although a common pattern is for men to become less involved in their children's lives after separation as part of a post-divorce 'package deal' (Kimmel 2000: 141), separated/lone parent men have become a significant political force (Gregory and Milner 2011) highlighting a diversity of ways men want to be involved in their children's lives. However, there are few unambiguous models of how shared caring works when relationships fall apart. In this study the way the men felt they should be involved was thrown into disarray for some men upon separation/ divorce. Non-resident fathers can find it very difficult to carve out a fathering role even though they are very committed in the face of economic, social, and institutional pressures (NESF 2001; Corcoran 2005). Unlike the conflict Paul experienced (see Chapter 4), Graham (26), who was also a separated father, felt 'happy with the amount of involvement ... I am still pretty much there in the front line ... as bad and all the break-up was ... When we were going through the break-up there was a lot of name calling and a lot of insults but [my involvement] ... was never ever brought into it, never, it was never an issue'. Yet Graham expressed how 'Emotionally for me I felt that I failed as a man, I felt it is my job to keep the family together and I couldn't. So for me I felt absolutely worthless ... I felt for ... [my daughter] and I suppose for her mother ... I see it as the job of the man to keep the family together and I failed.' In a similar way, Simon (48) felt he had failed in his role as protector:

When my marriage broke up ... my biggest sense was how do I protect the kids, how do I have a relationship with them ... Things happen that shouldn't happen, shouting, and perhaps it turns; it can get ugly, they are part of it due to the dynamic in our family. But what happened actually really hurt me enormously not being able to prevent them from being exposed to what was going on. (Simon, 48)

Lone/separated fathers can feel very conflicted not only because they have 'failed' to keep the family intact, but also because they are unsure about their role in any reconstituted family arrangements (Smart and

Neale 1999). This was also true for Paul who felt very conflicted about the caring role he would take in any reconfigured family arrangements:

> [D]oes that mean [my children's step-father] is half a father and I'm the other half? Do they have two full fathers? Is he a step-up or step-down on me? Is he stepping on me, or over me, or under me? How do I feel about that or how does he feel about that? How do I feel about the fact that I might be doing it to some other man? Now that's a struggle for men! (Paul, fathers' rights activist)

Smart and Neale (1999: 72–4) propose that men in post-divorce situations can find themselves in 'a chain of relationships' rather than a 'discrete family unit' and the arrival of another man 'seems to be linked to an understanding of what a father's role is meant to be. What most fathers seem to dread was the thought of another man parenting their children or their children calling another man "Dad"'. Paul recounted this anxiety when he said: 'There's the role play of what will happen in that new model. In other words, will that new partner of mine become a replacement mother of my children? ... Will I be man of that relationship and do the non-caring things like provision of resources and will she now do the tactile things? How do we unravel those struggles?'

Here Paul is unsure about whether to do feminine nurturing, although in some ways he feels obliged to. Yet he sees a step-father taking on his masculine role as provider in conflict with the ideal he holds about his legitimate role. Combined with the practical struggles over issues like housing and access, this can have a very negative impact on the self-identity and self-esteem of men who hold these beliefs. The politics of lone fatherhood is often portrayed as reactionary, and though it can manifest as anti-feminist and anti-equality, lone fatherhood contains significant contradictory experiences. For example, lone fathers comprise a wide variety of diverse men with different experiences. Barker (1994: 239) claims that differences between lone fathers are best understood as expressions of different forms of masculinities. In his study of lone fathers he found that some men continue to operate as traditional patriarchs and pursue patterns consistent with hegemonic masculinity, but some men felt they were unable to because of the situation of what caring involved for them. Some fathers he defined as 'gender pioneers' who 'were living their lives in ways which implicitly or explicitly challenged hegemonic masculinity'. Similarly, Risman (1998: 154) finds that lone fathers often consider themselves to have caring traits that would be traditionally defined as feminine. Barker

(1994: 13) asserts there is a clearer shared definition of what is involved in mothering than there is in lone fathering. Lone fathers, he notes, respond in various ways to the incongruence between the reality of lone fatherhood and dominant definitions of masculinities in respect of the different circumstances in which they have become lone fathers (through separation, divorce, and widowhood or unplanned pregnancy). Johansson's (2003) study of Swedish non-resident fathers found that non-resident fathers experience problems in developing paternal caring identities. He found that non-resident fathers reflexively choose between pursuing hegemonic norms and primary caring ones because to pursue both is incompatible. Many non-resident fathers, he claims, avoid primary caring and become less involved in their children's lives. He argues that it is more compelling for these men to pursue hegemonic goals because by not doing so they have to let go goals that are socially valued for men and because they have not internalised a model of what is involved in non-resident caring. And men in these situations may have to face the disappointment from their children that they are not more available, an emotional dynamic that can often bring forth men's own emotional relationships with their own fathers.

Smart and Neale (1999: 146) identify the complexity of how power operates in intimate family relations upon separation/divorce. They explain how men's and women's experiences of powerlessness can differ in post-divorce situations by distinguishing *situational* power from *deliberative* power. Situational power arises from the fact that women are generally the primary carers. It is separated/divorced men who are, therefore, more likely to experience this form of powerlessness, but it is also the more commonly recognised as injustice, as the inability to exert control and to being denied rights. Debilitative power is much less recognised as injustice. It occurs where one partner tries to prevent the other from constructing a new identity, often by denying them independence and space (ibid.: 139):

Women's sense of powerlessness ... seemed to be embedded in their inability to become their 'own' person again. Men's sense of powerlessness was quite different; it usually manifested itself when they were unable to control others. It was other-directed rather than inwardly directed. (Smart and Neale 1999: 144)

Smart and Neale maintain that men can feel powerless post-divorce because feeling powerful is related to having a traditional fathering status. When men lose this sense of masculinity through family breakdown it becomes very challenging for them to re-establish because having to negotiate with their former wives and this can give a sense of powerlessness. By only recognising one type of power, family law neglects mothers' desire to develop a new identity. This also affects men because fathers' rights discourses express a loss of rights but they do little to articulate the sense of loss of both identity and love which occurs when complex intimate care relations are fractured. Consequently many non-resident fathers' sense of loss is expressed as anger at the loss of rights or as despair and hopelessness (ibid.: 195–6). Where conflicts occur in care relations men tend to employ an ethic of justice (favouring similar outcomes or joint custody) whereas women tend to emphasise responsibilities and only to deploy an ethic of justice when referring to fathers' rights or to children's (ibid.: 171). Solutions to the difficult moral–emotional dilemmas of post-divorce parenting need to be guided by the 'practical realities' of family circumstances, including who the primary carer has been, the relationship between parents and children, and whether there was violence in the family, rather than on an ideal of what a family should be (ibid.: 193). From a (pro)feminist perspective it is easy to dismiss the angry rhetoric of fathers' rights advocates. Affective equality offers the chance to get beyond this and understand both the loss and sadness of these men as well as the issues of rights and obligations.

Feminine masculinities

Normative prescriptions that men should care in 'masculine' ways were less evident in the conversations than the ambivalence surrounding whether men should care in stereotypically feminine ways. As Chapter 5 has emphasised, nurturing care was primarily depicted in terms of feminised expressive characteristics in terms of 'soft' emotions, intimacy, sensitivity, and 'tactile' physical caring. Good carers, in the modern sense, are expected to be emotionally intelligent; to have proficient intrapersonal and interpersonal skills including being attentive, receptive, and responsive, emotionally attuned, good listeners, empathetic. They are also expected to process feelings, develop relationships, manage emotional bonds, and maintain social networks (Goleman 1996; Egan 2009; Richard 1990; McQueen 2004). Men are widely expected to be more emotionally present and expressive within interpersonal relations (Giddens 1992; Seidler 2006: 63; Craib 1998). In Ireland the silence and emotional awkwardness surrounding intimate personal relations are being surpassed by greater expectations for men to be emotionally communicative (Ferguson 1998; Inglis 1998a), with even traditionally conservative farmers developing 'qualities involving more emotional openness and less rigid gender divisions' (Ní Laoire 2002: 25–6). Connell (2011: 45) cites Ferguson as evidence for the emergence that 'Softer masculinities, more equal marriages, and more engaged fatherhood, have become hegemonic' in postcolonial Ireland. However, this claim should not be mistakenly applied to support the view that men and gender equality are hegemonic. Certainly these contemporary emotional norms have enabled men to enter emotionally caring spaces, but these spaces can be fraught with tension and anxiety when they clash with hegemonic ideals (Henwood and Procter 2003; Wall and Arnold 2007). Traditional breadwinner models of family man have declined and newer more caring masculinities are observable in daily life but they have not become hegemonic or culturally ascendant (Gregory and Milner 2011).

Despite the fact that many men have reconfigured more intimate and emotionally expressive masculinities, men continue to be stereotypically characterised as emotionally inexpressive or emotionally illiterate. Many men are found to conform to stereotypes for being emotionally hollow (Duncombe and Marsden 1998) and to experience difficulty when monitoring their internal emotional states and feelings. They also tend to intellectualise and rationalise as a defence against experiencing particular emotions (Rubin 1983). In general men are said to be good at organising events and spending time together but poor at emotional communication when doing so; their relationships are often depicted as shallow, superficial, and emotionally unsatisfying compared with women's, which are portrayed as deep, intimate, meaningful, and lasting (Messner 2001). Male emotional inexpressiveness occurs within wider cultural and social contexts where it is not socially acceptable for 'real men' to display emotion (Blye 1996: 119). Public displays of care and intimacy are relatively taboo among men crossing class and other boundaries because men actively police and control the boundaries that define the norms of masculinity for emotional content lest they signify femininity (Rubin 1983; Polce-Lynch et al. 1998). Consequently, men experience discomfort in recognising and expressing emotion, and grief and vulnerability is replaced by emotional 'stoicism' (hooks 2004). Even at times of crisis and vulnerability men carefully manage the expression of emotion and the revelation of vulnerability in order to preserve one's masculinity (Bennett 2007).

This contradictory and ambivalent relationship between masculinity and 'feminine' emotion was exceptionally evident in the conversations.

Some of the men expressed feeling comfortable with contemporary norms favouring emotional intimacy and considered it better for men in general to develop emotional skills and expressive attributes. Others expressed feeling uncomfortable with these norms, feeling uncertain about whether they were appropriate for men, whilst a few men forthrightly rejected them. Douglas (48) described feeling uncomfortable expressing concern about his children's well-being even when they are ill which he described as 'making the fuss' commenting 'Some fathers can be like that. I would be concerned but I may not be the greatest at showing it...I don't like them situations.' Some men highlighted the situational context that affects how awkward expressing emotion could be, especially within the context of caring for their mothers. John (47) found caring for his mother 'Emotionally...a heavy weight on me because the relationship I had with my mother...I feel I should be doing my best for her as she did for us. My mother never used the love word but always did the best for us...I find it much easier looking after the children than looking after my mother.' Similarly Dave (34) described how 'stressful' he experienced providing intimate physical care to his mother. He thought it an uncomfortable emotional space for men to occupy because men are generally not expected to do because it 'doesn't always sit well...I don't fully understand it...I'm not entirely comfortable being in that space with her...lifting her or being able to help her to dress, I'm not really comfortable with that at all.'

Many of the men in the conversations proposed men would be better off to develop more expressive emotional skills, but this view was not universally or uncritically endorsed. Based on his experiences as a community worker, Eddie maintained that the men he worked with in community development were pressurised to develop feminine expressive emotional attributes as a means of coping with problems they faced in life but he was sceptical about whether this was either a better way of coping or appropriate for men. Eddie didn't 'necessarily think that it's a case men need to be more like women in terms of mental health because...women are very heavily socialised to be emotional and weak...[M]aybe [masculine] coping skills, you know, deserve more recognition as positive things'.

Public health perspectives widely support the view that men are better off developing nurturing attributes but Eddie's beliefs are supported by researchers who emphasise the importance of gender differences in how men care and cope for their well-being or that gender is irrelevant and coping merely an individual phenomenon (Zwicker et al. 2010). Masculine identity, defined by separate and marked emotional boundaries, is claimed to be positive for men while feminine identity is claimed to be negative because it is characterised by passivity, self-effacement, irrationality, and sentimentality (Kraemer 1995; Kelly et al. 2008). Similarly Paul (fathers' rights activist) felt that men were inappropriately pressurised to become more feminine. He was angry at what he defined as the 'feminisation' of the word 'care' because it presents men as 'feelingless' and emotionally 'inarticulate' and denounced norms that pressurise men to develop feminine attributes and undervalued masculine ones. Paul believed 'Society needs men to go to war; they need men to drive trains and fix the roads. The role of care [as] intimacy ... [is a] simplistic view of care presented in the soft imagery of media and it denies other caring roles that men are playing.' Men, he claimed, are losing a sense of masculinity and becoming 'more like women' and he wanted to see a revaluation of 'providing' as caring which he described in somewhat heroic terms: 'You know I could be in here caring for my kids all night but if I don't get money to put the heating on then we'll all be cold and we'll die, we'll die, my children will die in my arms but they will die nonetheless.'

Bowers (1999) proposes that traditional masculine ways of coping and caring are psychologically healthier for men but that this does not mean that all types of caring alienate men. She argues that although social definitions of caring as nurturing are incompatible with masculine identity, many aspects of caring are not, such as organising and 'taking charge'. However, on the one hand, even if Bowers' claim supports the contradictory lived experiences of providing care for many men, care nonetheless involves emotions, intimacy, sensitivity, and touch. These are traditionally seen as feminine and thus this presents a major obstacle to men who do not feel they can care in this way. On the other hand, Paul was rejecting the popular stereotype that defines caring purely as emotional nurturing work. This very stereotype, however, hides the complex and multifaceted activities that comprise caring that women do, including its mental (organisational/managerial) and physical aspects (Lynch 2007). Therefore, this 'feminised' understanding of caring makes it seem more inaccessible to men than it might be since managerial and organisational attributes are traditionally thought of as 'masculine' virtues. The fact that evidence for emotional stereotypes can be found in gender relations should not overlook how men care differently in both feminine and masculine ways. Neufelds and Harrison (1998), for example, conducted research on relationships of reciprocity among carers, their social supports, and care recipients. They found that differences between men and women were broadly in keeping with

Gilligan's (1982) theory of different gendered moral orientations in that most of the men were less receptive and sensitive to non-verbal signs of reciprocity, or what they referred to as 'constructed reciprocity'. Most of the men based a sense of reciprocity on principles (justice) and role obligation, for example, as husbands. The study indicated how women displayed 'a greater propensity' to establish a sense of reciprocity arising from the caring process. However, there were differences among the men with some men more skilled than others at decoding non-verbal cues and those who were better decoders were found to have a more positive caring orientation. The point is that emotional norms and stereotypes construct gendered patterns of caring, but there are many men who do not conform and there are alternative discourses of emotionality among men within diverse cultures of masculinities. It may be true that some men cope better in stereotypical masculine ways but writing out emotional competence from the script of masculinity limits involvement in nurturing when relationships require emotionally expressive reciprocity.

The belief that men are unnaturally under pressure to become 'more like women' and that their gender differences should be left alone are broadly critiqued by constructionist orientated gender scholars. Within this tradition, many studies find that men experience the social pressure to avoid expressive emotional practices including nurturing ones out of fear that they will be perceived as feminine (Courtenay 2000). Furthermore, many studies attest to the detrimental effect these emotional constructions have for men's health and well-being. Men reject emotional intimacy because they perceive it as unmanly, they project weakness and vulnerability onto others, and they engender macho and competitive relations in order to prove they are real men (Clare 2000). Kahn (2010: 71) suggests that it is not that men should become more 'like women' but rather they should let go essentialist and binary understandings of gender and recognise diversity among men. They should also help men to appreciate their privileges, so that men can understand how their lives are constrained by dominant masculinity.

It can also be a trap to analyse men's ways of caring and coping in a dualistic way, as either good or bad. Men can develop different 'styles' of intimacy based on time spent doing things rather than talking. Male bonding, for example, can contain contradictory experiences of being 'meaningful' for the men involved, by creating a sense of love, support, and solidarity among men, yet at the same time they can distance male–female relationships (Messner 2001: 254). Sport

can provide opportunities for men to express emotion and overcome fears about physical and emotional intimacy with other men
(Westwood 1990 : 69). Love and care labour may also have conflicting
intent in the sense that solidarity bonding between certain individuals or groups may preclude solidarity for others. An example is seen
in stereotypically misogynistic male bonding and homophobia where
bonding is based on denigrating 'Others' (Curry 1991). Love relations
can be strained by a tension between separation and attachment and
raise negative and destructive emotions including fear, jealousy, and
hatred. Subjective feelings of love and care do not preclude a structural
relationship of exploitation (Lynch and McLaughlin 1995). Solidarity
relations can be not only framed positively as a basis for identity and
belonging but also framed negatively on the basis of difference and
division (Woodward 1997a).

As a community worker, Eddie perceived a focus on emotions as a
source of oppression for marginalised men, and a way of minimising
class-based inequalities:

> [T]he lads should be able to access services, education, proper
> housing and health without first having to go through a process
> of de-masculinisation ... [N]o-one asks businessmen to sort out their
> feelings towards homophobia before they can access loans or busi-
> ness meetings ... [I]n community work settings the first thing on
> the agenda seems to be getting around talking about your feel-
> ings and sitting around counselling [rather than] why there is no
> accommodation or why there are twenty courses for women and
> none for men ... I think there's a real danger in focusing on men
> and emotional stuff in isolation from the context of where men's
> lives are at ... It's like focusing on one aspect of an oppressed group's
> behaviour without seeing it all; you'd actually be playing a part in
> the oppression. (Eddie, community worker)

Eddie draws our attention to the dangers of class bias when working
with men in social care or community settings; settings which can see
middle-class practitioners setting the agenda for marginalised men.
Viewing all men's lives through the prism of gender power can overlook
the class and racial oppression that marginalised men encounter. Again,
this view fails to account for the privileging of class-based inequalities
over those based on gender and sexuality. Peter's community work lens
was different. He recognised men's problems with emotional communication especially in their friendships with other men, and believed that

becoming 'more like women' would improve men's lives and gender relations for Traveller men and women:

> Traveller men are still not at the stage where Traveller women are at in terms of talking about very personal issues ... Friendship among Traveller men is very limited in that it's either a football buddy, or a drinking buddy, or somebody you might go hunting with or horseracing ... [It is important to] arrive at a situation where Traveller men would be engaging with other Traveller men the same way women are engaging with each other ... That it doesn't diminish who you are and it doesn't make you less of a man if you talk about children to another man, or talk about sexual relations to another man.
>
> (Peter, Traveller and a community worker)

Yet even men who did not want to see men becoming 'more like women' in terms of emotions recognised intimacy and care as major issues for men. Eddie saw the men who he worked with as men who were often excluded from intimate care relations, and he saw that this lack of intimacy as a major social problem for them, noting there is 'a lot of pent up sexual, emotional frustration in a lot of the lads ... [I]t would be 10 or 20 years since they have had a relationship with a man or a woman so there's a lot of pain there that's probably feeding the alcoholism and a lot of other stuff'.

Sattel (1998) is critical of theories that emphasise the emotional ineptitude of men as an oppression. He suggests that men assume power through the credibility of the rational persona whilst simultaneously warding off emotional pain by distanced emotional involvement. He argues that it is in men's interests to become inexpressive not because of the constraints of culture but because of the expectations that men should wield power. Here emotional inexpressiveness is theorised as a manipulative tool used to guard and maintain a dominant social position. Men police caring qualities in themselves and in other men because of what is at stake for them in losing power and privilege (Bubeck 1995:165). Women's emotional work in marriage supports men's competitive relations in public life (Duncombe and Marsden 1998; 1993), while male 'emotional inexpressiveness' and 'domestic incompetence' are merely a resource used by men to avoid nurturing work (Coltrane and Galt 2000; McMahon 1999; Sattel 1998). Avoiding emotion means that men are able to develop a dominant subjectivity by maintaining the illusion of power and control and they can also commit to the demands of capitalist production (Frosh 1994).

Craib (1998: 113) also reminds us that complying with masculine feeling rules about managing stress, dissatisfaction, expressing anxiety, and intimacy is also intensely emotional. This indicates not only how men are often highly skilled emotional actors, but that complying with masculine emotional codes is itself gendered emotional work. Men use emotional work to actively manage the impressions and reactions of others. Johnston and Morrison's (2007) study of white, middle-class heterosexual college-age men in Ireland found that the 'hegemonic model operates as a superordinate organising influence' but masculinity is also situational involving a 'contextual masculine presentation' that allows men to switch to different modes of masculinity, depending on the relationship context. They propose that this allows men to present a macho front in particular situations while being expressive and sensitive in others. Other studies have also identified how men use emotional labour to recreate dominance and realise their interests. Sattel (1998) suggests that men can be situationally expressive when necessary – a finding Pierce (1998) noticed for male lawyers in litigation cases, and Hyde et al. (2005) found in how young Irish men negotiate access to sex. The use of emotional intelligence is also well established in (men's) corporate business relations (Freshman and Rubino 2002), which although sometimes overstated (Zeidner, Matthews, and Roberts 2004), nonetheless co-opts 'feminine' emotionality for productivity and profit (Lewis and Simpson 2007). The suggestion here is that there are many contexts and situations, and perhaps increasingly so, where emotional expression is a prerequisite for dominance (Korobov 2011). Therefore, dominant masculinity does not necessarily write out emotional labour from men's lives but may in a particular situation implore it. What dominant masculinity does write out, however, is nurturing labour, the other-centred emotional disposition of care.

Emotional inheritances

Victor Seidler has written extensively about masculinity, power, and emotion. He argues the dominant masculinity of Western societies (based on the power of white, middle-class, Judeo-Christian men) bears a rationalistic heritage that has split emotion from rational thought. The formation of Western masculinity can be traced through its roots in Judeo-Christian culture and later Carthesian distinctions between emotions and bodies (*cogito ergo sum*) (Seidler 1989: 18). Following a Weberian argument he proposes that this rationalist inheritance was solidified by Kantian Enlightenment ethics and Protestant work practices which became institutionalised within the spirit of Capitalism. Masculinity became associated with the rules and principles of rationalistic justice ethics and emotion with femininity, unreason, irrationality and, consequently, inferiority. Dominant masculinity bears the signs of rationality marked by self-control and mind-over-matter and the suppression of emotion, feeling, and desire (Seidler 1998; Williams and Bendelow 1998).

Seidler (2006: 26, 2003, 1998) acknowledges that dominant rationalistic inheritances affect different cultures of masculinities in varying ways, but, nonetheless, the dominance of rationalistic thought alienates from emotions and affective relations. Men develop a distrustful and ambiguous relationship with their emotions because emotionality contradicts the sense of mastery and control which reason symbolises. Experiencing the feeling of control and mastery requires men to repress, suppress, or rationalise emotion and treat their bodies as machines. The rationalisation of emotion and the dominance of cognitive thinking mean that men need a reason to justify the experience and expression of emotions, particularly those signifying weakness (Seidler 1989: 187). Instrumental language use enables men to avoid the pain involved in emotional self-revelation and inner lives are silenced in order to achieve instrumental ends.

The association between rationalistic thought and dominant masculinity means men experience emotion as a moral weakness and a threat to their identities. Moreover, this perception of difference and superiority becomes a deeply held disposition for many men. Consequently men tend to distrust women's sense of justice and morality based on a care ethic where moral judgements are grounded within the context of affective relations rather than rational rules and principles (Seidler 1989; Gilligan 1982; Fisher and Tronto 1990). The result is men subordinate women and repress signs of femininity within themselves and among men.

Disavowing emotion, however, does not mean men do not need care and nurture. The loss of 'tenderness' in men is the price that has been paid as a result of the construction of patriarchy (Kraemer 1995: 204). For hooks (2004: 66), it is viewed as a 'psychic self-mutilation' that kills off the emotional side of men. Men's strong sense of self in public is often at the expense of a private weakened sense of individual identity (Seidler 1989). Specifically, the needs and characteristics of empathy, receptivity, nurturing, and compassion are suppressed because they are inconsistent with the demands of masculinity (ibid.: 148). Seidler argues that this can produce unwillingness to talk and a block to intimacy and consequently a vicious cycle of isolation and loneliness as Buchbinder (1994: 38) writes '[t]he condition of men' as 'lonely, traversed by tension, conflict and confusion'.

Men's fear of emotion means men project unconscious feelings onto others, especially women. This results in women becoming the emotional workers. Women's emotional work becomes the embodied gender division of labour (Seidler 1998). Women take on the job of emotional management creating and sustaining relationships, negotiating intimacy, and appeasing tension and aggression (Shilling 1997; McMahon 1999; Buchbinder 1994). Despite this men tend to misrecognise and take for granted women's emotional work in relationships as work because they perceive themselves as independent and not needing nurture (Seidler 1997: 46–7). Men do not always understand that relationship building does not occur in the same fashion as their often-instrumental acting in the world because men are often without language to articulate what is missing emotionally and they only recognise particular emotions are legitimate and feel the need to rationalise emotional reactions (Seidler 1989: 63; hooks 2004). Therefore, men are often blind to the love and care that they receive, devaluing the work that partners do because doing so would convey need and acknowledge dependency. Ironically, men's repression of emotion and denial of vulnerability often result in a lost 'emotional common sense' and greater emotional dependency on women (Kaufman 1994: 149). Men come to expect and demand intimacy from women but the same intimacy and tenderness can contradict the dominant modes of masculinity. This amounts to a psychic conflict between emotional need and perceived emasculation (hooks 2004: 70).

Men's identification with self-sufficiency and independence means they find it difficult to accept and realise the importance of interdependency within relationships. Women also become frustrated with men within heterosexual relationships when they cannot identify their emotional and care needs (Seidler 1989: 109). As hooks notes:

Usually rage, grief, and unrelenting disappointment lead women and men to close off part of themselves that was hoping to be touched and healed by male love. They learn to settle then for whatever positive attention men are able to give. They learn to overvalue it. They learn to pretend that it is love. They learn to speak the truth about men and love. They learn to lie...So many of us have felt that we could win male love by showing that we were willing to bear the pain, that we were willing to live our lives by affirming that the maleness deemed truly manly because it withholds, withdraws, refuses, is the maleness we desire (hooks 2004: 2–3).

Conclusion

A masculine sense of self that is dependent on public success can blind men to the affective aspects of relationships and they can come to associate affective needs with emasculation. The contradiction is that men want and need love from both men and women but find it enormously difficult to seek and establish relations of love because of these 'imperatives of masculinity' (Buchbinder 1994: 38). The conflict between men's desire for intimacy with women and dominant definitions of masculinity as care-free and independent can lead to a 'tacit dynamic' that contributes to male violence (hooks 2004). Men can confront this conflict with emotional stoicism, by denying and shutting out their emotional need for intimacy, or by a push and pull relational dynamic which manifests rejection and abuse within the relationship (Buchbinder 1994).

These dominant emotional inheritances affect men's involvement in nurturing, especially in public. Public displays of feminine masculinity can threaten dominant emotional norms and this distanced instrumental masculinity prevents fathers from developing emotional closeness and intimacy with their children and partners (Ferguson 2002). Bodily images can act in a self-fulfilling way becoming internalised. 'Boys don't cry' becomes an embodied and seemingly natural disposition (Shilling 1997). Caring and loving attributes become internalised in bodies through the senses, in touch, posture, feeling and texture, muscle tension, and in terms of smell (e.g. aversion to nappy changing) observation and hearing sensitivity, contributing to inability and incompetence.

8
Childhood Care Stories

Childhood experiences, especially the ones based on our intimate care relations, have been held responsible for the development of personality traits and lifelong relational dynamics. Within sociology and developmental psychology our primary socialisation experiences derived from our family life are understood as especially significant, and psychoanalysis gives great weight to the complex outcomes of interpersonal parental-child dynamics. Attachment theory has been particularly influential in linking early loving bonds to lifelong abilities to form loving relationships (Bowlby 1969). Attachment and separation issues are explicitly linked to gendered personality development within feminist object relations theories in how early childcare dynamics shape lifelong caring identities (Chodorow 1978). Within sociology, gender role theory has framed our understanding of how parental roles model behaviour for boys and men to follow (Pleck 1976). Simplistic accounts of object relation or role influences on behaviour and identity are no longer viewed at tenable (Chodorow 1994; Carrigan, Connell, and Lee 1987), primary childhood socialisation experiences are nonetheless significant in how we construct a narrative of self, including a caring self, throughout our lives (Giddens 1992). This chapter considers how the men narrate their intimate lives as children, how these stories frame their present understandings of care, and it speculates as to how these understandings have shaped their caring practices and equality in their lives.

Care experiences

The majority of the men in the study claimed to have experienced good basic care as children as a minimum, meaning they felt their basic needs to food, shelter, and safety were met. There were, however, considerable generational differences in how the men defined what basic care entailed. Several factors were seen to have shaped both the quality and the quantity of the care they experienced including poverty and social class, family size, issues of disability, and mental and emotional health within families, the marital harmony of their parents, religious beliefs, rural and urban social environments, and the culture of care within the community at the time. For older men, good basic care meant being 'well looked after', having 'plenty of good plain food', and 'never [getting] too badly beaten', and there was an acknowledgement that 'things were hard' and care was often 'no frills'.

Some of the men evaluated the quality of the physical and emotional care they received as children against the standards and expectations of the social milieu at that time and, as Rory (55) put it, were reluctant to evaluate these experiences with 'more informed eyes'. Cathal (58) recounted experiencing care that was harsh and paltry. He didn't 'think there was very much love and care demonstrated in the fifties in Belfast [where he grew up]. If you weren't in ragged clothes and you had food in your belly that was considered care you know'. Yet he accepted it as the standard of the day suggesting 'I really don't think it was going to get much better than that...working class families...in the fifties was fairly rough you know...A child today wouldn't have an idea.' These experiences contrasted those of the younger men like Graham (26) who described having a much less impoverished childhood, though it was gendered nonetheless. He described how 'My father worked, my mother stayed at home and done the usual things; provided for us, put clothes on our backs, fed us, taught us right from wrong, manners. That is pretty much all you want, you know, if you can do that, you know, you are a good parent.'

Childhood care experiences were defined by the men as having a significant influence on their caring attitudes, behaviours, and values. Sometimes care experiences were said to have provided a model that the men copied in their own lives, but more reflective accounts of complex and contradictory influences were also recorded. Several men emphasised being generally influenced by a culture of care which they felt pervaded the society at the time as well as being influenced by how their parents embraced that culture through charity, 'selfless' caring, compassion, and generosity or in general ways by 'doing your best for others' or 'looking out for others'.

Angus (43), Tommy (49), and Adam (73) described being strongly affected by very neglectful or otherwise traumatic childhood care experiences. Angus recalled 'a typical example' when he was 'seven or eight' when his mother said 'I am going to kill myself.' He explained 'the way I was cared for' was 'not particularly good psychologically... I mean I have had treatment for depression and alcoholism'. Tommy described being deprived of the love and care of his father, who was an alcoholic, uninvolved and sometimes violent. He reflected that 'Looking back on it now, how I survived is just beyond me but I think it happened because you just get resilient in that way, ... you just become very strong, you are able to cope with the things that normal kids wouldn't be able to cope with, you just develop these strategies to be able to cope with things.' The problems that Tommy and Angus experienced as children contributed to addiction problems they spent many years trying to overcome. They also believed their experiences had a profound effect on the caring and emotional relationships throughout their lives:

> [It affected me] profoundly!... I suppose I didn't like conflict because there was so much of it at home. I didn't want to be experiencing at home sort of passive aggression as well, then... I became like that rather than being assertive and standing up for myself. I couldn't do that because you weren't allowed to do that or there were a lot of secrets like 'Don't say anything to your Da.' It was all learned stuff... even now... I wouldn't say haunted, but it still affected me... I am still scarred by it. (Tommy, 49)

Care deprivation

Tommy's and Angus's experiences resound with the conversations with the community workers (Eddie, Tom, and Peter) about the emotional impact of poverty and marginalisation on the men they worked with. They too perceived many of the problems of the men they worked with arising from their negative care histories, and they understood these negative care experiences to be a primary source of this marginalisation. A major difficulty for the men was their inability to construct conventional paths to valued masculinity through paid work or fulfilling normative affective relationships. They also saw these negative histories reinforced on a daily basis not only through economic marginalisation and other oppressions including racism for some, but also due to the hostility, isolation, and exclusion they felt within the community. They explained how being marginalised from employment affects men's self-worth and this can affect the men's ability to contribute to fulfilling care relations, or to reproduce oppressive ones through; for example, gender-based violence. Affective inequalities were perceived as mutually reinforcing of material and symbolic inequalities. Their point was that these men are not only marginalised from the power, resources, and status that accrue to men but also from affective aspirations.

What is interesting is that both Angus and Tommy drew on their negative care experiences to reconstruct more caring masculinities in later life. Paradoxically, rather than blame their parents, they both attributed this to their feelings of guilt and shame because they had not taken greater care of their families during their childhood. Tommy wanted to be more involved with his own children whom he had himself neglected through his addiction:

> Some of the stuff that I was brought up to believe ... I was conditioned in a certain way, women done certain things and men done certain things. Then I started taking an interest in the kids, I wanted to be around them all because ... I don't remember my Da being around a lot, so I wanted to be around a lot and I thought that was important for the kids. Because even then through my madness and through my sickness that I wanted to be there for the kids at some level ... and I wanted to change nappies [diapers] and I didn't mind wheeling the pram [stroller], and that was like whoa! (Tommy, 49)

Angus felt morally obligated to care full time for both his parents. He felt his caring identity was 'negative' in the sense that it was derived from 'a need to please, a need never to lose my temper, never get out of control, never fall out with anybody if possible'. He thought that he had developed a 'caring role' as a result of trying to keep his family together as a child as a result of 'the destruction wrought by alcohol in our family'. At this point in his life he wanted to enter paid labour by working in a caring occupation as addiction counsellor 'partly giving something back'.

It is plausible to conclude, as they understood themselves, that Angus and Tommy became hands-on-carers because they were fighting feelings of guilt and shame. The emotional and addiction problems that related to their care experience meant that they have been unable to construct a conventionally legitimate masculinity through paid work and careers which also meant that they had no conventional masculinity to lose by becoming carers. By writing a new caring narrative they convert their negative care experiences into something positive as a new source of strength and inspiration.

For very different reasons (disguised here to preserve anonymity), Adam (73) also experienced a traumatic childhood being raised in institutions from the age of seven having been separated from his family. He recalled surprisingly positive experiences of institutional care, but he always felt the loss of his family and in his narrative he expresses high regard for the familial ideal. His experiences also led him to construct a caring masculinity as an adult. However, in contrast to Tommy and Angus, Adam did pursue a conventional masculinity by becoming a successful businessman and constructed a caring masculinity, not by doing hands-on-caring but through his charitable work and by defining himself as a good breadwinner. In constructing himself as caring, Adam does not question the gender order of caring since he idealises the extended family based on traditional gender divisions as the best form of care for families:

> Generally in all kinds of respects a traditional family and a traditional way of holding a unit together is best...This is a traditional passing on support from one to the other to where younger generation and back to the older is good for society and maybe I'm right and maybe I'm wrong, it might not be able to be done in modern society. But if it could be done we are losing something vital. I think the unit that holds together is the proper fabric for society as a whole. (Adam, 73)

Adam felt that his valuing of traditional gender divided caring is due to his life experiences:

> I became a father and husband and maybe self-consciously I avoided thinking about it...I don't know if people reflect on things as getting married or having children but with me it was maybe because of my past experiences; a lot of things did happen in my life. (ibid.)

The conversations suggest there is no clear or automatic link between missing out on care during childhood and doing primary caring, but these men did hold caring dispositions ('caring about') even though it did not easily or in every case translate into primary caring ('caring for'). Being deprived of care as children is associated with constructing oneself as caring as an adult. However, this can occur in contradictory ways and need not result in a questioning of the gender division of caring labour. The neglect that Angus and Tommy experienced resulted in them struggling with personal issues that meant that they could not care for themselves let alone for others for significant periods of their young to mid-adult lives. Subsequently the emotional dynamics of family life have drawn them back in a cathartic way to heal past pains by both becoming full-time primary carers. The stereotypical path to masculinity through paid work has not been emotionally accessible to them and they had not been preoccupied with establishing a conventional masculinity in their lives, thus making it relatively easy for them to construct a caring masculinity since they have not experienced the power of this conventional masculinity to lose. Additionally Angus and Tommy have internalised and accepted their status and identity as carers. Accepting these deviant self-definitions of masculinity psychologically equips men to deal with the loss of power and construct caring sensibilities (Bubeck 1995: 165). In contrast Adam pursued a hegemonic ideal defined by his success within his business and paid work and by having a prominent role in the public sphere, which was facilitated by having a conventional gender division of caring labour in his family. However, although the masculinity that Tommy and Angus pursue is widely different to Adam's breadwinner business masculinity; what they have in common is their caring intentions. The difference is that Adam's conventional masculinity exists alongside a caring identity which supports rather than challenges his sense of himself as a man, but one which is at odds with the belief that caring should be shared equally between men and women.

Care-free childhoods

As well as good and bad caring experiences, having to do (or not) care and household work as children was believed to have influenced the future caring orientation of these men. The majority of the men did not have primary caring responsibilities as children. Many of the men described having lots of freedom when they were children and not having too many 'demands' made on them besides some basic household chores. Some of the men described being 'spoilt' and being 'pets' in the family and admitted how never being 'forced to do any major jobs at home' had made them 'quite lazy', 'sit back', and 'let it happen'. Dave (34) associated his care-free experiences during childhood with a learned helplessness and dependency on women's practical and physical caring as an adult:

> It was only in later years when my mum started working that we saw ourselves as having to do these things ourselves and for a long time

I kind of realised I didn't know how to negotiate the world generally you know that kind of sense of how do I do this or how do I operate this machine. How do I put a washing machine on; basic ordinary things at the age of 19 or 20 it's kind of very traditional way of looking at it. (Dave, 34)

He also felt this affected his capacity to negotiate intimacy and sharing in relationships:

It had a profound affected in my current relationship ... I think I have very much been moulded in the traditional fashion and I'm very aware of it and I have tried my best to not let the frustration of it not turn my way to get to me ... sometimes I don't even know it is happening ... in spite of myself. Yeah and unconsciously the things I would say, like a hole in a pair of pants recently I said to [my partner], 'You wouldn't if you get a chance patch it up' ... It's always about questioning my own assumptions ... I have come to terms with the idea that it is about my own self. (ibid.)

In general, the inequality in how caring was divided within families of origin was described in innocent terms but sometimes the detrimental nature of gender socialisation was acknowledged as Tommy recounted:

I had very fixed views that women were just the main carers for children, around the home, they had a certain degree of freedom but they hadn't much of a voice either, whatever a man said, that was it and that was the way it went. That was the way I was brought up ... I was very chauvinistic you know and I just saw women as second class citizens to me anyway; they were there just to provide for the men, that was how I was conditioned. (Tommy, 49)

Tommy (49) grew up within a socially disadvantaged inner-city working-class community. His mother was both primary carer and provider for their large Catholic family and his father, though not entirely absent, was usually unemployed and often prone to violence and alcohol abuse. Against this background Tommy's mother felt it was important that Tommy live up to masculine expectations for boys because to fail to do so or to resist this conditioning placed his masculinity at stake. Whether her belief was legitimate or not is a mute point because she was more concerned that he would be victimised for failing to perform conventional masculinity and he would thus require more care and attention from her, something she was stretched to provide:

> Even my mother used to say to me 'Ah now you are not to be going to the shops all the time, and you shouldn't really be doing that all the time, bringing the baby.' I used to have the youngest fellow strapped on in one of these strap-on things and she didn't like that, she used to see men as men, she didn't see them going to the shops and sharing in the responsibilities at home and cooking dinners and all of that stuff...It was breaking outside that mindset...they were the most difficult ones for me...I used to think about it for a while and say 'Ah shit, so what?' (Tommy, 49)

The stories of men who experienced neglect as children exemplified the irony that sometimes boys were expected to care in a negative sense by not being needy. The expectation that boys contribute to the family by being externally focused is perhaps ironically demonstrated by the expectation that they can best contribute by not creating trouble or by being a care burden on their parents. Tommy, who came from a large poor family of eleven children, was encouraged by his mother to be 'independent' and to 'care for [him]self' at a young age so that he would not be a further burden for his mother, whereas Angus's main task was to 'keep [his] mother happy and not upset her'. Tommy and Angus had what can be described as a negative or passive emotional work to do as children. While neither boy was expected to do much hands-on caring, they were expected not to demand care. Thus the 'boys don't cry' narrative that many men internalise is circulated by the child's caregivers on the grounds that it is in the child's best interest and because the carer does not have sufficient resources to meet his care needs.

hooks (2004) maintains that patriarchal socialisation is a form of abuse which inflicts psychological damage on men and boys who are victimised and brutalised into patriarchal ways of relating. Citing Anakin in Star Wars as an example of repressed loss, she argues that men repress the loss of intimacy and grief arising from mother separation, thus constructing an emotional (Darth Vader) dynamic for men to take up patriarchal positions in society. She argues further that a process of splitting occurs when boys learn that expressing loss and pursuing intimacy are unacceptable in patriarchal society. Boys experience a more emotionally conflicted process of identity formation because boys are constrained by social expectations and punished for role deviance. Clare holds the same analysis locating the source of men's denial of emotional need in the developmental process of separation from their mothers which is said to create 'impermeable ego barriers' and an opposition to women and femininity:

> boys and young men are consciously or otherwise coping with an early intimate identification with their mother which threatens their identity as men and compromises their sense of self ... the seeds for men's avoidance of intimacy and self revelation. In protecting himself from the pain of future separations men construct protective emotional barriers around themselves. (Clare 2000: 151)

Men are said to experience greater difficulties in establishing intimate relationships because of a fear of re-abandonment and this results in a continuous testing in interpersonal relationships.

Care-full childhoods

The gender order within families was evident in the division of care responsibilities among children. By the men's own accounts having caring responsibilities as children were said in general to have opened them to do more caring as adults. However, these responsibilities were few in the men's childhoods and sometimes having caring responsibilities contributed to a flight from caring as adults. For some care responsibilities are seen to have 'rubbed of somewhat' and are viewed as important in 'bring[ing] out a good side of a human being'. Dermot (35) grew up within a working-class community in a large family. He recalled how caring for his sisters when he was young nurtured not only a feeling that he was a capable and responsible carer but also a sense of feeling trapped or overburdened by the responsibility:

> You realise when you get older now, like you want your own independence, ... I should have my act together I should have my own car, I should have a job and a mortgage ... you kind of feel a bit more mature and a bit more independent if you have those things yourself ... [As a child] you never felt independent because you never had your own room or you never had time to yourself because you were either doing odd jobs or going to the shop; cleaning out the fire you know washing the delph. I've washed delph for 25 years and I'm sick of washing them ... you didn't have the independence back then because you had to help out otherwise your mum and dad wouldn't have been able to cope. (Dermot, 35)

Though these experiences of caring were for Dermot a source of confidence about his care capabilities, he felt that they also led him to avoid care responsibilities in his adult life:

> I'm glad I did it because it did kind of…I want to become a parent myself one day and I know changing nappies [diapers] and bottles and stuff like that you know all of that has changed…I remember making up the bottles…I remember changing their nappies…I remember winding them…it's a kind of good life-experience for you because if you haven't planned to become a father and this is suddenly thrust upon you this can freak you out but it makes you kind of nearly ready to become a mother or father yourself…We'd look after them watch them on the road, go up to neighbours go to the shop for them and stuff like that…Looking back on it now it was a good experience but at times I felt like I didn't really have a childhood…I wished my parents didn't have so many kids…I wouldn't have that many kids myself.' (ibid.)

Dermot also felt his particular working-class experiences being very significant in his present day view of what comprised good care:

> I think the experience I had bringing up my younger brothers and sisters when I was 10, 11, 12 gave me the experience of looking after [my step-child]…I think I'm strict but fair…the reason I'm strict is that my parents were strict on me because if they weren't strict on us we probably would have went down the wrong path we would have got in to drugs,…breaking into houses…joyriding stuff like that…My parents put the fear of god into me…[because I would get] a hiding off them. (ibid.)

It was felt by some of the men that not having to do caring work as children and having all one's care needs provided by women created an expectation that they were entitled to be cared for by an 'Irish mammy'. This was true even for Conor (57) who held very traditional views about gender roles:

> [It]…would come from practice as well, I didn't have to do it when I was younger. And this is what I see in my own chaps now and they would be cooking, they went to College…and they had to cook for themselves and it would be no bother to them. They would probably leave it there for the mother to tidy up after them if they

got away with it all right, but then that is men for you I suppose. (Conor 57)

A similar perspective was held by Fran (Catholic Priest) who proposed that men's sense of superiority was related to 'an inherent self-understanding' related to men's 'preferential treatment in a family'. This was 'building his identity... feeding into his male dominant ego'. Men's sense of superiority, he argued, contributes to emotional problems they experience because it actuates their feelings of inferiority and powerlessness when they confront their own vulnerability. When the men did identify having caring responsibilities in their childhood they generally referred to more supportive care roles such as 'looking out for' siblings. Their contributions to household labour were sometimes recalled in provisional rather than as caring or domestic terms:

> I think I had my first part time job when I was about 15... I was always very independent... I'd put aside X amount working over the Summer... there was a period of about two years where [my dad]... was in and out of jobs and money wasn't as easily come by... all of us kind of just pulled up our socks... And you become a better person yourself because you become more independent and you are learning life's experiences... and learned about the power of money and the value of money. (Fionn, 25)

Nurturing role models

Although the extent and nature of gender divisions of caring varied, all of the men describe their parents as having highly gendered work practices in their families of origin with mothers (and sometimes grandmothers, sisters, or other females) as primary carers:

> The Irish mammy... when we were growing up she would have your breakfast ready for you, the clothes were always clean. She'd stop short of cleaning your own room... but always made sure your hair was brushed, your teeth were clean, she always had the dinner ready, you know, just a mammy. Dad... he cared for us in different ways, he was the provider, he brought the money in for mammy to provide the dinner and all that. He did care for us, of course he did, just in different ways... Dad would be bringing you to football practice and picking you up and on days off school he'd bring us off to work with him, that sort of thing... I suppose there was no end to

what mam done ... putting plasters on the knee and the whole thing. (Graham, 26)

Though some of the men's mothers were primarily seen as homemakers, many were part-time breadwinners working within family enterprises or in formal or informal labour-markets. Fathers' role as primary breadwinners generally excused them from hands-on caring, steering them more towards supporters and facilitators of care at family outings, encouraging education, and as disciplinarians. Rory (55) described the 'separation of labour ... my father ... kept the tent in place in which my mother exercised care. If he hadn't the tent would have collapsed you know ... he cared enough to provide that structure'. With some exceptions most of the men relied on their mothers to do the emotional work. Rory said 'I remember if I was upset I'd go to my mother for comfort you wouldn't go to my father ... you would get a hearing from my mother ... in that sense she was the primary emotional carer. She could deal with emotional material.' In contrast many of the men's fathers are described as being 'distant', lacking in 'affection', or that emotion 'wouldn't come as natural', although sometimes they are described as 'fun'. Showing emotion verbally, saying 'I love you' or 'hugging', is said to be especially problematic for many fathers who were more likely to have 'man to man chats'.

Whilst gendered experiences of caring are not without contradictions and tensions, in general they establish for the men an 'ideal' blueprint that structures primary-care relations. They establish the desire and expectation that women will be the carers meeting familial care needs. Charlie (28) grew up in a single-parent family in England with three older sisters who he claimed doted on him. He claimed to have 'definitely taken that in to later life. I look to be cared for, I don't do it on purpose but I find people mothering me you know. Over here [Ireland] I've got my Irish mummy ... what it is about me that maybe people do think I need mothering. It's strange so I never actually cared for anyone when I was very young up until I left home'.

'Traditional' Irish family relations are stereotypically characterised as community embedded, highly patriarchal, and emotionally distant (Hillard 2007: 83). The clichéd image of traditional Catholic Irish family life depicts the intensive mothering of Irish 'mammies' who 'pamper' their sons socialising an expectation that women will care for them throughout their lives, with a wife simply replacing the role of mother upon marriage. This is accompanied by the stereotype of the emotionally distant breadwinner father (Ferguson 2002) who models men's caring incapability. Indeed these emotional patterns were clearly identifiable in the men's narratives but so too were dissenting or alternative stories. None of the men described having fathers who were hand-on-nurturers in any significant respect although mothers were not universally nurturing and some were also breadwinners. Many of the men were influenced by the caring that they felt their fathers express either as breadwinners or through other caring roles:

> I always want to emulate my father because he is kind of an unsung hero...because he has done a lot for me and my family...And he has achieved a lot and I don't think he has got the recognition that he deserves in work...he has obtained so many skills in his life. Like he is self sufficient in nearly everything, he can do the plumbing, the electrics, he can build a wall, he can do the whole lot. So I always feel like a white collar worker...never get my hands dirty kind of thing...Who is going to fix something if there is a problem?...I'd like when I get older that I could emulate what he has done, he is just as good a father...he can hold his head up high. (Fionn, 25)

Although the majority of fathers are described as distant or unemotional, caring identity and parental caring practices are further complicated because some mothers were also viewed as less emotionally caring while a minority of fathers were depicted as strong care models. One of the fathers was also seen to be more emotionally caring. And fathers' were commonly defined as caring arising from different expectations for mothers and fathers. Liam (36), for example, defined his father as caring because he 'never lost his temper with anyone at work' or Greg (51) because his father did not physically chastise his children. Angus (43) 'always looked up to' his father who was 'a hero...the most stable influence....always very kind in that he would never shout at me or demand anything of me'. Cian (49) had a similar story of his father's stable influence. He spent 'a huge amount of time' in hospital during childhood. This arose from the nature of his disability, and having been primarily cared for by women either as nurses or as home carers, nonetheless he admired his father's efforts enormously to keep him a 'part of the family'. Expressing great admiration he commented how 'here was a man...who had lost his brother and his wife and then had taken in other kids from that family' yet he only ran 'a small little grocery shop'. All of these men appreciated their fathers caring in various ways and sought to emulate these ideals.

There again some men described their fathers as emotional and nurturing even through they fulfilled breadwinner roles. Simon (48) described his mother as emotionally 'cold' in comparison to his father who he saw as the emotional carer, but ironically he identified the object of this emotional care in his father's work:

> I think I learnt it from my father. I think that's why he died early I think he gave enormous amounts in his business for example ... He was enormously caring towards all of those [employees] like in ways you wouldn't believe it was a kind of extension which came out of his own family experience. He even gave the same care in his family for his siblings looking after people making sure they were alright, giving them money ... for me certainly ... [it is] partly learned ... how you be, it is the kind of gender identification that this is what it takes to be a man, to take these responsibilities. (Simon, 48)

Simon describes being influenced by this sense of masculine caring that is focused on ensuring 'outcomes' and that does not shrug off responsibility. He describes this as 'dealing with [caring responsibility] like a man' which is akin to combining elements of caring with a masculine or 'manly' and perhaps machismo ethic. It is a kind stewardship or paternal gregariousness that he feels rose above self-interest and pettiness by keeping an eye on the bigger picture with regard to the outcomes for the entire family. To be a sole breadwinner then did not necessarily mean the men perceived their fathers as any less caring than their mothers as Douglas (48) explained:

> So a man, definitely at that time, he was regarded as the man and his meals were on the table because he had to rush back out to do his work ... It is not that men were selfish beings ... [like a] big country man that came in and just growled at the table ... he done his fair share as well ... You wouldn't tie it in with ignorance or anything like it ... Occasionally ... you had a bully of a man at that time that took advantage of the situation as well, because if he is not kind hearted or he is carrying a chip, no matter what, he is still going to take it out. (Douglas, 48)

The various ways that parents' modelled care was seen to shape the identities of the men in different ways. Some men felt that they defined their own sense of caring in opposition to the models their father's offered, and they identified more with the care that mothers provided. Several men felt uncertain about how to be caring as men because they had absent, neglectful, or abusive role models to follow in their fathers.

Charlie spoke about his father's alcoholism and his absence physically and emotionally from the family home:

> There was something missing at the end of the day…it made me respect my mum a lot more…She is one of the strongest people I know and it's from what she had to go through so I suppose that is one good thing to come out of it…I wished my dad could take me up and play football…[but]…I got everything that I needed at the time. Just now as you get older a couple of my mates are going out to have pints with [their dads] now I suppose I think I have tried to replace that with my friends [by having] a more grown up relationship with somebody male. (Charlie, 28)

Tommy's father was also an alcoholic and was emotionally absent as a carer but he had a physical presence that had a toxic effect on the family dynamic:

> I think if [my mother] had the support of her husband maybe that possibly there would have been more attention given to the children because she had to worry about where the next meal was coming from or if he was going to come home or be violent or some type of verbal or emotional or mental abuse, or physical at some stages. That was always on her mind, having to worry about that and it was so hard for her if you think about all the stuff that she had to endure. (Tommy, 49)

John's father was also absent as an emotional carer though he was not physically abusive:

> I suppose sometimes I find the whole fatherhood thing quite diffi-cult not knowing whether you are going too much the one way or too much the other way. Role models are very poor, I don't really have a role model as my father wasn't around when I was younger and then he died…So from that I have to build up my own idea of what a father should be. (John, 47)

The love men need from their fathers can be distant or emotionally or physically absent. Additionally fathers can perceive their sons as rivals for mothers' love, or seek to develop a 'real' masculinity in their sons, one that represses the feminine. Buchbinder (1994) argues that this emotional minefield for men results in denial, repression, and displacement where emotional need is articulated in less positive ways. This can become a major tension in men's lives. Although the majority of the men accept the social norms that prevailed when they were children and resisted evaluating their father's love in the light of contemporary standards, increasing social expectations on men to be emotionally intimate (Giddens 1992) do affect how some of the men judge their fathers (Holter 1995: 120) (e.g. Pascal (48), Dessie (46), Dave (34)). This desire for love and intimacy is a source of change among men even if it is not hegemonic. Occasionally the emotional inexpressiveness of fathers was presented as a model against which a caring sensibility was constructed:

> A few years ago I would have said a huge priority was to be as unlike my father as possible. And I guess by that I mean that I would try to be more emotionally literate and available to other people and indeed in some ways to pursue things that would make me happy as opposed to feeling I hadn't the time or opportunity to do that. (Pascal, 48)

But there again, these emotional inheritances were perceived by Fionn (25) to be difficult to disconnect from:

> The males in my family can take a lot of things on the chin, on the shoulder and then eventually too many of them take over and then there is a big bang of, you know, I am not happy with this or whatever, as opposed to dealing with it on an ongoing basis. And I just tend...probably because we just grow up looking at your father or whatever and mimicking him and I think we have all done that. But I think we have all realised that we have done that and now it is kind of phasing out...we would actually realise that this is building up inside us and then take action as opposed to letting it take over you. (Fionn 25)

Rory refused to use contemporary care values that emphasise emotional intimacy as a lens to view his father's caring because he felt that this made invisible the care of his father:

> I'm conscious of saying that my father was more distant and my mother being closer you know.....There's an Irish poet that talks about putting the shoes on the child for the first time and the child stamping the foot and then she realises this is the first step away

from her...I think my parents protected us and they put shoes on our feet...I always felt a sense of gratitude towards them but there is some bit of me that's always reluctant to look at them through more informed eyes. (Rory, 51)

Some of the men identified more with their mothers or other female cares and were influenced by their view that caring and domestic work should be shared equally:

I think the way I was brought up definitely shaped my views. My grandmother was a very strong woman and independent view that was ahead of her time...[She would say] 'Men have to make dinner and share the work; there's nothing wrong with your uncle washing his own socks' that type of thing...There was a general feeling...that there's nothing wrong with the man washing his own socks. (John, 47)

While there was admiration for their fathers' ways of caring and for other reasons, there was often recognition and high regard for the emotional capabilities of their mothers:

My mum is very emotional, probably like myself, like she would actually get upset much easier whereas men kind of have more backbone and that kind of thing. And the other side of it...there is something about my family but they can let a lot of negatives hit them and they build up inside you and then there is an explosion. As opposed to, like my mum, one negative will hit her, there is a small explosion and it is gone, it is dealt with. (Fionn, 25)

Not all female carers fall into the stereotype of 'feminine' emotionality with some described as taking a 'material approach' to caring. John suggested he constructed his caring identity in some respects in opposition to the emotional 'harshness' of his grand mother:

I can see the way your parents parented you, you learn from them. And my grandmother...if you fell and hit your head on the ground it was 'Ah get up what's wrong with you' kind of thing...There was two sides to her, you always knew that there was a soft side to her, a very soft side actually...I have ended up the same and I am conscious of it and I have to work at being a father...if I fell in to the traditional role in which I was reared I would be very different. But I had to work at it and it is hard labour to break the habits of years. .... I would have been shouted at as a kid and I would have been slapped quite a lot ... so you could very easily fall into that way of dealing with your own children. I have never hit my own kids and I find myself shouting at them quite a lot sometimes ... I do have to consciously stop ... and put yourself in to the other mode of doing things. I do find it hard. (John, 47)

Although stereotypes of fathers as being distant and mothers being nurturing are evident, there are significant contradictions and counter-identifications. It is not possible to definitively know how the various roles and identities play out for these men in practice but in these stories we can say that they are significant in how the men define care.

It is plausible to speculate that the 'traditional' gender division of caring within emotionally secure families established care norms as the default care relationship. Against this background there does not seem to be any reason for men to challenge their masculinity or disrupt the gender order they have inherited. In this context, men are less likely to challenge their masculinity and the privilege of not having to do caring work equally. The stories show how men assume that they will be cared for by their mothers and this privilege, as the default expectation, can easily be carried though one's life and transferred on to other relationships if unchallenged and facilitated.

Similarly, the stories show much greater identity among the men with the breadwinner caring roles of their fathers. One of the important findings here is that men's practices are often defined as caring because of their breadwinning and because their intentions are viewed as caring. In other words, for many of the men, their fathers caring practices are not judged on the basis of how involved they were in hands-on-caring. This adds a layer of complexity to men's identifications with their father's practices because these practices are evaluated separately to their father's caring feelings and intentions, whether they did much caring work or not. In other words, just because a parent did not do caring work does not imply that their intentions were unloving or uncaring or judged to be so. Thus fathers' roles are often defined in affective terms and legitimated as caring and this gives many men no reason to reject these roles as they construct masculinity in their own lives.

However, some men do judge their fathers' caring practices in terms of their involvement in nurturing. This is most evident when fathers are judged to be unemotional, uncaring, or distant, perhaps because generational expectations about the level of emotional intimacy in families have altered (Giddens 1992). Where men had either no father figure, or their fathers were physically and emotionally absent, there is a greater identification and empathy with the caring roles of their mothers and there is more reason for them to construct a different caring masculinity. These experiences are related to sons who construct an oppositional caring masculinity by empathising with feminine caring attributes.

Overall the men were more likely to identify with their fathers as breadwinners and sometimes to identify with the caring they were seen to do in their role. The emotional dynamics related to being neglected in childhood and experiences of emotionally distant fathers, and indeed mothers, are associated with the desire to create more caring and emotionally nurturing masculinity. However, disruptions of caring in families can contribute to a commitment to reproduce a more 'successful' model of family, or they can make one sceptical of this model as an entrapment for women.

Conclusion

Not to discount the structural factors influencing men's role in caring (Calasanti and King 2007; Risman 1987), family dynamics do appear to be important in how these men construct gender and caring. Nonetheless, caring identity cannot be read off in any simple way from these experiences. Other studies have found how having a gender-equal family of origin increases the likelihood of being positively disposed to gender equality in one's life but there are several additional intervening factors shaping practices including gendered educational regimes and the distribution of resources between women and men within the culture which can erode the benefit of egalitarian family experiences (Holter, Egeland, and Svare 2009: 8). Risman (1998: 92) argues that family and work contexts are more significant than early gender socialisation in shaping caring practices, and even though people face several material constraints such as low incomes and few care options, some parents are nevertheless not entirely constrained and do make choices about work and family practices (ibid.: 73). Men can participate in caring as parents by either modelling or compensating for the level of involvement that they experienced from their own parents, but caring identities are drawn from multiple sources (Masciadrelli, Pleck, and Stueve 2006). The emotional dynamics derived from early childhood socialisation can be deeply rooted and resistant to change through rational reflection, but they are held in check by conformity to gender ideologies that are shaped through ongoing interactions involved in doing gender (Duncombe and Marsden 1998: 217–18). Despite dominant gender socialisation some men can overcome the cognitive dissonance between their role in caring and their identity as men. Hirsch (1996: 107) argues that 'psychological dispositions, such as gender role identity, allegiance to ethical standards or ideologies, and levels of affect for the dependent person all appear in the personal space of men and influence their choice to act in non-normative ways'. Masculine identity does not always or equally debar men from participating in caring. The men's reflections on their childhoods demonstrate how images of masculinity are passed on and re-imagined. They show that when men experience a conventional gender order as loving and secure, it forms a default model for affective relations in their lives. The love and security they attach to this model gives them no reason to question its expectation or aspiration; it bestows life with emotional meaning. When this gender order in families is disrupted, however, men are more likely to question a traditional gender division of labour in their lives, although some men will try and reconstruct it in their lives. And their reflections contain significant evidence of a subjective dialogical narrative as they try to make sense out of conflicting meanings about what it means to be a (caring) man.

9
Care-Free Masculinities

Gender equality is widely regarded as a central value of Western societies. It is often contrasted with the more gender divided cultures both
historically and contemporaneously. Present-day egalitarian values are
founded on the liberal concept of equal opportunity and access without
discrimination to various freedoms and resources widely available and
valued in the public sphere. The objective of liberal equality of opportunity is not to eliminate inequalities altogether but to regulate competition to them so that differential outcomes are accepted as free and
fair, but in practice there can be many conflicting and contradictory
beliefs about what is free, fair, or equal (Baker 1987, 1999). Western
welfare states are similar in so far as they contain gender inequalities in resources, opportunities for paid work, and responsibility for
unpaid work, and in that they inadequately support caring. However,
they vary in how they support combined paid work and motherhood,
the extent and nature of inequalities among women, how they support
different types of family forms, and support for women and families in
poverty (Daly and Rake 2003: 153–5). The majority of the men in the
study defined equality broadly in liberal terms but there was a spectrum of opinions: some held relatively radical views advocating a more
equal distribution of resources while others, holding more conservative
outlooks, opposing greater levels of equality in peoples' lives.

Care recognition and equality

Among European societies, Ireland and Italy traditionally took a particularly conservative stance on the role of women as carers, because policy
foreclosed employment opportunities for women along with strong
gender norms that made care a private issue for families (Daly and Rake

2003; Daly 2001b: 45). There was some appreciation of this among most of the men in the study. Generally there was a shared understanding that traditionally Irish society was conservative in respect of gender roles, and most (but not all) men believing that greater freedom for women has been a good thing. This was true also for many of the more conservative men like Conor (57) who acknowledged that historically in Ireland 'The men got away lightly...that women in the country got a raw deal...they worked hard, they went nowhere...the women never had access to the money...The only outing they had was going to Mass on a Sunday or something like that...they had no choices.' Paddy was an older men's support worker who himself was in his 80s; he made a similar point:

> [Traditionally in Irish society men believed] that's women's work and that's men's work, ...especially as far as the children was concerned. Rearing the children was left to women only and the men went out to work in the morning especially in the rural areas where there were farmers. They went out to work in the fields in the morning and they came in when it was dark, and they were working so hard and tired. And women to a certain extent let that happen because women felt 'ah well he is working all day with a spade and that he's tired'. They didn't realise they were probably working twice as hard inside looking after the children, cooking meals, preparing meals, looking after livestock around the house. And they did maybe give that status to men that maybe they didn't really deserve. It should have been more as it is now with everybody shares and shares alike you know male or female. (Paddy, 80s)

Favourable attitudes towards gender equality have been increasing in Western societies (Wilcox 1991) including Ireland (Fahey, Hayes, and Sinnott 2005) and despite considerable differences in their attitudes towards equality, the majority of the men nonetheless expressed support for gender equality and did not want to be presented as antiquated or anti-equality. Tommy (49) suggested equality 'would be great...people would get on a lot better...the world would be a better place...There wouldn't be any power struggle...we would all be equal'. Younger men like Charlie (28) tended to perceive beliefs that men should not be sharing and caring as simply ridiculous and anachronistic: 'I don't know if they think it's below them or they think it's a woman's job which is completely Neanderthal I don't know who thinks like that nowadays. No it should be equal really.' Among these younger men it was believed that equality in caring has been achieved. Graham (26) felt 'Society is changing; a lot of chores or jobs that were...gender specific...it is not that way anymore...I am doing a lot of things that my Dad wouldn't have done, you know, but that is just the way it is, that is just the changing face of society.' If not totally achieved, they were certainly optimistic that gender equality was a positive and progressive inevitability. Fionn (25) said: 'I think in my workplace there are actually more women than there are males in the lower tier at the moment and then in the bigger tier there are more males, but they are all aged 50, 60, 65. I think in time it is going to be more equal because from the 25 to 35 bracket I think there are actually more females than there are males.' Angus (43), a full-time primary caregiver to his elderly parents, suggested that older men were sometimes doing more of the care than women. He noticed how 'In a rural community the amount of single men who are looking after their parents would probably be higher...than woman actually...there would have been an awful lot of men who might have been the youngest, who stayed in the house and looked after their parents and never got married.' There again there were men who felt that equality, whilst bringing some benefits for women, has simply gone too far:

> Men are, in the country places, doing it more now than...the generation before me...they didn't do it at all I thought, very few...it was the man's job, the breadwinner, and the woman was the homemaker and that is the way it was...We were in the generation where...the wife wasn't solely seen as the homemaker and the husband wasn't solely seen as the breadwinner, there was a little bit shared. But now it has nearly gone, the women are all working now, that they are as important to the income now, or maybe more important in a lot of cases, than the man. And maybe some women, I don't know...I think it has gone too far. (Conor, 57)

There were also men who held more sceptical views. Pascal (48) questioned whether 'generational' change was occurring, observing 'my youngest sister's friends seem to have married fairly unobstructed heterosexual guys who don't lift a finger and those are situations where these women are working full-time as well so it's not simple enough to say there has been a generational shift.' John (47) proposed that women 'got a very raw deal to the whole equality thing' because 'they expect there to be sharing the breadwinning role 50% with their husbands and to have a career but they are also supposed to...come home, make the dinner, look after the kids, put them to bed, even look after their own elderly mother down the road, whereas men don't take on that role automatically'.

The decline of the male breadwinner model has seen the emergence of two distinct discourses surrounding caring (Lewis 2001b: 59). On the one hand, one has a conservative–communitarian discourse that rails against the erosion of the traditional family (with women as unpaid carers). This coincides with the growth of individualism, with an emphasis on turning back the clock to reinstate a male breadwinner model. On the other hand, a feminist care-centred discourse argues for an 'ethic of care' that recognises our relationality rather than our assumed individual self-interest. This divergence between valuing care and gender equality was also notable for some of the men; valuing care did not necessarily translate into valuing equality in caring. Douglas (48) talked about care needing to be 'looked into' on the grounds that the younger generation were becoming less caring. Although he didn't favour people being 'weighted down with responsibilities' he suggested that 'values should be taught to them' as this was the only way they would 'practice it'. Jamal (32) went further to argue that care should be compulsory for anyone whose 'behaviour is normal' (not for 'paedophiles' or 'violent people') through compulsory education programmes or community service work and 'career breaks' that facilitate care as a 'civic duty' (see Kershaw 2006, 2005).

Quite a few of the men felt that care was debased when equated with material rewards. Dave (34) also felt that care was undervalued 'politically' but questioned whether care could be 'built in to our economy', that 'maybe there's another way of valuing people's lives other than just a monetary value'. Similarly Cian (49) considered material incentives to compromise the essence of caring. He suggested that 'We are just after letting the thing go too far and people have no sense of responsibility, everyone is too much looking at what they are getting paid...Unfortunately in this country...it has just got so materialised...big car, big mortgage...it really has destroyed our family values, our neighbourly values which meant an awful lot.' Rory (55) was one of the few men to advocate caring and saw it as undervalued because it received inadequate monetary incentives and was suspect about attempts to symbolically recognise caring as simply rhetorical:

> Certain aspects of caring are seriously undervalued...You can earn so much money for playing football or playing music or if you just happen to buy a house at the right time...There is a kind of spurious valuing [and] exploitation of people who care intensively for others...in a sense of people praising it...Jesus they wouldn't fucking pay for it, they wouldn't create the society that rewarded

care properly you know ... the caring function is valued verbally but not otherwise. (Rory, 55)

Discussions of the role of the state in providing, regulating, or supporting care also exposed ideological differences among the men. Conor (57) argued 'the government are held responsible for everything. If the bulb blows in someone's council house kitchen, the Government is nearly supposed to go and change the bulb for them. How far can the Government go?' Although he was prepared to acknowledge 'maybe the government could do more in regards to looking after older people, like care has gone very expensive ... the government do pay a certain amount of that for people who can't afford it themselves. I don't know what more they can do really'. In contrast men with greater home care responsibilities like Angus (43) were more likely to endorse state involvement in supporting caring because 'In a society where people are having very small families and people are living much longer I think the state needs to play a much bigger role, in day care especially for the elderly, in crèches.' Angus was aware of the resource implication of valuing care explaining 'we need to pay a lot more tax and we need to get a lot more services for children, for people with any disability and for the elderly in my own case. As a society we need to take the pressure off individuals and share it more in the community'. In contrast Liam (36), who was unmarried and had no children and no care responsibilities, considered state involvement in the provision of caring services as a luxury that could not be afforded:

I consider things like the cost of services in a society and how a society can honestly sustainably provide services. So I have always gone for the idea that since the resources must be there to provide the services and since it must be honest resources, resources that you can say hand on heart will be there next year and will be there the following year, it is what a society can afford rather than what the ideal of what you would like society to provide. (Liam, 36)

Liam spoke candidly about his privileged class background and acknowledged that life is unfair for some people, yet he did not see the state having any role in altering structural inequalities:

I do accept that it is most unfair on specific individuals who therefore have to take a much greater sacrifice and responsibility, financial and emotional ... What strikes me is that life is unfair but ... I have always benefited from its unfairness. I may not have particularly wanted to do so, but I am not changing it so [that] I am not benefiting from its unfairness. (ibid.)

The stories contain contrasting and conflicting perspectives about men's evaluation of equality in caring, as they transverse across moral conservative and radical viewpoints as well as libertarian-left or right and socialist-interventionist standpoints. But their central thrust overall displayed considerable resistance to substantive equality in caring. As other studies have found men draw on various discourses to support their gender ideology (Gough 1998; Thomas 1990). In different ways the men drew on four care-free gender discourses in writing out primary caring from masculinity. Men's care-free designation was rationalised on the basis that it was *unnatural* by conflicting with men's evolutionary and biological nature; *dysfunctional* by disrupting the natural social order; *impractical* by contradicting sensible economic considerations; and *abnormal* by deviating from normative values and conventions.

Caring masculinity as unnatural

The belief that men and women are essentially different types of human being is perhaps the most common and deeply held discourse about gender. Biological and evolutionary essentialist gender discourses downplay the shared basic human capabilities which men and women have in common whilst exaggerating common sex-based differences (Nussbaum 1995a, 1995b; Kimmel 2000; Connell 1987). Essentialist beliefs were endorsed by several men in the study in the way they define primary caring to be unnatural for men based on biological and evolutionary understandings. Caring was said to come naturally to women whereas men's caring capacity was understood to be 'naturally' limited. Men were described as 'not as equally equipped', 'not naturally good at mothering', 'not naturally bred to do it', needing to be 'taught' because it was not 'nature's way'. Women were defined as 'naturally more capable', possessing 'a maternal thing', 'a natural instinct', were 'better cut out', and had 'a far greater instinct'. It made 'logical sense' for caring to be women's 'set up in life' because of 'human nature' with women's 'genetic make-up' making it 'fall into place'. Cian (49) argued that gender differences in caring 'just comes from Mother Nature, there is not a fucking thing we can do about that... Inherently, females are probably better carers than males... I am only going on the last 60 million years of history... that is just probably a fact of nature'.

Typically the essentialist views conveyed by the men were flexible; it was not believed that men could not, or should never, do caring. Gender difference was perceived more as a continuum with infant mothering placed at the feminine end of the caring spectrum closest to women's innate instincts. This meant that men could do some caring but not 50% of it as to do more would go against the biological and evolutionary grain of men's natural abilities compared with women's natural propensity to care. Ironically some held the view that more egalitarian societies are dangerous because they tamper with fixed and natural human nature:

Niall: 'Do you think that men can learn to be good carers?'
Douglas (48):   'Of course, certainly yes. But I wouldn't like to see the female species losing their abilities either...they are better equipped for it; not that it is to come out that you think I am a male chauvinist because that is not the case, but we can take anything to its limits. Like evolution takes 100s and 1,000s and maybe 1,000,000s of years, we better not try to change it all over night.'

At times men who employed this discourse contradicted themselves by arguing that not all women make natural carers. Greg (51) admitted to having very conventional views throughout his life, and perceived caring as women's role, but his direct experience of providing hands-on care both to his children and as a care assistant began to change his view to the extent that he considered he was more willing to do some forms of caring than his wife:

Hands-on care, there are very, very few men that would be willing to do that type of thing. Care of the elderly or care of young people or whatever, men are not naturally bred to do it, they should be made to do some of it...some women couldn't do the hands on care work either because my wife has told me straight out that no way in the world could she do that [referring to the intimate personal care for people with high physical dependencies] and she has a much stronger stomach than I have. (Greg, 51)

Gender difference ideology circulates in many different forms. Popular psychology transmits accounts of gender differences which support the idea that men and women, beneath the social and cultural exterior, are bodies biologically coded and primed for difference (e.g. Gray 1993). Child development theories have promoted the ideology that men are designed to provide and women are designed to care (Bowlby 1969; Woodward 1997b). Conservative religions, especially fundamentalist ones, promote the belief of the primordial family as a natural social formation (Coltrane 1996). Even gender studies, long dominated by strong social constructionist perspectives, contain some essentialist perspectives within men's studies (and men's political and religious movements) (Kahn 2008; Clatterbaugh 1997) as well as some versions of Difference, conservative, or Radical feminism (Tong 2009; Crompton and Lyonette 2005). Yet this is also rejected as a misinterpretation of feminism (Richardson 1996). Biological accounts of social life continue to dog academic discussions of gender and the discourse of evolutionary-psychology and socio-biology is widely taken up uncritically by popular media (Jackson and Rees 2007; Ging 2009). Genuine biological differences related to sexual reproduction and infant nurturing do influence aspects of caring, but these differences cannot account for gender inequality and the unequal division of domestic and caring labour or the diverse ways that men can be involved in love labour (Stockard and Johnson 1992).

Caring masculinity as dysfunctional

Closely associated with essentialist beliefs in gender differences was the discourse of caring masculinity being dysfunctional. The academic legitimation for these beliefs can be found with the American Functionialist sociology of the 1950s which proposed an integrated and functioning society which depends on a traditional gender division of caring work assigning men and women different functional roles (Parsons and Bales 1953). Similar to the idea that equality in caring work is dangerous because it tampers with our essential nature was the view that it was also dysfunctional and damaging to the social fabric which holds society together. Conor (57) claimed that women's retreat from caring roles would have adverse effects on the common good:

> Definitely the men, they should be doing their fair share, but I do see them doing a good bit more than they were doing and I would see men doing more than their share even...Maybe I am old fashioned, but I wouldn't be as old fashioned as to say that the woman

should be tied to the kitchen sink... Definitely women are entitled to their freedom and all that kind of a thing... [but] ... are the families suffering because of it? (Conor, 57)

The functionalist belief in the complementarities of gender was shared by Adam (73) who emphasised the importance of men holding different and corresponding care roles. He proposed that 'children take instructions from the father because the mother is too close to them... I think naturally a solution would be for men to become the primary provider for women to be primary carer for the family... There is a natural order of things and men primarily start by providing things and women naturally give the children care'. Valuing gender symmetry did not, however, preclude men from having a role in caring because

> [a] father has to show a certain amount of intimate attention to the children... the loss of purpose... that must come from lack of instruction from a father to his son [on] how to make his own way in life. The young people see their competitors and society. They don't really feel any good and they haven't made anything of themselves and I think this is the main reason for suicide. (Adam, 73)

Adam understood the gender division of caring to be essential for the appropriate socialisation of sons into the competitive masculine world:

> There is a job to be done between the two parents... the mother should provide the warmth and the care and presence of the home you see for the children and the man should be the one that goes out... He is a creative individual who brings security to the home because he is doing well or having his own business at the same time his role is to be the authority you see... There should be a parent at home but a father should remain a father and should go out and hunt for the wild animals... the competitive world... The woman should provide presence, care, attention, and love. (ibid.)

Functionalist perspectives uphold the value of patriarchal family relations with fathers taking on an authoritarian role, to say 'no', to lay down the 'law', and instil 'rational' discipline. This understanding fuels a moral panic that men's absence from an active fathering role is leading to feminised or delinquent sons who are alienated from their innate masculine character (Ferguson, McKeown, and Rooney 2000; Rush 2004; Carrigan,

Connell, and Lee 1987; Bly 1990). It also supports a conservative politics endorsing a rigid separation of spheres between men and women, and consequently the gender inequalities which this gives rise.

Caring masculinity as impractical

Caring was also written out of men's lives by the way that primary caring was defined as impractical for men based on rational economic considerations. Men's care-free practices are explained in respect of the practical economic decisions that men and women make. All the farmers drew on this discourse arguing that farming offered few opportunities for men to be involved in caring. Dessie (46) noted 'As a self employed farmer...I think of paternal leave and maternal leave and I say without a doubt there are certain professions that make it easier than others.' Douglas (48) suggested:

> Different careers can only allow a person to be as caring...you take for instance the truck driver...he has to put bread on the table. He can't be compared with the lad that is finished at 4 o'clock in the evening and measured against him...So you can't divide it up equally then...understand a person's career because not everybody can say, 'I can take an hour off now or an hour off then.' (Douglas, 48)

Conor (57) mentioned that traditionally in Ireland 'The men did do the farm side of it, they were out on the land and they were working and times were hard and they worked long hours to make ends meet...There wasn't many opportunities and the women would stay at home until they got married...It was a kind of a viscous circle then.' Conor rationalised breadwinning on the grounds of the economic well-being it provided his family, and this enabled him to justify being less involved in nurturing:

> You might wonder would I regret it or something like that...Well to a certain extent but not really because it kind of...[gave me] a sound footing financially...a better standard of living...It is kind of a balancing act...I could have stayed at home and been with the children here all the time but sure I wouldn't have been able to educate them then...They'd probably have ended up labouring on building sites or something like that or working in a shop or something like that. (Conor, 57)

Practical rationality can, however, potentially serve to undermine men's care-free practices. For example, Tommy (49) suggested 'The other half is saying "Look I am bringing in as much money as you, why should I have to clean when I come home. You are coming home doing the same thing, what is the difference", which is only fair, it is fair dues.'

Economic rationality only partly explains the care decisions people make (Hearn and Pringle 2006a; Bubeck 1995: 146). Many studies have shown how men generally prioritise their work over care, especially when developing and securing their careers, even when it defies economic rationality such as when wives earn more (Ranson 2001; Kimmel 2000; Cheal 2002: 93–102; Thébaud 2010; Lynch and Lyons 2009b). Men can experience difficulty in not being a primary breadwinner (Lynch and Lyons 2009b) and encounter a dilemma when their commitment to paid work clashes with intensive demands of love labour (Lynch, Baker et al. 2009). For their part women's care rationalities may also trump economic rationalities even when women earn more (Duncan and Edwards 1997; Lynch, Lyons, and Cantillon 2009b), but couples also jointly negotiate class-based strategies in their choices and bargaining for care responsibilities (Shows and Gerstel 2009).

Caring masculinity as abnormal

Caring was also written out of the masculine script when caring was defined as abnormal for men. Simon (48) argued men are affected by dominant media representations that depict men to be incapable of providing care, noting 'There is an enormous gender injustice that takes place around this issue in that men are not capable because of social conditioning and how we are brought up and how society is structured that men are denied access to experiences that could otherwise be quite enriching for them.' Dessie (46) argued that men continued to be subject to social stigma when doing feminine tasks because stereotypes that caring and domestic work is 'a woman's job' and 'below them' are widely promoted particularly within the media:

> Even if you look at television ads for washing powder and things like this, that doesn't help in the role of men taking over because in an awful lot of situations it is women that are there. Or there is food to be prepared on the table it's, 'Mum I don't like the taste of this' or whatever. An awful lot of advertising actually still shows the mother as the real caregiver and that is a huge influence....That needs to

be gender balanced...Maybe we can put a photograph of a man in washing the clothes. (Dessie, 46)

John (47) proposed that people can have an interest in promoting these norms because they find alternative norms threatening. Having a caring orientation went against the 'tradition' and 'image that the wife does everything':

> Elements within society want to believe that men are...[incapable of caring]...They are not able to care whether it be for children or for elderly parents and there is maybe that in the feminist view of things. They don't want men to take that role you know because traditionally they are seen as the emotional ones, the caring ones. It's a little bit unspoken of a threat from men if we are seen as actually quite caring. I don't' look after my children as easily as my wife can you know but it's like a threat to womanhood. (John, 47)

Jamal (32), an African-Irish Muslim, spoke about care in Ireland with a sense of distance from the prevailing culture. He identified his Islamic religious views as a major influence on his attitude to care, compassion, and charity. And he felt that care-free norms can vary in different cultural settings:

> You can see a man doing a superb motherly job, you know, kissing, hugging, everything that you need...[However], it depends on where you come from, if you are conditioned as a human being...I have seen middle class traditional countryside people reacting and interacting with their kids in a totally different way than a family that have lived here in Ireland from a very affluent background...The countryside people are totally different from the Dubliners...Catholicism would have an influence on you...the behaviour of each person coming from the two backgrounds would be totally different. (Jamal, 32)

Restrictive gender norms surrounding caring were said to affect both private familial and public care work for men. In the public sphere these restrictive gender norms were said to give women an 'advantage' when pursuing caring occupations because women are defined as naturally caring and trustworthy and by contrast gender norms for men are said to define men and masculinity as dangerous, violent, and sexually predatory. Conor (57) explained that he had given up doing voluntary work with young people, something he had done for much of his life, because it was shrouded with suspicion:

> Maybe it is a kind of suspiciousness or something ... being involved with any group of youngsters you can never be on your own. Like at one time I could take ... a bunch of chaps, in the field on my own but now you'd never let yourself in that situation. And you would never have a child in the car on his own. Everyone is watching everything now; I think it is not the way it should be ... at my age now I don't want that hassle ... You just can't be on your own with youngsters. The enjoyment is nearly gone out of it. (Conor, 57)

Conor was experiencing what Doucet (2006: 209) describes as 'residues of a social fear around close relations between men and children, particularly between men and the children of others. Such suspicions differ from rural to urban areas and are expressed in other ways for low-income fathers and gay fathers'. Reflecting on his experience working as a community volunteer, Nevan (74) also felt 'A lot of females would have preferred to be cared for by females ... I have come across that [in my voluntary work]. Some people say after calling "could some of the ladies call?" maybe because they can relate better.' Angus (43) reflected on this from his own experience as a caregiver to his parents. He found providing intimate personal care especially challenging because it was not seen to be appropriate for a man to undertake. It was difficult 'Overcoming what is not natural ... like helping your mother, not helping them dress, but bringing them to the toilet ... that takes a lot. They are the physical demands of ... of seeing, I suppose, your parents naked in a sense, both physically and psychologically, and their need.'

Some of the men certainly felt that their engagement in caring was limited or constrained by the restrictive gender norms and images. This perspective contrasts with those like Paul's mentioned earlier that men are constrained in their traditional roles because feminine expressive norms for men are ascendant. Much of this seems to hinge on the kind of masculinity and caring men wish to practice. Perhaps reflecting (as well as constructing) these differing views, there is a great deal of ambiguity in contemporary images of caring for men circulated within the media. The discourse of 'new fatherhood' masculinity is as Gregory and Milner (2011: 14) observe, 'riven with tensions' by pessimistically, on the one hand, echoing moral panic about the fathering practices of marginalised men and their effect on children, while, at the same time, failing to offer a meaningful alternative for these men and, on the other hand, optimistically suggesting that men have changed more than they have in actuality. Their study of cultural representations of fathers in France and the United Kingdom shows that '"subordinate" forms of masculinity have found their way into mainstream cultural products and the newer model of shared parenting has made inroads in dominant cultural representations', yet there continues to be 'cultural doubts and uncertainties about the role of fathers within the family' (p. 15). Media representations of men as intimate carers can give the impression that men are more involved in caring than they are in practice whilst, at the same time, in a subtle manner they confirm that men are secondary carers in supportive roles to women (Wall and Arnold 2007). Instead of these images necessarily undermining the femininity of caring, contemporary images of nurturing masculinity can portray the ambiguity of caring for men by placing an emphasis on the 'machismo' of men's caring and hence reinforcing that men should care differently (Wall and Arnold 2007: 521; Romano and Dokoupil 2010). Norms and media stereotypes presenting it as inappropriate for men to care can be internalised by men and manifest as an uncertain relationship with caring. But it is important to state also that it is not just confusing or stereotypical representations of men doing care that limit masculinity but also images which ignore care altogether. The ignorance and invisibility of care in images of masculinities are shown in how men's interests are represented in entirely different ways than women's, in terms of sports, heterosexuality, cars, technology, violence and aggression and danger, some of which (although not all) are in many ways the antithesis of caring (Brandth 1995; Dill and Thill 2007; Ricciardelli, Clow, and White 2010).

Gender difference and equality

Overall the ways in which primary caring was written out of the script of masculinity centred on the understanding that the men and women are either innately or socially constructed as different. Men's interests, roles, identities, and basic capabilities were seen to be at odds with primary caring and dissimilar to women's interests and identities. Whether innate or socially constructed, these differences are said to make doing care difficult for men. Liam (36), who was unmarried and had no caring responsibilities, perceived caring as a responsibility he should avoid because he felt incapable of doing it. Liam expressed being disinterested in caring because he felt both incapable and selfish saying 'I feel that if I were a parent I would probably do a bad job of it and since

I would have a huge responsibility to a child, to my child...I think it would be selfish to try to take it on because it is not something I could afford to fail in because it wouldn't be me failing, it would have direct consequences on someone else.' Referring to the intimate personal care for people with disabilities, Liam considered it relevant that men would care differently based on possessing different physical capacities:

> I think that there will probably always be a majority of women in nursing and care of that sort, care of the sick. But it is not necessarily a woman's occupation and that men can be prepared to take a greater role in it. Whereas possibly male nurses would be used more where there may be a mental illness and the possibility that staff could be intimidated, could even be assaulted on occasions. (Liam, 36)

Despite claiming that people should be compelled to care, Jamal (32) noted how 'you feel about it' is a primary criterion for how to judge how drawn one should be. Angus (43) considered it something he should take on board positively as a choice although it was evident that he felt he had little choice: 'Generally it is just I have chosen to do what I do, I do it well, it is hard to say I don't mind doing it but I suppose I cannot see it being any other way so.' Angus considered caring to be more difficult for men because they have not learned to do it:

> I think it is slightly more difficult for me and maybe for a man that wouldn't have, say cleaned children, bathed children regularly and be used to bathing other people...I don't think you would find as many male home helps or male carers looking after women in the same way that women bath and shower and clean men...It is not something as usual in society for men to be in that role. (Angus, 43)

The stereotype that men are unemotional was presented as evidence of men's incapability to care. Stereotyped masculine emotionality is said to leave men 'somehow lacking' and 'preclude [men] from having a caring nature'. John (47) felt that men restrict themselves to bread-winner roles not only because it is 'expected' but also because 'men may feel sometimes trapped in breadwinner roles because they do not know what to do with their emotions'. This 'gender trap where women are expected to do the caring' is believed to be 'a trap for men as well':

> Because men think in a different way and view emotions in a different way than women do there is an assumption we're not

able to do that sort of stuff...I think men deal with emotions quite differently...Men...make a decision and go do it...about 30 seconds...whereas women have a different approach to it...There is a presumption made that we can't handle caring and that sort of stuff that we are somehow lacking when it comes to giving whether it's emotionally or caring. (John, 47)

Dave (34) noted that men focussed more on political rather than personal and intimate dimensions of caring:

Women I think are more focused on the person. Men can get obsessed with the system around the person that they are caring with or for...They are consumed by access and payment systems and benefits whereas women tend to think more about how the person is within the world...helping someone in a wheel chair... [If] I'm a woman then I'd say 'Well there's no ramps on this building' as opposed to 'There just aren't any ramps'...Men...see it in the abstract in that they want to change it all as opposed to the particular situation. (Dave, 34)

Rory (55) was a strong believer that men and women have different ways of showing care. He felt that men care in lots of ways since 'I can't imagine there's a job in the world that couldn't be done with caring.' Rory worked in a managerial capacity that often involved facilitating groups and managing group conflict in organisations. Like Dave, he described how the men in his workplace care in more political ways than women. While 'we all intensely care for this organisation, the two men here have led the battle in many ways...it's a game and the women find the game hard to be part of in a different way...It's like, as men we have access through our own social organisations, we know the posturing...maybe it was the whole caring in different ways you know'.

These views that men care differently were generally (though not exclusively) presented as an argument that men are, or can be, caring in their differences, in how they demonstrated and expressed their caring, or in their roles as workers and breadwinners. Rory (55) explains the desire to create caring equality as overlooking men's and women's preferences, interests, and competences to do caring work, and he claims this places a higher value on equality than it does on respecting peoples' differences. Rory makes the point that calls for equality in caring threaten masculine and feminine identities and are morally and 'ideologically driven' rather than grounded in people's experiences, capabilities, or the needs of the care recipient. In that sense his rationale appears to be grounded in a feminine ethic of care rather than a feminist or social justice ethic. Rory argues that sometimes people are comfortable with the care that they provide and they like doing it because they feel that is their way to make a contribution. He describes caring for his mother-in-law: 'I cook and shop and do all that so am I caring for her? Of course I'm caring for her! Am I washing and cleaning her? No! My wife is doing that. So I'm saying I'll get her a bit of liver she'll like that.' Rory maintained 'people should do what they are good at doing', explaining 'it is my wife who cares for her mother. I'm not as skilful' and 'she wouldn't be comfortable'. He recounts how his wife's brother 'wants to share some of those duties' but 'he gets in the fucking way because it's his need to do certain caring duties that it just doesn't fit. He's not as good'. Despite his brother-in-law's 'good heart' Rory finds his caring inept because being 'ideologically driven' he has not learned to be 'skilful' at caring. This dilemma characterised some of the tensions and practical realities around caring and men, who have not learned to undertake caring from an 'innate' disposition.

The tension between feeling skilful and comfortable at caring and feeling obligated to be more involved was a running theme for several of the men. Some of them admitted limiting their caring practices in order to remain within their 'comfort' zone by doing 'practical' care tasks rather than more 'intimate' tasks. Not to discount the lived complexities, practical difficulties, and personal preferences on the part of both care recipients and carers, from a gender equality perspective however, remaining within one's comfort zone is a privilege that allows many men to avoid the subordination of caring. As one participant recounted men are generally not seen to take the 'energy, time and effort' to fulfil caring because they have the option to 'just sit back and watch ... if you can get away without doing it'. A major problem from the point of view of gender equality is that men can afford to define caring as a choice (a 'route that you want to take in life') because men are more likely to have the privilege of not having to do the caring unless women are not available (Lynch, Baker et al. 2009). Many men have developed restrictive caring abilities because they have not learned to do caring in an expressive way (Lynch and Lyons 2009b), but men can also feign incompetence and mess up when called on to participate as a way care avoidance (McMahon 1999: 30).

Educators understand how desiring to learn is the first major hurdle to be overcome in learning anything. Many of the men claimed that men can become carers if they are willing to challenge their identities by developing a sacrificial 'disposition' that made them 'suitable' for caring. It is, however, an identity that one must embody since they need to 'enjoy' caring and actively 'set their mind' to caring having 'taken an honest appraisal of what a task entails' including the 'sacrifice for other people', 'selflessness', and 'the responsibilities'. To do caring men must have 'the level of patience...effort, enthusiasm and ability' and 'the motivation not to feel depressed'. However, in practice, becoming a carer means that men often struggle with their identity. Simon (48) explains that there is a strong caring side to him that was other-centred and giving, but he still found this 'a journey', 'a difficult area', a 'tension' with 'an opportunity cost'. He claims he 'found [him]self probably having to give too much more than [he] should have perhaps'. In practice then becoming a carer entails rejecting the stereotypical goals of masculinity, the forms of capital that legitimate hegemonic masculinity, by accepting the low status of caring confirmed by carers' invisibility and insignificance especially among men. Put simply, becoming a carer can be experienced by men as emasculation because it asks them to stop being a man (Lynch, Baker et al. 2009). In other words exiting one's comfort zone can be experienced as exiting one's identity.

Claims that men's caring is overlooked when using a 'feminine yardstick' (Thompson 2000) risk both essentialising differences in caring and hiding inequalities in the division of love and caring work. Although socially constructed gender differences in how men and women care can be found (Kramer and Thompson 2005), and doing gender and doing caring are intimately related (Simpson 2009), differences in emotional work are situational, strategic, and embodied rather than essential. This is not to deny how deeply held the emotional disposition of masculinity can seem (Seidler 1997). Men do caring in diverse ways including in ways typically defined as feminine despite the fact that there are some discernible patterns to how men engage in caring overall (Marsh and Musson 2008; Pierce 1998; Sattel 1998; Hyde et al. 2005; Freshman and Rubino 2002). Certainly studying men's caring through a maternal lens can limit our view of fathers' caring and the ways that fathers promote playfulness, independence, risk-taking, and physicality (Doucet 2006: 222). It can also be presumed that feminine ways of caring are necessarily superior. Therefore, it is important to keep an open mind about difference where difference doesn't make for disadvantage, but unfortunately all too often difference does make for disadvantage and the view of difference can reinforce essentialist beliefs and overlook the malleable and socially constructed nature of caring and how traditional patterns of caring derive from privilege.

The rationale that men and women inhabit different caring worlds because they have different capabilities is also deployed to argue that women act as gatekeepers to men's greater involvement. Charlie (28), who had no children, but was in a committed relationship, had never reflected on whether he would become a primary carer because he felt his partner was 'so orientated around children' that he wouldn't 'get the chance'. At the same time he didn't feel he would be required to have the same level of involvement because 'She is so good with kids... it wouldn't bother me I would love to look after the kids all day but I don't know if that would happen.' Men are 'gatekeepers' for gender equality because of the resources they command collectively (Connell 2011), but women can act as gatekeepers to men's involvement in caring because they perceive it as their sphere of influence, seek to protect it from men's control, and because they perceive men as inadequate caregivers (Chapman 2004: 117–18; Kullberg 2003; Kraemer 1995). Women can also hold gender difference beliefs that perceive it inappropriate for men to care and make it difficult for men to change (hooks 2004) but men typically expect women to take caring roles (Doucet 2006: 135). Holter et al. (2009: 109), for example, identify a discourse that fathers are not 'given the change' to be significant for Norwegian men but even stronger for Norwegian women. While the actuality of whether men are 'given the change' in practice is not established, 'this explanation has become one of the most socially and culturally accepted and legitimate explanation of the significant differences in mothers' and fathers' practices when it comes to parental leave' (ibid.: 110).

Certainly there are many women who choose to care (Harkim 1995, 1991) but there are many factors shaping care preferences which, within male dominated societies, are generally limited (Jacobs and Gerson 2004; Lynch and Lyons 2008). Explanations why women 'choose' caring over paid work within the context of neo-liberalism where people are supposed to be free-thinking agents revert to biological essentialism that women simply prefer to care (Crompton and Lyonette 2005). Much of the argument about choice is based on market rationality (the hallmark of neo-classical economics and rational-choice theory) that assumes independent competitive individuals who make rational choices but care rationality is based on relationships, connections, and interdependence and, therefore, fails to account for how choices are not all equal (Lewis 2001b). Choices and preferences are constrained by the moral imperative for women to care which can be deeply internalised and regarded as an innate disposition (Lynch and Lyons 2009b; Kullberg 2003; Ungerson 1983), and which varies culturally even within European societies (Kremer 2007), in ways that outweigh material rewards for women (Lynch, Cantillon et al. 2009).

Conclusion

Care is recognised by these men as a valuable social good and the good society is one that nurtures a caring society. Many of the men support gender equality at least in liberal terms and some of them go beyond equality of opportunity expressing the more radical view that caring should be equally distributed between men and women. Recognising care and gender equality, however, does not necessarily equate; for some men care and equality are entirely different. In fact, good care for some men equates with an unequal gender division of labour. Despite this the gender equality is broadly endorsed and most men do not want to be perceived as out of date with contemporary norms. At the same time men are keen to rationalise inequality in caring, which they do so using four gender discourses that define caring in opposition to masculinity. The men describe a contradiction between their gender identity and caring, and this experience provides a rationale for the avoidance of caring. This symbolic devaluation of men as carers lets men off the hook to reproduce their privileges (McMahon 1999) and to avoid caring except as secondary carers, facilitators of care, or care commanders (Lynch, Lyons, and Cantillon 2009b). The men's gender ideologies enable them not only to avoid the burdens associated with caring but also to miss out on many of its benefits (Peterson 1998: 49; Segal 1997a).

10
Care-Full Masculinities

The study set out to understand how masculinity is defined in relation to care by exploring the ways that care is gendered for a small group of men in Irish society. Broadly the men in their personal conversations defined themselves either as *Conservatives* (Cian, Nevan, Adam, Douglas, Conor, Rory, and Liam), *Sharers* (Pascal, Jamal, Fionn, John, Dessie, Dermot, Dave, Charlie, and Graham), or *Carers* (Tommy, Angus, Simon, Cathal, Greg). The classification connects how the different men define caring and masculinity in relation to their accounts of their practices, and though there is a remarkable affinity between them, the fact that they are occasionally incongruent indicates certain tensions, contradictions and inconsistencies in how they imagine themselves as men and how they live their lives. Some of the men are difficult to place and they cross categories: Greg could be defined as formerly very conservative in his attitude to caring, but he is considered a *Carer* as he became a primary carer for his children and increasingly defines himself thus. Nevan also defines his life in conventional ways but feels positive about younger people sharing caring and might, therefore, be considered a *Sharer*. Although Rory defends gendered differences in caring, he also supports men having a much greater involvement in caring generally so he is considered a *Conservative* and a *Sharer*. What they have in common is a cultural context where the master narratives of *Nurturing Femininity* and *Breadwinner Masculinity* provide a conceptual blueprint or ideal type men identify with and compare themselves to in different ways and which produce varying degrees of not only conformity and commitment but also resistance amongst men.

Conservative masculinities

Conservatives understood caring most trenchantly in terms of a gender division of labour comprising complementary male breadwinner and female carer roles. They all experienced a stereotypical gendered division of caring in their families of origin and they all empathised with, and were reluctant to judge or criticise, these practices when reflecting on them. They saw their breadwinning and that of their fathers' as heavily constrained by practical and economic realities. They did not have to sacrifice paid work to caring nor did most of them experience these in conflict, either because they had no caring responsibilities, or because the women in their lives did the caring work. Most of them had a strong sense of duty towards family that included a paternalistic and commanding attitude to caring and a view that nurturing was women's work. At most, they expressed minor regrets for not being more involved in nurturing. When they reflected on the time they had invested in paid work compared with caring, they tended to justify its 'price' on the basis of its economic contribution to their family. They also defined breadwinning as caring by emphasising its loving motivations and outcomes. Rory, for example, suggested that breadwinning is the structure that facilitates other forms of caring. In the political conversations Paul (fathers' rights activist) goes further, arguing that breadwinning is a superior form of caring because, he claims, it keeps people alive. Conservatives were more likely to express apprehension about the decline in availability of the nurturing capital that caring femininity represents to them. They were most likely to privatise love and care labour as a familial responsibility and least likely to advocate for more care services to support love labour. The greatest degree of ideological resistance to equality comes from Conservatives, many of whom believe that equality has 'gone too far'.

Conservatives resist change in the gender order of caring by drawing on essentialist discourses that masculinity is incompatible with caring, but although they are most opposed to equality in caring, there are a number of contradictions in their accounts. On the one hand, some of these men make strong statements that masculinity is incompatible with caring. On the other hand, they often resist being labelled as uncaring by claiming that they are equally capable of caring as women. Nevan, for example, does not reject gender or caring equality outright:

Niall: Ok, so you wouldn't have any kind of objection if men started to care for say children, for elderly people, as much as women?

Nevan: None whatsoever.

Niall: And you think it might be a good thing for society?

Nevan: It could be good for the sake of society as well...Not...at times things enters your mind saying 'Well that shouldn't be done' but then when you go back and look at it again you'd say 'Well I wouldn't change that, I would leave it as it is, it is working out all right so why change it?'

Conor claimed to support equality stating 'Yes, definitely yes, sure why should it be different like, men should be as good I suppose. There is no aspect of it that men wouldn't do or couldn't do if they laid their mind down to it, or had to do it.' There are also tensions between the traditional caring practices that they espouse and socially valued ideals of equality. This is evident by the way that ideological dilemmas between traditional masculinity and gender equality are managed. Edley and Wetherell (1999) show how men use 'disclaimers' such as 'I'm not sexist but' as a means of separating the principle of equality from its practice, thus enabling men to proclaim liberal ideals of gender equality yet remain complicit with hegemonic masculinity. Similarly in this research, the discourse of gender equality is often a rhetorical device to defend their caring practices as Douglas does, for example, by saying 'not...that you think I am a male chauvinist...but!' In this way even conventional men try to manage tensions within gender relations and present an image of being modern men without contradicting the dominant ideology of gender equality (of access and opportunity). Finn and Henwood (2009: 560) propose 'a more complex mix of hegemonic and non-hegemonic masculinities as men adapt to different discourses and practices of fatherhood at different times and often deploying contradictory positions at the same time'. There is then a reflection occurring among these conservative men as they watch a changing gendered landscape. As they see men engage in caring and women enter the public world, the conservative view is undermined, placing their ideology under pressure to change, and there are instances where they resist conservative masculinities, see the benefits of love labour for themselves and desire to embrace it.

Sharing and caring masculinities

Men who professed a strong commitment to sharing care equally with others including the women in their lives were defined as Sharers. Most of the Sharers have not experienced a rigid gender division of labour in their families of origin nor did they empathise with gendered caring practices, and they were also more critical of them. They did not define their caring exclusively through their roles as breadwinners, although breadwinning continued to be very important for many of them. Nonetheless, paid work was a major way that their masculinity was defined. Sharers, therefore, had to balance paid work and caring responsibilities to maintain a sense of themselves as valued men. Sharers with caring responsibilities (some had none) had more negotiations and compromises to make around caring and paid work than Conservatives. While Sharers described aspects of caring to be rewarding, they were also very aware of its burdens and none willingly choose to do caring in place of paid work. Sharers, however, resist greater levels of caring equality on the grounds that it is impractical, uneconomic, or negatively sanctioned by their employment. Doing less care is rationalised on the basis that it means claiming less advantages in the public sphere or because of the material gain and well-being of their families. Sharers are prepared to do caring and be seen to do it, but they are opposed to sacrifice the work-based masculinity while doing it. A fear of emasculation was evident when men are asked to give up paid work to do primary caring because they can feel insignificant and invisible to other men when doing caring. This shows that men face the inferred moral judgement of other men when they do primary caring. Sharers masculinity is more conciliatory to gender equality but remains underpinned by the hegemonic belief that full equality can only be realised in an 'ideal world'. Sharers are not prepared to alter their own behaviour in any radical way so that they do not benefit from the gender order. Nonetheless, Sharers, as well as men like Fran (Catholic Priest), Peter, Tom, and Eddie (Community Workers), and Declan (Trade Union Official), and Paddy (Older Men's Support Worker) hold more egalitarian beliefs about sharing care. Their reliance on formal and informal care services enables them to balance paid work and care responsibilities and thus maintain a sense of themselves as men in the public sphere. Consequently they look more favourably on the provision of care services and public policy supports for caring.

Men who undertook primary care roles were defined as Carers. They typically resisted traditional gender ideology and maintained they did all aspects of caring. Since they have experienced both the burdens and benefits of doing caring work at first hand, these men have greater empathy with the caring work done by women and expressed a more compassionate and caring masculinity. They did not use essentialist discourses to the same degree as Conservatives because this ideology is undermined by their experience that they are competent carers. They did not define masculinity strongly through paid work and defined caring more in terms of nurturing, although they also experienced negotiations and compromises around paid work and the demands caring placed on them. While they noted how rewarding their caring work was for them, they were also acutely aware of its emotional burden. However, Carers and Sharers claim that there are also emotional payoffs in terms of 'knocking the corners' of one's masculinity and by deepening intimacies and affective relations. This included Greg (51) and Cathal (58), who, before undertaking caring, held conventional attitudes to the division of family caring. Sharers and Carers are also more likely to claim that oppressive social norms make it hard for men to care. Sharers and Carers sometimes claim that women resist men's caring by the labelling of men as 'emotionally unstable' and 'unable to plug in to their emotional side' in contrast to the labelling of women as 'naturally' caring.

A further distinction can be drawn between 'No Choice Carers' and 'Nothing to Lose' Carers. 'No Choice' Carers had sacrificed having a full-time commitment to paid work when becoming carers, since there were no women willing and available to do it for them. 'No Choice' Carers (Simon, Cathal, and Greg) became primary carers for their children when their marriages broke down or when their wives were unable to perform caring work. Cathal described having to fight to gain custody of his children and explained that the main barrier was that being a primary caring single father goes against institutional norms and expectations for men. These experiences were much lessened when men (such as Graham and Simon) were able to negotiate informal agreements about caring with mothers. Nonetheless, family breakdown was a major life adjustment for the men because their new identity as single or shared parents was the antithesis of heteronormative care relations. The experiences of separated fathers show how feeling good about themselves as fathers and overcoming their sense of 'failure' is about accepting and constructing new definitions of caring masculinity and negotiating new affective roles and responsibilities.

Angus and Tommy could be considered 'Nothing to Lose' Carers. They claimed to have had emotionally deprived childhoods and they maintained that dealing with this emotional legacy left them poorly equipped to establish a conventional path to masculinity through paid work. Since they have not constructed a conventional masculinity through paid work, they did not sacrifice a conventional masculinity when they became carers. In contrast to dominant care-free norms of masculinity, both Tommy and Angus felt morally and emotionally obligated to become primary carers even though this denied them the opportunity to construct themselves as paid workers and, therefore, as dominant men in these terms. To cope with the low status and emotional burdens of being a full-time carer Angus took on board a professional caring persona and defined his caring as would a paid worker. Both Angus and Tommy experience emotional gain by constructing an identity as primary carers and feel competent and accomplished in that role. Ironically, through this process, they experience an emotional catharsis which enables them to begin re-establishing a path to paid work and perhaps a more conventional masculinity. Tommy noted that since he had the 'experience' and 'invested some of my time' he could 'develop a career from it'. 'No Choice' Carers on the other hand had established a conventional masculinity through paid work and they did sacrifice their careers and their participation in public life while doing caring. This sacrifice was not as much as it might, however, because they retained a semblance of masculinity through paid work because they were all able to negotiate care time in their work.

There is a clear affinity between having to do caring work and professing a *Conservative, Sharing* or *Caring* ideology. Having caring responsibilities as children is related to men feeling more capable of doing caring as adults, even though many other factors intervene to influence the caring one does in life. Doing caring work is associated with having a more flexible definition of masculinity, men's roles, and men's caring capabilities. Men who do caring have a greater appreciation of the minutiae of the physical and emotional burdens and complexity of caring. Even men who formerly held conservative attitudes to the sharing of care work, such as Tommy (49) and Greg (51), constructed a more caring masculinity from doing primary caring. Although men find caring to be emotionally burdensome and although it contradicts dominant imperatives of masculinity, they also find caring to be fulfilling and rewarding. Sharers and Carers provide evidence of gender convergence by demonstrating increased levels of intimacy and sharing of care responsibilities. Men like Fionn (25), for example, show how their involvement in the care of their children leads them to reflexively reconstruct their masculinity.

Nurturing caring masculinities

Perspectives that advance essentialist differences between men and women in respect of care face the contradictory evidence that men can care (Segal 1997b: xv; Pringle 1995) and that equality in care itself generates wider social and psychic change among men (Chodorow

1978; Dinnerstein 1977; Balbus 1998). Coltrane (1996) argues that care practices are ways that people do gender either in how they form conservative practices or deny them. Coupled with increasing individualism and the fact that peoples' identities are so intimately tied to the division of caring, he notes, it is unsurprising that the dual spheres ideals persist. Yet he claims dual-income couples are compelled to negotiate new gender patterns and this leads to ideological change. Men who share care more equally tend to define men and women as basically similar whereas those who do not tend to 'attribute special skills and intuitions to women and mothers ... when domestic activities are shared equally "maternal thinking" develops in fathers as well as mothers, and the social meaning of gender begins to change' (Coltrane 1996: 83). Being involved in childcare can help men to feel good about themselves as carers and develop a more other-centred and caring personality (Kraemer 1995; Palkovitz, Copes, and Woolfolk 2001).

Despite the care-free designation of men, their personal stories showed also how care-free masculinity is undermined by the experience of doing caring work. The stories conveyed how doing caring work helps men to develop a more nurturing and compassionate masculinity. This is turn enabled men to develop caring capabilities including practical, emotional, and cognitive caring attributes, and nurture caring values. Doing caring also appeared to support men to develop a 'softer' masculinity, to reform their lives and construct other-centred sensibilities, and to engage with fears surrounding vulnerability. It also enabled them to identify women's caring burdens and appreciate how difficult, complex, and underappreciated caring work can be. Cathal (58) said caring 'knocks the corners off you. You become much more ... reasonable ... [it becomes] easier for you to understand someone else's perspective, get on in a group ... learn to get along ... and indeed care ... for other human beings ... soften you up a little bit ... compromise and make allowances ... be far more amenable'. Upon becoming a father Jamal (32) explained 'I do things that I have never thought that I'd do like smelling her and just hugging her and start kissing and so on, things that I never thought that I'd do, it is just beyond ... I can't describe it, it is very hard to describe.'

To do nurturing work for men is to actively integrate feminine characteristics into masculinity (Doucet 2006: 237) and to embody a feminist masculinity because it involves men developing relational skills and learning to express emotions without oppression or fear (hooks 2004). Intimate caring allows men to learn non-erotic forms of gentleness and touch as they get used to the bodily care of others (Hearn

2001). It enables the re-embodiment of practices that are necessary to accompany institutional changes:

> Baby work is very tactile, from getting the milk in, to wiping the shit up, to rocking a small person to sleep. To engage with this experience is to develop capacities of male bodies other than those developed in war, sport or industrial labour. It is also to experience other pleasures. (Connell 2005: 233)

And it permits men to reconnect with capabilities that have been repressed:

> As we learn to appreciate the time we spend with young babies and infants it can be a way of accepting love and nourishment that we too easily reject from adults. In its own way it is part of the initiation into manhood, for it potentially awakens us to qualities of care and love that we might not have thought ourselves capable of. (Seidler 1997: 111)

Child care can allow men to explore emotional intimacy in relative safety, more so than with other intimate care relations. Though some men find it uncomfortable to have to 'serve' children, it can also prove easier for men to enter a relationship based on unconditional love and innocence (Coltrane 1996). To be involved in nurturing care for some men is to 'experience a relationship with their children which is usually available only to mothers... to experience a different kind of love, one which carried caring responsibilities and not, just distant affection' (Smart and Neale 1999: 105). Greg (51) described the impact of caring responsibilities on his appreciation of caring:

> I had to be a more hands on father... there was extra to be done... my wife definitely does I'd say easily ten times more work at home that I do.... But basically it did change my outlook... I wouldn't just stop and ask the kids how you are; I'd say 'well is there anything you want to say to me?'... active listening kicked in big time... it possibly has made me a better parent... I have learned that you have to treat them with respect. (Greg, 51)

Tommy (49) explained how caring enabled him to empathise with women's caring burden:

> I realised how difficult it was for women when I was left with the children... I had only two children and my mother had eleven

children and I was struggling to do the basic stuff and I realised how difficult it was for a woman to manage and how resourceful and how creative and how strong they were. And only then could I identify with their struggle and then I had a different opinion on the roles and how brave they were and how much they were getting short changed...so I began to identify with them. (Tommy, 49)

Fionn (25) noted how emotionally and physically wearisome caring could be especially with young children: 'The first four months were very difficult...you are sleep deprived...then everything aggravates you...a lot of stress...a lot of tension...[now] we're better equipped to deal with it.' Dessie (46) spoke about his appreciation for the complex and draining nature of caring:

> If I have the kids for a full day...getting your work done, organising phone calls, getting the kids to school, getting back, making sure medication is taken and whatever. The multifunctional tasks are just...you really have to schedule yourself and I find I am often with a pencil and paper at the table writing everything down and saying, 'Gosh, this is quite demanding.' (Dessie, 46)

Men also realise how undervalued caring is when they experience their caring being unappreciated. Simon (48) emphasised how 'isolating' it can be and how 'The reward is not really that apparent...you are doing all this stuff day after day and not getting any reward out of it...you are just getting worn out. And it would be nice to get some strokes...you are not going to get it from the kids because they are not going to see it that way.' Tommy (49) found an appreciation of caring in the dependencies others had on him:

> I know it has to be done, I mean it is a difficult job at the best of times but when I sit and talk about that or if I put my head down at night and I think...you have done the best you can today...If I wasn't in the equation, I don't know where my children would be, and I know their Ma would probably struggle with having them all on her own. (Tommy, 49)

These experiences help men to appreciate the privilege of being care-free. Angus (43) talked about forgetting to take time for himself: 'I have to remind myself when my mother went in [to respite care]...that I could close my bedroom door, I had to stop myself locking the side door, I have to remember that I can put music on...so I have to remind myself of freedoms when she is in.' Sharing care work is 'a real cultural revolution' because it allows men to empathise with the invisibility, lack of recognition, and the emotional burdens of gendered and subordinated world of caring (Castelain-Meunier 2002: 187). Smart and Neale (1999: 93) maintain 'when fathers were placed in the same structural position as that more commonly associated with mothers, they began to care about things like, table manners and house work and bedtimes. They objected as much as mothers to being keep up late or being taken to the pub'.

Men's care for children is especially significant in reconstructing nurturing masculinities but other care relations are also important. Many older men reshape their masculinity as a result of experiences caring for their wives even though they may struggle with it and may hold on to aspects of hegemonic masculinity (Applegate and Kaye 1993; Campbell and Carroll 2007). Dave (34) reflected on how difficult it was for his father to reimagine himself as a carer for his wife upon retirement. He said his father 'was very comfortable in the breadwinner role,...very comfortable with the kind of split between the home and work...he doesn't know where to place himself in what is home and what is work now that he has retired'. Growing old, experiencing illness, or retirement can challenge men's sense of masculinity and contribute to a feeling of emasculation (Arber and Ginn 1990; Chapman 2004:189). Older male carers can become unhappy and depressed because of the dissonance between their masculinity and the status, isolation, and disempowerment of caring work (Kramer 2005; Applegate and Lenard 1993: 155; Russell 2007). Dave (34) explained how difficult it was for his father to leave paid work and become a primary carer to his mother, noting 'it hasn't always been easy...he was the breadwinner in the house...it has been hard to see him struggling'. Despite these challenges Dave perceived his father's transition to be 'actually quite rewarding because he sees a bigger picture than when he was at work...I see him as kind of developing different sides to himself which I didn't see when I was growing up'. Dessie (46) told a similar story about witnessing his father's transition from being a breadwinner to being a carer:

> It is quite interesting to see how dad has changed now that he is in his 70s. Mum died of cancer and he was an absolute brilliant carer for her in hospital. And my twin brother...had cancer...and now he has rheumatoid arthritis and dad goes to the hospital everyday to see him. And he has three young children and my dad takes them to

birthday parties and he helps take them in to school... You adjust to change when it happens... when I think of him as my dad earlier and now to see him doing maybe what might have been frowned upon earlier. (Dessie, 46)

Having to do caring work is viewed by some men as one of the most important ways of valuing caring work as Rory (55) noted 'If we all work at care we begin to see the value of specific caring things. It's because it's a less caring society that we find that... [the] caring thing is less valued'. Becoming a full-time carer could mean having to cut yourself off from oppressive norms and relationships among men that subordinate caring:

> Their attitudes, it is the way we were brought up, it is the world we were brought up in, you know. It is they just don't fuckin' want to take responsibility, pawning it off like, 'ah it is a woman's thing, I don't want to be doing it' laziness and arrogance and can't get humble enough to say 'Listen, I should be taking responsibility for this.' Maybe they might appear weak and vulnerable to other men, I don't know, but I don't be around men like that anymore so I don't have a problem with it but I am sure there are people who are like that, you know. (Tommy, 49)

Graham (26) was 22 when he became a father. He commented how this marked a major transitional phase in his life that made him reassess what he saw was typical yet care-free and irresponsible behaviour:

> At such a young age for me it was an overwhelming sense of responsibility, it was like it was time for me to start... I had better buck up and take stock. It was an amazing feeling but scary as well. I have a huge responsibility now, I can't be going around be a Jack-the-Lad or acting the maggot or getting up to any mischief that any other 21 year olds should be doing. This is my life now and I have to be responsible now. (Graham, 26)

Initially when Tommy (49) became a father he described how being self-absorbed with other concerns rather than having a transformational effect on his caring practices:

> Well I was just completely self-obsessed, I didn't really give much... I thought, yeah it was great and all... I have arrived, I have become

a father…but I had no great real interest in it…I wasn't in that place; I wasn't in a position to be the responsible father. Part of me wanted to be but I was just so obsessed with myself and drugs and drink, you know, that was secondary, my children were secondary. (Tommy, 49)

Having a caring masculinity is a contradictory social and emotional position for men because it is caught between the public imperatives of paid work and productivity, on the one hand, and intimacy and involvement on the other. One of the main contradictions is between men who seek to maintain superordinate identities, embodied as a gendered habitus (Bourdieu 2001), while, at the same time, reflexively renegotiating expectations of emotional intimacy and shared caring within contemporary relationships (Giddens 1992). Ferguson (2002) argues that the gender order in Ireland is both reconfiguring new masculinities based on reformed hegemonic practices and producing a counter trend of increasing individualisation, fluidity, and reflexivity among men. This study highlights how, as the care gap in society is increasing, and as new norms are defining men as Sharers of caring, men have to face even more the contradiction between traditional definitions of masculinity and caring. Many men are attempting to negotiate being more involved carers without losing their sense of masculinity but this ultimately depends on them continuing to have a role in the public sphere. The ongoing tension between hegemonic definitions of masculinity and prevailing conceptions of caring mean, however, that doing primary love labour for men equates with taking on board a more feminised and subordinated masculinity. Contradictions between masculinity and caring, nonetheless, occur within the context of a gender order that privileges most men with the choice of not having to become full-time love labourers to the neglect of their public persona. Hegemonic masculinities are held together by the underlying hegemony of the capitalist–patriarchal order which defines men as especially care-free. This gender order normalises male privilege which is taken for granted, expected, and is invisible to its beholders (Bourdieu 2001; Kimmel 2000). Men are structurally positioned to defend privilege rather than embrace change and because of this they continue to be 'laggards' in the transformation of intimacy (Giddens 1992: 59–60 and 67). Men's insecurities about their position in gender relations are accentuated during periods of rapid social change, characteristic of modernity, and neo-liberal capitalism (Giddens 1991; Hayward and Mac án Ghaill 2003; Hearn 1999).

Insecurities are experienced at the level of identity as the old certainties of gender and heterosexuality are eroded (Ashe 2004; Buchbinder 1994) creating a crisis for patriarchal men in particular (Segal 1997b) that feeds reactionary politics among men (Frosh 1995).

Letting go of paid work for many men also means 'softening' or letting go of the harsher aspects of masculinity as Simon (48) noted 'Looking after my kids...it really re-focused me on what I wanted out of life rather than working for organisations...I'm not an organisation man...And I didn't like the fact that I took a lot of the work home with me in my head, it was with me 24/7.' John (47) felt if men rely less on paid work as a source of identity then it means they are positively disposed to undertake more love labour if economic circumstances permit explaining 'I was always the major breadwinner...but it wouldn't be an issue for me if [my wife] got a job in the morning that was earning more than me; I'd say off you go. I would not have a problem staying at home all day minding the kids.' Caring practices help men to experience personal change, appreciate how skillful and important caring is, and critique the care-free structures in paid work (Doucet 2006: 207). Men can care in emotionally intimate ways but these feminine-defined emotional practices are subject to negotiation, contestation, and resistance in different ways and in different places, and internally within men themselves. This is all the more reason why men's nurturing love labour is a form of heroic resistance to hegemonic masculinity (Aitken 2009). Resisting hegemonic masculinities involve a dialogue with self amid conflicting pressures to conform (Kahn, Holmes, and Brett 2011), which itself is emotional labour. The transformation men experience while doing caring challenges the gender division of labour. Along with restrictive gender stereotypes and gender identities men's caring should be supported as a gender equality intervention itself (Morrell and Jewkes 2011).

The intersection between masculinity and caring confronts men with a contradiction; to be a valuable man is to be powerful, and to be human is to be vulnerable. How can men acknowledge their masculinity when feeling vulnerable and how can men acknowledge their vulnerability when feeling masculine? Whilst we cannot do anything about our human vulnerability except to deny it, we can change the script of what it means to be a man. Caring helps to resolve these internal and external tensions and contradictions (Doucet 2006: 238). Equality in caring can create opportunities for men to deepen caring relations with others and create a healthier and caring society (Connell

1987: 4; Hearn 1987: 185, 1989). The relational gain men can experience as a result of becoming caring (Lynch, Lyons, and Cantillon 2009a) can help to compensate men for the loss of power (May 1998: 23; Kaufman 1994). When men acknowledge love and dependency it shows that they are vulnerable and needy and challenges their identities based on power, independence, and commanding (Seidler 1989: 40; Donaldson 1993). Experiencing one's vulnerability means men have to realise their limits to performing hegemonic masculinity and this can open spaces for change (Gray et al. 2002). This is all the more reason why men can benefit from support to help them meet caring expectations and cope with the loss of privileges as a result of change. For example, Tommy felt the need for

> Men...should seek some type of support in other men doing it [care]...If there is a fear around doing it just check out...men's support groups around the country...They should maybe look to that and look to life experiences of men who are caring for their children or whatever...Generally men don't fuckin' see it. They are, you know 'Get out of that, I'm not doing that.' (Tommy, 49)

The research shows that there is a hegemonic masculinity but it is a contested site. Care-free hegemonic ideals and practices operate among men and within gender relations more broadly. Different ideals and justifications for care-free practices may compete for hegemony too, but they are complicated by alternative internal and external voices, images, and a desire to develop more meaningful caring relations. Men are changing and the more they do caring the more they change. These changes are occurring even though many men resist. Whether individual men are sole breadwinners, shared carers or primary carers, hegemonic masculinity in the lives of these men is underpinned by the care-free assumption that underpins differing hegemonic ideals and practices. In order to pursue the gendered symbolic capital that secures one's legitimacy as a dominant man one must live a life that is free of the burdens of primary caring responsibilities, whether a traditional breadwinner, the transnational business man, or the rational economic worker; being care-free is assumed natural and inevitable for men. Care-free assumptions are encoded in the gender order by being institutionalised in political and economic life. Men do not expect to become primary carers, and, therefore, do not prepare for it and feel hard done by when they have to do it. Within this framework of care-free masculinities there are variations in gender ideologies and practices among men. The hegemony of care-free masculinities is true even though there are differences and diversities among men with some men being more or less care-free than others; there are those who have to do primary caring as well as a majority who do not. How care-free men are in practice can also involve an internal dialogue and a struggle for many men, although it may not for some, because the expectation to be successful and committed to the public sphere is also defined as caring. Nonetheless many men make some sort of trade off between their investment in hegemonic masculinity in the public sphere and the love labour of primary care relations but the gender order rarely calls on men to reject masculinity outright for love labour. Several factors are important when men do confront care choices including the rigidity of gender difference ideology which they hold, the extent that they define caring as unmanly, and the degree to which these definitions are institutionalised; the extent that masculinity is defined and structured through paid work means that men have much to lose by reneging on it.

Conclusion

Debates about the causes of men's uncaring practices generally lie somewhere along a spectrum of views between structural constraints related to the economy and ideological factors related to psychological and socio-cultural issues (Bjornberg 2002; Chesler and Parry 2001; Reay et al. 1998). Some observers are most sympathetic to a basic materialism underpinned by men's dominance and exploitation of women (Gerstel and Gallagher 2001; McMahon 1999; Delphy and Leonard 1992). However many analyses suppose a complexity of dynamic interfacing factors. Holter et al. (2009: 157), for example, argue that several factors are complexly correlated with more gender-equal care practices, including age, childhood gender socialisation, education, and gender ideology, but overall they find resource equality and material issues matter more than attitudes. Kremer (2007), on the other hand, acknowledges the material incentives and disincentives which welfare states impose are important in shaping preferences, but cultural ideals of care are crucial factors. There again others have emphasised significance of status differences in the organisation of work as crucial. When thinking about men's resistance to caring, for example, Delphy and Leonard (1992: 136) argue that caring activities per se are less significant than the relations of care production. The key issue, they claim, is that caring is subordinated work most often done by women who have a subordinated status in society compared with men. The tasks of caring are less important to appreciating men's practices than are the relations of production within which caring takes place:

> What we have within the family is not a division of tasks, but a division of jobs – by age, gender and relationship. 'Jobs' comprise typical tasks plus their conditions of performance and remuneration and status ... This is why debates about whether or not say, cooking is 'really interesting' or 'really important' can remain endlessly unresolved ... Men virtually never do cooking in the same conditions as women, that is, routinely, for household consumption, as economically dependent housewives ... It is not household tasks but the job which is not valued; and this is because it is work done in a subordinate position by people who have the general status of subordinates in society. (Delphy and Leonard 1992: 136)

Some commentators are a little circumspect about the value of old modernist dualisms for accounting for emerging masculinities and femininities and they argue for a greater dialogue between materialist and post-structuralist accounts (Mac án Ghaill and Hayward 2007). There again, others propose a complex interaction between material and symbolic practices, cultural beliefs, and structural constraints (Coltrane and Galt 2000). The care study provides reasonable evidence for the role of material issues in altering men's practices and attitudes to caring, but these practices are moulded by gender ideologies and discourse about masculinities and femininities within a relational dynamic which in turn is embodied through practice. We should not, therefore, overlook material explanations in term of understanding men's pursuit of power and status in public, as well as the importance of resources in shaping practices and ideologies, but we must also appreciate the symbolic and emotional interrelation between feeling respected and recognised as a man and feeling cared about and valued. In this respect I am inclined to agree with Finch and Mason (1993: 172) among many others who argue that moral and material elements of caring obligations are 'finely interwoven'. Therefore, I suggest that relational identities are significant in so far as they help us to appreciate the personal domain. While fleeting in some respects, identity positions can also be deeply held and embedded within particular sets of social relations especially within family and workplace structures of which care relations transverse both. Moreover the field of masculinities studies has broadened our appreciation of the material and social construction of men's bodies. Whether understood as bodily reflective practices, the embodiment of cultural inheritances, or the somatisation of social structure, the reconstruction or transformation of masculinities calls for an engagement by men in caring and for the nurturing of caring masculinities.

11
Towards Affective Equality

This study has considered the care-free dynamic of Irish masculinities, but within a wider global context wherein men are expected to have fewer caring obligations than women. Chapter 4 explained how care-free and care-less masculinities result from men's practices constructed to avoid feeling inferior in the face of the hegemonic imperatives men encounter. Chapter 5 emphasised men's recognition, esteem, and dependence on nurturing femininities as a valuable caring social good as well as their anxiety arising from their fear that they might not be able to access it. Chapter 6 demonstrated men's ongoing ambivalence about their involvement in caring against a background of breadwinner expectations and the pressures of paid work. Chapter 7 highlighted how the men negotiated the meanings of masculinities against the dominance of care defined as feminine nurturing. Chapter 8 exposed how the men narrated their childhood care stories in accounting for the caring practices in their lives and how these recollections are used to both reform masculinity as well as defend care-free practices. Chapter 9 defined how men defend their caring practices by drawing on four care-free gender discourses. Chapter 10 outlined the men's perspectives about how influential caring practices were in transforming masculinities and creating more caring men. In this final chapter I offer some brief concluding thoughts and reflections on the study and on the prospects for affective equality.

Care and the good society

The focus of this book on care occurs against the backdrop of the failed neo-liberal project in post-Celtic Tiger Ireland (Ging, Cronin, and Kirby 2009; Coulter and Coleman 2003). The ideologies of productivity, competitiveness, and consumerism that privileged a narrowly defined concept of economic growth above equality in the conditions in people's lives marginalised caring social goals. The relentless pursuit of economic growth and the attendant income inequalities neo-liberalism has brought about has created more dysfunctional societies with much higher rates of a variety of social problems. These include teen pregnancies, violence, imprisonment, poor mental and physical health making life for the majority shorter, unhealthier, and more unpleasant (Wilkinson and Pickett 2010). The growth-at-all-costs logic suggests that the resources that support public welfare, health, and care are dependent on exceptional and ever increasing economic growth patterns. It assumes that the resources that are required to produce the collective well-being will automatically trickle down to the poor or to anyone who has not insured their welfare on the private market. Accordingly, any intervention or direction by the state to regulate inequality is seen to erode wealth creation by dampening an individualistic entrepreneurial culture (Kirby 2002).

The idea that public wealth is about public choices is lost in a climate that favours neo-liberal, privatised, and individualised market solutions (O'Sullivan 2007). The crisis of global capitalism and the self-interest, independence, greed, and individualism underpinning it stand in conflict with other humanistic secular and spiritual–religious values of care and altruism that derive from our dependence on, and commitment to, others (Lynch 2007). Neo-liberalism frowns on welfare dependency and caring altruism because it values competitiveness and greed, and rewards self-interest and supposed individualism (Kiely 2004). Within neo-liberalism poverty and other social ills are easily rationalised on the basis that the poor are idle, lazy and, therefore, undeserving. Not only have these neo-liberal values failed but they also overlook the ironic fact that any putative entrepreneurial self is dependent on the care institutions of society for their existence. Human beings are not only economic, political, cultural, and moral but also affective and relational and not merely rational-economic actors; people draw on a care rationality when making decisions (Finch and Mason 1993).

It would be nice to think that the current crisis of global capitalism, and the European debt crisis more specifically for Ireland, has produced a reassessment of narrow economistic business models. If anything, within Ireland, it would seem to have enhanced them. A more competitive, aggressive, 'slender' 'Ireland inc.' is being called for in response to the crisis and the caring institutions of society are being asked to downsize to pay off public and private debt through (care) austerity.

Neo-liberal masculinities have not been undermined by the crisis; arguably they have been enhanced. Care was not prioritised during the boom years and is certainly not being prioritised during the bust. For example, one of the earliest acts of the new political administration following the economic collapse was to postpone the development of a National Carers Strategy (Minister for Social Protection [Deputy Joan Burton] 2011). There are, however, alternative voices even from within the political establishment. Although one can be cynical about anti-materialist discourses arising during times of austerity, there are voices challenging the narrow economic model that has prevailed (see Higgins 2012), and there is now a political interest within the EU in increasing men's involvement in gender equality (Brodolini and Fagan 2010).

Placing care and equality as central–social and economic objectives offers a radically different view of society. Baker, Lynch, Cantillon, and Walsh (2004: 34) proclaim the good society is one which values equality of condition in economic, political, cultural, and affective relations. Equality of condition in economic life, they propose, means 'having a range of resource-dependent options that is of roughly the same value as those of others'; in political relations it 'means the roughly equal enabling of each person to influence the decisions that affect their lives'; in cultural life it means having 'the freedom to live one's life without the burden of contempt and enmity from the dominant culture'; and in affective relations it 'means promoting circumstances in which everyone has ample scope for forming valuable human attachments'. Affective equality necessitates the fair and equal distribution of both the burdens and benefits of caring obligations as well as creating a society where people have fulfilling ways of experiencing care.

Men and caring citizenship

Gender and caring inequalities will not be altered substantially without men's greater involvement in unpaid care work in families, especially since men's very economic independence and greater earning power are based on their avoidance of care (Daly and Rake 2003: 137). Men must be held equally accountable and responsible for the moral work of care for the 'crisis of caretaking' to be resolved (Gerson 1993: 284).

Affective equality includes women and girls having men equally share in the burdens of caring work; it also includes the right of boys and men to have access to more emotionally fulfilling relationships. Men need to be understood as needing care too! While men are feeling a greater degree of responsibility to provide care, there is also a greater expectation that men should have the opportunity to care, along with the benefits that it offers (Daly and Rake 2003: 178).

Equality in caring, however, is more than simply choosing on the basis of preferences which are themselves the product of unequal social positions embedded within material and symbolic hierarchies. Equality in caring requires having meaningful choices based on a much greater range of care options (Daly and Standing 2001: 5; Lewis, Campbell, and Huerta 2008), based on social and economic policies that are geared to realise care as 'balanced reciprocity' (Standing 2001: 30). Pursuing gender justice in affective relations involves a 'complex equality' that depends on abolishing compulsory heterosexuality and the stigma arising from sexual difference and creating a non-hierarchal and reciprocal heterosexuality (Connell 2005: 230).

A major obstacle for gender equality is how to address the institutionalised hegemony of men (Hearn 2004) and the ascendancy of care-free masculinities. The care-free assumption for men means that men do not pursue a politics of care that seeks ways for people to manage, balance, and share caring obligations. What would our society look like if men were expected to undertake caring equally? What creative institutional and legal solutions would be embedded in the social fabric if men (as wielders of political power) had self-interest in creating them? Political and economic changes are needed to ensure men and women can share caring and participate in public life equally (Lewis 2006b; Pascall and Lewis 2004; Rush 2006; Fanning and Rush 2006).

The liberal state, by defining care as a private concern, ignores the needs of carers and reinforces the dominance of men. Citizens need to be defined as relationally dependent and interdependent rather than necessarily autonomous and capable of realising social, civil, political, and economic rights (Lanoix 2007; Lynch and Lyons 2008). Care dependents and informal unpaid caregivers are denied full access to citizenship because the citizen is primarily defined as an economically productive and participative worker (Walby 1997: 4; Lanoix 2007; Rantalaiho and Heiskanen 1997). Public policy is then designed to meet the needs of citizens as producers and consumers rather than as carers effectively encoding patriarchal values in the structure of employment (Lynch, Lyons, and Cantillon 2009b). Affective equality demands we reject the zero-load worker and the care-less model of the citizen (Lynch and Lyons 2009a), and the focus on gender equality in the labour market can overlook the importance of care as a social good. Nonetheless, care-friendly workplaces and social policies need not be perceived as a net cost on economic life. Apart from the fact that care is integral to economic life more broadly, gender equality policies and practices in the workplace including ones which accommodate caring obligations are linked to greater participation, satisfaction in work and productivity, not least by allowing for the greater utilisation of women's talent (The Gender Equality Project 2012; Monks 2007). But care must accrue citizenship rights equal to employment rights (Standing 2001: 28). Inclusive citizenship should be defined in terms of the participation of men and women in both employment and in care, and care should be resourced by right, to give and to receive (Kremer 2007: 44).

Care and affective change

Affective relations are primarily responsible for generating inequalities of love, care, and solidarity (Baker et al. 2004), but they can also be a focus of change (Knudson-Martin and Mahoney 2009). Most informal carers lack power in economic, political. and cultural terms but carers can be involved in reflexive processes of change through negotiation and responsiveness that involve skill and agency, and this makes care relations a site of change and not merely responsive or reflective of external changes. Smart and Neale (1999: 20) note how this makes women into 'sociological agents', but this study also shows how masculinity is transformed through caring. Deconstructing dominant masculinities raises personal and political challenges for men because it requires a fundamental 'reconstitution of patriarchal relations and dominant forms of men's subjectivity' (Hearn and Pringle 2006a: 368). Doing care work helps to achieve this even though men will resist change both ideologically and emotionally. Deconstructing dominant masculinities, however, also involves emotional and bodily reflective changes which are deeply personal. Men must be afforded opportunities to alter their practices and not just have their attitudes criticised, and key to this is to consider the wider condition of resource allocation between men and women (Holter, Egeland, and Svare 2009). Additionally ideological changes in how men are represented as carers in the cultural sphere are important in legitimating new models of masculinity for men to emulate (Henwood and Procter 2003), even though they can contain cultural stereotypes and patriarchal subtexts (McMahon 1999: 105). The care and economic rationalities that men and women are socialised into are not socially inevitable (Lynch, Baker et al. 2009). Many men are constructing more caring masculinity and realising the importance of affective relations in their lives. Moreover, though gender equality improves women's quality of life more than men's, men also benefit in a variety of ways (Holter, Egeland, and Svare 2009). Masculinities studies need to examine more closely the benefits of equality in men's lives and the ways in which diverse caring masculinities can be nurtured.

Conclusion

Two major changes have occurred in my life during the time it has taken to write this book. First, I became a father to two children and despite my long interest in care a steep learning curve ensued. Secondly, a global crisis in capitalism began as the financial banking sector collapsed (prevented mainly by the socialisation of private debt), with Ireland being particularly badly impacted. Writing this book has always been a personal journey as well as a political one. Becoming a parent has helped men realise the intensity, commitment, and cooperation that equal caring demands, while the latter has alerted me to the wider resource constraints and social stressors which many people care under. A caring society is one which appreciates the social construction of care and understands that private care experiences are also public issues. It is also a society which legitimates caring masculinities as valued identities for men and recognises that care and masculinity need not be mutually exclusive. It is a society that socialises care as a common concern.

References

Abel, Emily K., and Margaret K. Nelson. 1990. *Circles of Care: Work and Identity in Women's Lives*. New York: SUNY Press.

Agadjanian, Victor. 2002. Men Doing 'Women's Work': Masculinity and Gender Relations Among Street Vendors in Maputo, Mozambique. *The Journal of Men's Studies* 10 (3):329–342.

Aitken, Stuart C. 2009. *The Awkward Spaces of Fathering*. Farnham: Ashgate Publishing.

Aldous, J. 1998. The Changing Concept of Fatherhood. In *The Family: Contemporary Perspectives and Challenges*, edited by K. Matthijs. Belgium: Leuven University Press.

Allatt, Patrica. 1993. Becoming Privileged, the Role of Family Processes. In *Youth and Inequality*, edited by I. Bates and G. Riseborough. Buckingham: Open University Press.

Allen, Davina. 2001. The Implications of Healthcare Reforms for the Profession of Nursing. *Nursing Inquiry* 8 (2):64–74.

Alvesson, Mats, and Kaj Skoldberg. 2000. *Reflexive Methodology: New Vistas in Qualitative Research*. London: Sage.

Applegate, Jeffrey, and Lenard Kaye. 1993. Male Elder Caregivers. In *Doing 'Women's Work': Men in Nontraditional Occupations*, edited by C. L. Williams. London: Sage.

Arber, Sara, and Nigel Gilbert. 1989. Men the Forgotten Carers. *Sociology* 23 (1):111–118.

Arber, Sara, and Jay Ginn. 1990. The Meaning of Informal Care: Gender and the Contribution of Older People. *Aging and Society* 12 (4):429–454.

Arendell, Terry 1997. Reflections on the Researcher – Researched Relationship: A Woman Interviewing Men. *Qualitative Sociology* 20 (3):341–368.

Arksey, Hilary, and Peter Knight. 1999. *Interviewing for Social Scientists*. London: Sage.

Ashe, Fidelma. 2004. Deconstructing the Experiential Bar: Male Experience and Feminist Resistance. *Men and Masculinities* 7 (2):187–204.

———. 2007. *The New Politics of Masculinity: Men, Power and Resistance*. London: Routledge.

Bacik, Ivana. 2004. *Kicking and Screaming: Dragging Ireland into the 21st Century*. Dublin: O'Brien Press.

Bacik, Ivana, and Eileen Drew. 2003. *Gender Injustice: Feminising the Legal Professions?* Dublin: Trinity College Dublin Law School.

———. 2006. Struggling with Juggling: Gender and Work/Life Balance in the Legal Professions. *Women's Studies International Forum* 29 (2): 136–146.

Badgett, M.V. Lee, and Nancy Folbre. 1999. Assigning Care: Gender Norms and Economic Outcomes. *International Labour Review* 138 (3): 311–326.

Bagilhole, Barbara, and Simon Cross. 2006. 'It Never Struck Me as Female': Investigating Men's Entry into Female-dominated Occupations. *Journal of Gender Studies* 15 (1): 35–48.

Baker, John. 1987. *Arguing for Equality*. London: Verso.
———. 1999. Equality. In *Social Policy in Ireland: Principles Practices and Problems*, edited by S. Healy and B. Renolds. Dublin: Oak Tree Press.
Baker, John, Kathleen Lynch, Sara Cantillon, and Judy Walsh. 2004. *Equality from Theory to Action*. Hampshire: Palgrave Macmillan.
Balbus, Isaac D. 1998. *Emotional Rescue: The Theory and Practice of a Feminist Father*. New York: Routledge.
Banyard, Kat. 2010. *The Equality Illusion: The Truth about Women and Men Today*. London: Faber and Faber.
Barker, Richard. W. 1994. *Lone Fathers and Masculinities*. Aldershot, UK: Avebury.
Barrett, Michele, and Mary McIntosh. 1982. *The Anti-Social Family*. London: Verso.
Barry, Ursula, ed. 2008. *Where Are We Now? New Feminist Perspectives on Women in Contemporary Ireland*. Dublin: TASC.
Bartkowski, John P., and Xiaohe Xu. 2000. Distant Patriarchs or Expressive Dads? The Discourse and Practice of Fathering in Conservative Protestant Families. *Sociological Quarterly* 41 (3):465–485.
Bartolomei, Maria Rita. 2010. Migrant Male Domestic Workers in Comparative Perspective: Four Case Studies from Italy, India, Ivory Coast, and Congo. *Men and Masculinities* 13 (1):87–110.
Baxter, Janeen, Belinda Hewitt, and Michele Haynes. 2008. Life Course Transitions and Housework: Marriage, Parenthood, and Time on Housework. *Journal of Marriage and Family* 70 (2):259–272.
Beasley, Christine. 2005. *Gender and Sexuality: Critical Theories, Critical Thinkers*. London: Sage.
———. 2008a. Reply to Messerschmidt and to Houson. *Men and Masculinities* 11 (1):114–115.
———. 2008b. Rethinking Hegemonic Masculinity in a Globalised World. *Men and Masculinities* 11 (1):86–103.
Beck, Ulrich. 1992. *Risk Society: Towards a New Modernity*. London: Sage.
Beck, Ulrich, Anthony Giddens, and S. Lasch. 1994. *Reflexive Modernisation*. Cambridge: Polity Press.
Bem, Sandra, L. 1993. *The Lenses of Gender: Transforming the Debate on Sexual Inequality*. London: Yale University Press.
Bennett, Kate M. 2007. 'No Sissy Stuff': Towards a Theory of Masculinity and Emotional Expression in Older Widowed Men. *Journal of Aging Studies* 21 (4):347–356.
Berry, Patrica, ed. 1987. *Fathers and Mothers*. Dallas: Spring Publications.
Bettio, Francesca, and Janneke Platenga. 2004. Comparing Gender Regimes in Europe. *Feminist Economics* 10 (1):85–113.
Bjornberg, Ulla. 2002. Ideology and Choice between Work and Care: Swedish Family Policy for Working Parents. *Critical Social Policy* 22 (1):33–52.
Bly, Robert 1990. *Iron John: A Book about Men*. Reading, MA.: Addison-Wesley.
Blye, Frank. 1996. Masculinities and Schooling: The Making of Men. In *Systemic Violence*, edited by R. Juanita and Watkinson, Ailsa. London: Flamer Press.
Bond, John. 1992. The Politics of Caregiving: The Professionalisation of Informal Care. *Ageing & Society* 12 (1):5–21.
Bondi, Liz. 2008. On the Relational Dynamics of Caring: a Psychotherapeutic Approach to Emotional and Power Dimensions of Women's Care Work. *Gender, Place & Culture* 15 (3):249–265.

Borchgrevink, Tordis, and Oystein G. Holter, eds. 1995. *Labour of Love: Beyond the Self-evidence of Everyday Life*. Aldershot: Avebury.

Bourdieu, Pierre. 1986. The Forms of Capital. In *Handbook for Theory and Research for the Sociology of Education*, edited by J. G. Richardson. New York: Greenwood Press .

———. 1990. *The Logic of Practice*. California: Stanford Univeresity Press.

———. 2001. *Masculine Domination*. Cambridge: Polity Press.

———, ed. 1997. The Forms of Capital. In *Education: Culture, Economy and Society*, edited by A. H. Halsley. Oxford: Oxford University Press.

Bowden, Peta. 2000. An 'Ethic of Care' in Clinical Settings: Encompassing 'Feminine' and 'Feminist' Perspectives. *Nursing Philosophy* 1 (1):36–49.

Bowers, Susan. P. 1999. Gener Role Identity and Caregiving of Widowed Men. *Sex Roles* 41:645–655.

Bowlby, John. 1969. *Attachment*. New York: Basic Books.

Bowlby, S., L. McKie, and S. Gregory. 2009. *Care and Interdependency across the Lifecourse*. Abingdon, Oxon: Taylor and Francis.

Bradley, Harriet. 1997. *Fractured Identities: Changing Patterns of Inequality*. Cambridge: Polity Press.

Brandth, Berit. 1995. Rural Masculinity in Transition: Gender Images in Tractor Advertisements. *Journal of Rural Studies* 11 (2):123–133.

Brandth, Berit, and Elin Kvande. 1998. Masculinity and Child Care: The Reconstruction of Fathering. *Sociological Review* 46 (2):293–313.

Brannon, Robert. 1976. The Male Sex Role: Our Culture's Blueprint of Manhood and What It's Done for Us Lately. In *The Forty-Nine Percent Majority: The Male Sex Role*, edited by D. David and R. Brannon. Reading, MA: Addision Wesley.

Braun, Virginia, and Victoria Clarke. 2006. Using Thematic Analysis in Psychology. *Qualitative Research in Psychology* 3:77–101.

Brid, Sharon S. 1996. Welcome to the Men's Club: Homosociality and the Maintenance of Hegemonic Masculinity. *Gender and Society* 10 (2):120–132.

Brittan, Arthur. 1989. *Masculinity and Power*. Oxford: Basil Blackwell.

Britzman, Deborah P., Stephen Frosh, and Wendy Luttrell. 2009. Affective Equality: Love, Care and Injustice. *British Journal of Sociology of Education* 30 (6):773–787.

Brod, Harry. 1987. The New Men's Studies: From Feminist Theory to Gender Scholarship. *Hypatia* 2 (1):179–196.

———. 1990. Pornography and the Alienation of Male Sexuality. In *Men, Masculinities and Social Theory*, edited by J. Hearn and D. Morgan. London: Unwin Hyman.

Brodolini, Fondazione G., and Colette Fagan. 2010. *Men and Gender Equality: Tackling Gender Segregated Family Roles and Social Care Jobs*. Brussels: European Commission, Employment, Social Affairs and Equal Opportunities.

Broom, Alex, and John Cavenagh. 2010. Masculinity, Moralities and being Cared for: An Exploration of Experiences of Living and Dying in a Hospice. *Social Science & Medicine* 71 (5):869–876.

Broom, Alex, and Philip Tovey. 2009. *Men's Health: Body, Identity and Social Context*. Chichester: Wiley-Blackwell.

Brown, Leslie, Marilyn Callahan, Susan Strega, Christopher Walmsley, and Lena Dominelli. 2009. Manufacturing Ghost Fathers: The Paradox of Father Presence and Absence in Child Welfare. *Child & Family Social Work* 14 (1):25–34.

Bubeck, Diemut. 1995. *Care, Justice and Gender*. Oxford: Oxford University Press.

Buchbinder, David. 1994. *Masculinities and Identities*. Melbourne: Melbourne University Press.

Burawoy, Michael. 2010. Eight Conversations with Pierre Bourdieu: An Outline Discussion paper http://www.swopinstitute.org.za/node/187. University of Witwatersrand.

Butler, Judith. 1990. *Gender Trouble: Feminism and the Subversion of Identity*. New York: Routledge.

Calasanti, Toni, and Neal King. 2007. Taking 'Women's Work' 'Like a Man': Husbands' Experiences of Care Work. *Gerontologist* 47 (4):516–527.

Cameron, Claire. 2001. Promise or Problem? A Review of the Literature on Men Working in Early Childhood Services. *Gender, Work & Organization* 8 (4):430–453.

Campbell, Elaine 2003. Interviewing Men in Uniform: A Feminist Approach? *Social Research Methodology* 6 (4):285–304.

Campbell, Lori, D., and Michael P. Carroll. 2007. The Incomplete Revolution: Theorising Gender When Studying Men Who Provide Care to Ageing Parents. *Men and Masculinities* 9:491–507.

Canaan, Joyce E., and Christine Griffin. 1990. The New Men's Studies: Part of the Problem Or Part of the Solution? In *Men, Masculinities and Social Theory*, edited by J. Hearn and D. Morgan. London: Unwin Hyman.

Carlson, Melanie. 2008. I'd Rather Go Along and Be Considered A Man: Masculinity and Bystander Intervention. *The Journal of Men's Studies* 16 (1): 3–17.

Carmichael, Fiona, and Susan, Charles. 2003. The Opportunity Costs of Informal Care: Does Gender Matter? *Journal of Health Economics* 22 (5):781–803.

Carney, Tanya. 2009. The Employment Disadvantage of Mothers: Evidence for Systemic Discrimination. *Journal of Industrial Relations* 51 (1):113–130.

Carrigan, Tim, Bob Connell, and John Lee. 1985. Toward a New Sociology of Masculinity. *Theory and Society* 14 (5): 551–604.

——. 1987. The 'Sex-Role' Framework and the Sociology of Masculinity. In *Gender Under Scrutiny: New Enquiries in Education*, edited by G. Weiner and M. Arnot. London: Open University.

Carter, Keith, and Sara Delamont, eds. 1996. *Qualitative Research: The Emotional Dimension*. Aldershot, UK: Ashgate Publishing.

Castelain-Meunier, Christine. 2002. The Place of Fatherhood and the Parental Role: Tensions, Ambivalence and Contradictions. *Current Sociology* 50 (2):185–201.

Cemlyn, Sarah, Margaret Greenfields, Sally Burnett, Zoe Matthews, and Chris Whitwell. 2009. Inequalities Experienced by Gypsy and Traveller Communities: A Review. In *Equality and Human Rights Commission Research Report Series*. Manchester: Equality and Human Rights Commission. Chambers, Clare. 2005. Masculine Domination, Radical Feminism and Change. *Feminist Theory* 6 (3):325–346.

Chapman, Tony. 2004. *Gender and Domestic Life: Changing Practices in Families and Households*. Basingstoke: Palgrave Macmillan.

Cheal, David. 2002. *Sociology of Family Life*. Basingstoke: Palgrave Macmillan.

Cheng, Cliff. 2008. Marginalized Masculinities and Hegemonic Masculinity: An Introduction. *The Journal of Men's Studies* 7 (3):295–315.

Chesler, Mark, and Carla Parry. 2001. Gender Roles and/or Styles in Crisis: An Integrative Analysis of the Experiences of Fathers of Children with Cancer. *Qualitative Health Research* 11 (3):363–384.

Chodorow, Nancy. 1978. *The Reproduction of Mothering: Psychoanalysis and the Sociology of Gender*. Berkley: University of California Press.

——. 1994a. *Femininities, Masculinities, Sexualities: Freud and Beyond*. Lexington: The University Press of Kentucky.

——. 1994b. Gender Relations and Difference in Psychoanalytic Perspective. In *The Polity Reader in Gender Studies*, edited by Polity. Cambridge: Polity Press.

Choi, Heejeong, and Nadine Marks, F. 2006. Transition to Caregiving, Marital Disagreement, and Psychological Well-Being. *Journal of Family Issues* 27 (12):1701–1722.

Christie, Alastair. 2006. Negotiating the Uncomfortable Intersections between Gender and Professional Identities in Social Work. *Critical Social Policy* 26 (2):390–411.

Clare, Anthony. 2000. *On Men: Masculinity in Crisis*. UK: Chatto and Windus.

Clarke, Juanne N. 2005. Fathers' Home Health Care Work When a Child Has Cancer; I'm Her Dad; I Have to Do It. *Men and Masculinities* 7 (1):385–404.

Clatterbaugh, Kenneth. 1997. *Contemporary Perspectives on Masculinity: Men, Women and Politics in Modern Society*. 2nd edn. Boulder, Colarado: Westview Press.

Cleary, Anne. 2005. Death Rather Than Disclosure: Struggling to Be a Real Man. *Irish Journal of Sociology* 14 (2):155–176.

Cleary, Anne. 2012. Suicidal Action, Emotional Expression, and the Performance of Masculinities. *Social Science & Medicine* 74(4), 498–505.

Cleary, Anne, and Teresa Brannick. 2007. Suicide and Changing Values and Beliefs in Ireland. *Crisis* 28 (2):82–88.

Cleary, Anne, Maria Corbett, Miriam Calvin, and Joy Wall. 2004. *Young Men on the Margins*. Dublin: Katherine Howard Foundation.

Clifford, Derek. 1994. Critical Life Histories: Key Anti-Oppressive Research Methods and Processes. In *Rethinking Social Research*, edited by B. Humphries and C. Truman. Aldershot, UK: Avebury.

Cockburn, Cynthia. 1990. Men's Power in Organisations, 'Equal Opportunities' Intervenes. In *Men, Masculinities and Social Theory*, edited by J. Hearn and D. Morgan. London: Unwin Hyman.

Coffey, Amanda, and Paul Atkinson. 1996. *Making Sense of Qualitative Ressearch: Complementary Research Strategies*. London: Sage.

Coles, Tony. 2008. Finding Space in the Field of Masculinity: Lived Experiences of Men's Masculinities. *Journal of Sociology* 44 (3):233–248.

——. 2009. Negotiating the Field of Masculinity: The Production and Reproduction of Multiple Dominant Masculinities. *Men and Masculinities* 12 (1):30–44.

Coltrane, Scott. 1994. Theorising Masculinities in Contemporary Social Science. In *Theorising Masculinities*, edited by H. Brod and M. Kaufman. London: Sage.

——. 1996. *Family Man: Fatherhood, Housework, and Gender Equity*. Oxford: Oxford University Press.

Coltrane, Scott, and Justin Galt. 2000. The History of Men's Caregiving. In *Care Work; Gender, Class and the Welfare State*, edited by M. H. Meyer. London: Routledge.

Connell, R.W. 1987. *Gender and Power: Society, the Person and Sexual Politics*. Cambridge: Polity Press.

——. 1993. The Big Picture: Masculinities in Recent World History. *Theory and Society* 22 (5):597–623.

——. 1995. *Masculinities*. Cambridge: Polity Press.

——. 1998. Masculinities and Globalization. *Men and Masculinities* 1 (1):3–23.

——. 2000. *The Men and the Boys*. Cambridge: Polity Press.

———. 2001 The Social Organisation of Masculinity. In *The Masculinities Reader*, edited by S. M. Whitehead and F. J. Barrett. Cambridge: Polity Press.

———. 2002. *Gender*. UK: Polity Press.

———. 2003a. Masculinities, Change, and Conflict in Global Society: Thinking about the Future of Men's Studies. *The Journal of Men's Studies* 11 (3):249–266.

———. 2003b. The Role of Men and Boys in Achieving Gender Equality. United Nations.

———. 2005. *Masculinities*. 2nd edn. Cambridge: Polity Press.

———. 2007. *Southern Theory: The Global Dynamics of Knowledge in the Social Sciences*. Sydney: Allen and Unwin.

———. 2011. *Confronting Equality*: John Wiley & Sons.

Connell, R.W., and J. W. Messerschmidt. 2005. Hegemonic Masculinity: Rethinking the Concept. *Gender & Society* 19 (6):829–859.

Corcoran, Mary P. 2005. Portrait of the 'Absent' Father: the Impact of Non-Residency on Developing and Maintaining a Fathering Role. *Irish Journal of Sociology* 14 (2):134–154.

Costa, Ricardo L. 2006. The Logic of Practices in Pierre Bourdieu. *Current Sociology* 54 (6):873–895.

Coulter, Carol. 2007. Family Law Reporting Pilot Project: Report to the Board of the Courts Service. Dublin: Courts Service.

Coulter, Colin, and Steve Coleman. 2003. *The End of Irish History? Critical Reflections on the Celtic Tiger*. Manchester: Manchester University Press.

Courtenay, Will, H. 2000. Constructions of Masculinity and Their Influence on Men's Well-Being: a Theory of Gender and Health. *Social Science and Medicine* (50):1385–1401.

Craib, Ian. 1987. Masculinity and Male Dominance. *Sociological Review* 35 (4):721–743.

———. 1992. *Modern Social Theory: From Parsons to Habermas*. 2nd edn. Edinburgh: Pearson Education Ltd.

———. 1998. *Experiencing Identity*. London: Sage.

Craig, Lyn. 2006. Does Father Care Mean Fathers Share? A Comparison of How Mothers and Fathers in Intact Families Spend Time with Children. *Gender & Society* 20 (2):259–281.

Creighton, Colin. 1999. The Rise and Decline of the 'Male Breadwinner Model' in Britain. *Cambridge Journal of Economics* 23:519–541.

Crompton, Rosemary, and Clare Lyonette. 2005. The New Gender Essentialism – Domestic and Family 'Choices' and Their Relation to Attitudes. *British Journal of Sociology* 56 (4):601–620.

Cross, Simon, and Barbara Bagilhole. 2002. Girls' Jobs for the Boys? Men, Masculinity and Non-Traditional Occupations. *Gender, Work and Organisation* 9 (2):204–226.

Crowley, Niall. 2006. *An Ambition for Equality, Justice in Controversy*. Dublin: Irish Academic Press.

CSO. 2010. Women and Men in Ireland. Dublin: Central Statistics Office.

Cullen, Kevin, Sarah Delaney, and Petrina Duff. 2004. Caring, Working and Public Life. In *Equality Research Series* edited by The Equality Authority. Dublin: The Equality Authority.

Curry, Timothy J. 1991. Fraternal Bonding in the Locker Room: A Profeminist Analysis of Talk About Competition and Women. *Sociology of Sport Journal* 8:119–135.

Curtis, Sarah, Wil Gesler, Glenn Smith, and Sarah Washburn. 2000. Approaches to Sampling and Case Selection in Qualitative Research: Examples in the Geography of Health. *Social Science and Medicine* 50:1001–1014.

Daly, Mary. 2001a. *Carework: the Quest for Security*. Geneva: International Labour Office.

———. 2001b. Care Policies in Western Europe. In *Carework: The Quest for Security*, edited by M. Daly. Geneva: International Labour Office.

Daly, Mary, and Sara Clavero. 2002. *Contemporary Family Policy: a Comparative Review of Ireland, France, Germany, Sweden and the uk*. Dublin: Institute of Public Administration.

Daly, Mary, and Katherine Rake. 2003. *Gender and the Welfare State: Care, Work and Welfare in Europe and the USA*. Cambridge: Polity Press.

Daly, Mary, and Guy Standing. 2001. Introduction. In *Carework: The Quest for Security*, edited by M. Daly. Geneva: International Labour Office.

Davis, K., M. Leijenaar, and J. Oldersma. 1991. *The Gender of Power*. London: Sage.

Davis, Kathy. 2008. Intersectionality as Buzzword. *Feminist Theory* 9 (1):67–85.

De Beauvoir, Simone 1949. *The Second Sex*. UK: Penguin.

Dean, Hartley. 2004. *The Ethics of Welfare: Human Rights, Dependency, and Responsibility*. Bristol: Policy Press.

Deave, Toity, and Debbie Johnson. 2008. The Transition to Parenthood: What Does It Mean for Fathers? *Journal of Advanced Nursing* 63 (6):626–633.

———. 1996. Familiarity, Masculinity and Qualitative Research. In *Qualitative Research: The Emotional Dimension*, edited by K. Carter and S. Delamont. Aldershot, UK: Ashgate Publishing.

Delamont, Sara. 2001. *Changing Women, Unchanging Men? Sociological Perspectives on Gender in a Post-Industrial Society*. Buckingham: Open University Press.

Delphy, Christine, and Diana Leonard. 1992. *Familiar Exploitation: A New Analysis of Marriage in Contemporary Societies*. Cambridge: Polity Press.

———. 1994. The Variety of Work Done by Wives. In *The Polity Reader in Gender Studies*, edited by Polity. Cambridge: Polity Press.

Denscombe, Martyn. 2002. *Ground Rules for Good Research*. Maidenhead, Berkshire: Open University Press.

Denzin, Norman K., and Yvonna S. Lincoln, eds. 1994. *Handbook of Qualitative Research*. California: Sage.

Deutsch, Francine. 1999. *Halving It All: How Equally Shared Parenting Works*. Cambridge, MA: Harvard University Press.

Devine, Paula, Ford Hickson, Helen McNamee, and Mick Quinlan. 2006. Real Lives: Findings from the All-Irelalnd Gay Men's Sex Survey, 2003 and 2004. Dublin: Rainbow Project and Gay Men's Health Project.

DHC. 2008. National Men's Health Policy 2008–2013: Working with Men in Ireland to Achieve Optimum Health and Wellbeing. Dublin Department of Health and Children.

Dill, Karen, and Kathryn Thill. 2007. Video Game Characters and the Socialization of Gender Roles: Young People's Perceptions Mirror Sexist Media Depictions. *Sex Roles* 57 (11):851–864.

Dinnerstein, Dorothy. 1977. *The Mermaid and the Minotaur: Sexual Arrangements and Human Malaise*. New York: Harper Colophon Books.

Directorate-General for Health and Consumers. 2011. The State of Men's Health in Europe. Brussels: European Commission.

Dobash, Russell P., and R. Emerson Dobash. 2004. Women's Violence to Men in Intimate Relationships. *British Journal of Criminology* 44 (3):324–349.

Dominelli, Lena, and Tim Gollins. 1997. Men, power and caring relationships. *The Sociological Review* 45 (3):396–415.

Donaldson, Mike. 1993. What Is Hegemonic Masculinity? *Theory and Society* 22 (5):643–657.

——. 1997. Researching Ruling Class Men: Biography, Autobiography, Life History. *Journal of Interdisciplinary Gender Studies* 2 (1):93–104.

Donaldson, Mike, and Scott Poynting. 2007. *Ruling Class Men: Money, Sex, Power.* Bern: Peter Lang AG.

Doucet, Andrea. 2006. *Do Men Mother? Fatherhood, Care, and Domestic Responsibility.* Toronto: University of Toronto Press.

——. 2007. 'It's Almost Like I Have a Job, but I Don't Get Paid': Fathers at Home Reconfiguring Work, Care, and Masculinity. *Fathering: A Journal of Theory, Research, and Practice about Men as Fathers* 2 (3):277–303.

Doyle, James, A. 1995. *The Male Experience.* 3rd edn. Wisconsin: Brown and Benchmark.

Dragiewicz, Molly. 2011. *Equality with a Vengeance: Men's Rights Groups, Battered Women, and Antifeminist Backlash, Northeastern Series on Gender, Crime, and Law.* Boston: Northeastern University Press.

Drakich, Janice, and Carl E. Bertoia. 1998. The Fathers Rights Movement: Contradictions in Rhetoric and Practice. In *Men's Lives*, edited by M. S. Kimmel and M. A. Messner. USA: Allyn and Bacon.

Drew, Eileen, and Anne L. Humbert. 2010. Gender, Entrepreneurship and Motivational Factors in An Irish Context. *International Journal of Gender and Entrepreneurship* 2 (2):173–196.

——. 2010. Who's Minding the Kids? Work and Family Issues Among Owners of Small Business Enterprises in Ireland. In *Human Resource Management in Small Businesses: Achieving Peak Performance*, edited by C. L. Cooper and R. J. Burke. Cheltenham: Edward Elgar.

——. 'in press'. Men Have Careers, Women Have Babies: Unequal Parental Care among Irish Entrepreneurs. *Community, Work and Family* 15 (1):49–67.

Drew, Eileen., Ruth Wmerck, and Evelyn Mahon. 1998. *Women, Work and the Family in Europe.* London: Routledge.

Duindam, Vincent. 1999. Men in the Household: Caring Fathers. In *Gender, Power and the Household*, edited by L. Mckie, S. Bowlby and S. Gregory. London: Palgrave Macmillan.

Duncan, Simon, and Rosalind Edwards. 1997. Lone Mothers and Paid Work – Rational Economic Man or Gendered Moral Rationalities? *Feminist Economics* 3 (2):29–61.

Duncombe, Jean, and Dennis Marsden. 1993. Love and Intimacy: The Gender Division of Emotion and 'Emotional Work'. *Sociology* 27 (2): 221–41.

——. 1998. 'Stepford Wives' and 'Hollow Men'? Doing Emotion Work, Doing Gender and 'Authenticity' in Intimate Heterosexual Relationships. In *Emotions in Social Life: Critical Themes and Contemporary Issues*, edited by G. Bendelow and S. J. Williams London: Routledge.

Edley, Nigel, and Margaret Wetherell. 1996. Masculinity, Power and Identity. In *Understanding Masculinities*, edited by M. Mac án Ghaill. Buckingham: Open University Press.

———. 1997. Jockeying for Positions: the Construction of Masculine Identities. *Discourse and Society* 8 (2): 203–217.

———. 1999. Imagined Futures: Young Men's Talk about Fatherhood and Domestic Life. *British Journal of Social Psychology* 38: 181–194.

Edwards, Derek, and Jonathon Potter. 1992. *Discursive Psychology.* London: Sage.

Edwards, Rosalind, Andrea Doucet, and Frank F. Furstenberg. 2009. Fathering across Diversity and Adversity: International Perspectives and Policy Interventions. *The ANNALS of the American Academy of Political and Social Science* 624 (1):6–11.

Egan, Gerard. 2009. *The Skilled Helper: A Problem Management and Opportunity Development Approach to Helping.* 9th edn. Belmont, CA: Brooks Cole.

Ehrenreich, Barbara. 1983. *The Hearts of Men: American Dreams and the Flight from Commitment.* London: Pluto Press.

Ehrenreich, Barbara, and Arlie R. Hochschild, eds. 2003. *Global Women: Nannies, Maids and Sex Workers in the New Economy.* London: Granta.

Eichler, Margrit, and Patrizia Albanese. 2007. What Is Household Work? A Critique of Assumptions Underlying Empirical Studies of Housework and an Alternative Approach. *The Canadian Journal of Sociology* 32 (2):227–258.

Elliott, Anthony. 2000. Psychoanalysis and Social Theory. In *The Blackwell Companion to Social Theory,* edited by S. B. Turner. UK: Blackwell.

Elmore, Marcus. 2007. Masculinities and Men's Studies: The Literature of a Growing Discipline. *Choice* February:931–939.

England, Paula, Michelle Budig, and Nancy Folbre. 2002. Wages of Virtue: The Relative Pay of Care Work. *Social Problems* 49 (4):455–473.

Engster, Daniel. 2005. Rethinking Care Theory: The Practice of Caring and the Obligation to Care. *Hypatia* 20 (3):50–74.

Erikson, Erik. 1965. *Childhood and Society.* UK: Penguin.

Evandrou, Maria, and Karen Glaser. 2003. Combining Work and Family Life: the Pension Penalty of Caring. *Ageing and Society* (23):583–601.

Evans, Joan. 1997. Men in Nursing: Issues of Gender Segregation and Hidden Advantage. *Journal of Advanced Nursing* 26 (2):226–231.

Evans, Joan, and Blye Frank. 2003. Contradictions and Tensions: Exploring Relations of Masculinities in the Numerically Female-Dominated Nursing Profession. *The Journal of Men's Studies* 11 (3):277–292.

Evans, Mary. 1990. The Problem of Gender For Women's Studies. *Women's Studies International Forum* 13 (5):457–462.

Fahey, Tony. 2003. Marriage Bar. In *The Encyclopaedia of Ireland,* edited by B. Lalor. Dublin: Gill & Macmillan.

Fahey, Tony, Bernadette C. Hayes, and Richard Sinnott. 2005. *Conflict and Consensus: a Study of Values and Attitudes in the Republic of Ireland and Northern Ireland.* Dublin: Institute of Public Administration.

Fanning, Bryan, and Michael Rush, eds. 2006. *Care and Social Change in the Irish Welfare Economy.* Dublin: University College Dublin Press.

Fast, Irene 1993. Aspects of Early Gender Development: A Psychodynamic Perspective. In *The Psychology of Gender,* edited by A. Beall, E. and R. J. Sternberg. London: Guilford Press.

Fawcett, Barbara, and Jeff Hearn. 2004. Researching Others: Epistemology, Experience, Standpoints and Participation. *International Journal of Social Science Methodology* 7 (3):201–218.

Featherstone, Brid. 2009. *Contemporary Fathering: Theory, Policy and Practice*: London: Policy Press.

Featherstone, Brid, Mark Rivett, and Jonathon Scourfield. 2007. *Working with Men in Health and Social Care*. London: Sage.

Fenton, Lindsay T., and Robert Pitter. 2010. Keeping the Body in Play: Pain, Injury, and Socialization in Male Rugby. *Research Quarterly for Exercise and Sport* 81 (2):212–223.

Ferber, Marianne A., and Julie A. Nelson. 2003. *Feminist Economics Today: beyond Economic Man*. Chicago: University of Chicago Press.

Ferguson, Harry. 1995. The Paedophile Priest: A Deconstruction. *Studies: An Irish Quarterly Review* 84 (335):247–256.

———. 1998. Working with Men and Masculinities. *Feedback: Journal of the Family Therapy Association of Ireland* 8 (1).

———. 2002. Men and Masculinities in Late Modern Ireland. In *A Man's World: Changing Men's Practices in a Globalised World*, edited by B. Pease and K. Pringle. London: Zed Books.

Ferguson, Harry, and Fergus Hogan. 2004. *Strengthening Families through Fathers: Developing Policy and Practice in Relation to Vulnerable Fathers and Their Families*. Waterford: Centre for Social and Family Research.

———. 2007. *Men, Sexuality and Crisis Pregnancy: a Study of Men's Experiences*. Dublin: Crisis Pregnancy Agency.

Ferguson, Harry, Kieran McKeown, and Dermot Rooney. 2000. *Changing Fathers: Fatherhood and Family Life in Modern Ireland*. Cork: Collins Press.

Finch, Janet. 1984. It's Great to Have Someone to Talk to: the Ethics and Politics of Interviewing Women. In *Social Researching, Politics, Problems and Practice*, edited by C. Bell and H. Roberts. London: Routledge and Kegan Paul.

———. 1989. *Family Obligations and Social Change*. Cambridge: Polity Press.

Finch, Janet, and Dulcie Groves, eds. 1983. *A Labour of Love: Women, Work and Caring*. London: Routledge and Kegan Paul.

Finch, Janet, and Jennifer Mason. 1993. *Negotiating Family Responsibilities*. London: Routledge.

Fine, Michael. 2006a. *A Caring Society? Care and the Dilemmas of Human Services in the 21st Century*. Houndmills: Palgrave Macmillan.

Fine, Michael, and Caroline Glendinning. 2005. Dependence, Independence or Inter-Dependence? Revisiting the Concepts of 'Care' and 'Dependency'. *Ageing & Society* 25 (04):601–621.

Fine, Michelle. 2006. Bearing Witness: Methods for Researching Oppression and Resistance – A Textbook for Critical Research *Social Justice Research* 19 (1):83–107.

Fineman, Martha. 2004. *The Autonomy Myth: A Theory of Dependency*. NewYork: New Press.

———. 2008. The Vulnerable Subject: Anchoring Equality in the Human Condition. *Yale Journal of Law and Feminism* 20 (1).

Finn, Mark, and Karen Henwood. 2009. Exploring Masculinities within Men's Identificatory Imaginings of First-Time Fatherhood. *British Journal of Social Psychology* 48 (3):547–562.

Fisher, B., and J. Tronto. 1990. Toward a Feminist Theory of Caring. In *Circles of Care*, edited by E. Abel and M. Nelson. Albany: State University of New York.

Flood, Michael. 1997. Doing Research on Men and as Men: Politics and Problems. In Masculinities: Renegotiating Genders (Conference Paper). University of Wollongong.

Folbre, Nancy. 1994. *Who Pays for the Kids? Gender and the Structures of Constraint.* London: Routledge.

———. 2001. *The Invisible Heart: Economics and Family Values.* New York: New Press.

———. 2006. Measuring Care: Gender, Empowerment, and the Care Economy. *Journal of Human Development* 7 (2):183–199.

Folbre, Nancy, and Julie A. Nelson. 2000. For Love or Money – Or Both? *The Journal of Economic Perspectives* 14 (4):123–140.

Folbre, Nancy, and Michael Bittman. 2004. *Family Time: The Social Organization of Care.* London: Routledge.

Fontana, Andrea, and James Frey, H. 1994. Intrreviewing: The Art of Science. In *Handbook of Qualitative Research*, edited by N. K. Denzin and Y. S. Lincoln. California: Sage.

Foundation for Male Studies. 2010. *Men's Studies: A New Academic Discipline.* Available at http://www.malestudies.org/.

Fox, Barry. 1997. Reproducing Differences: Changes in the Lives of Partners Becoming Parents. In *Feminism and Families: Critical Policies and Changing Practices*, edited by M. Luxton. Halifix, NS: Fernwood.

Fraser, Cait, and Deborah J. Warr. 2009. Challenging Roles: Insights into Issues for Men Caring for Family Members with Mental Illness. *American Journal of Men's Health* 3 (1):36–49.

Fraser, Nancy. 1995. From Redistribution to Recognition? Dilemmas of Justice in a 'Post-Socialist' Age. *New Left Review* (212): 68–93.

Freshman, Brenda, and Louis Rubino. 2002. Emotional Intelligence: A Core Competency for Health Care Administrators. *The Health Care Manager* 20 (4):1–9.

Frosh, Stephen. 1994. *Sexual Difference: Masculinity and Psychoanalysis.* London: Routledge.

———. 1995. Unpacking Masculinity: From Rationality to Fragmentation. In *Gender Power and Relationships*, edited by C. Burck and B. Speed. London: Routledge.

Gallagher, Alanna. 2008. Wanna Be in My Gang. *The Irish Times*, 4th December, 18.

Galligan, Yvonne. 1998. The Changing Role of Women. In *Ireland and the Politics of Change*, edited by W. Crotty and D. E. Schmitt. London: Longman Publishing Group.

Gatrell, Caroline. 2005. *Hard Labour: The Sociology of Parenthood.* Maidenhead: Open University Press.

Gerson, Kathleen. 1993. *No Man's Land: Men's Changing Committment to Family and Work.* New York: Basic Books.

———. 2003. A Few Good Men: Overcoming the Barriers to Involved Fatherhood. In *Family: Critical Concepts in Sociology*, edited by D. Cheal. New York: Routledge.

———. 2010. *The Unfinished Revolution: How a New Generation is Reshaping Family, Work and Gender in America.* New York: Oxford University Press.

Gerstel, Naomi, and Sally Gallagher, K. 2001. Men's Caregiving: Gender and the Contingent Character of Care. *Gender and Society* 15 (2):197–217.

Giddens, Anthony. 1991. *Modernity and Self-Identity: Self and Society in the Late Modern Age*. Cambridge: Polity Press.

———. 1992. *The Transformation of Intimacy: Sexuality, Love and Eroticism in Modern Societies* Cambridge: Polity Press.

———. 1994. Men, Women and Romantic Love. In *The Polity Reader in Gender Studies*, edited by Polity. Cambridge: Polity Press.

Gilbert, Rob, and Pam Gilbert. 1998. *Masculinity Goes to School*. London: Routledge.

Gilligan, Carol. 1995. Hearing the Difference: Theorizing Connection. *Hypatia* 10 (2):120–127.

———. 1982. *In a Different Voice: Psychological Theory and Women's Development*. Cambridge: Harvard University Press.

Ging, Debbie. 2009. New Gender Formations in Post-Celtic-Tiger Ireland. In *Transforming Ireland: Challenges, Critiques, Resources*, edited by D. Ging, M. Cronin and P. Kirby. Manchester: Manchester University Press.

Ging, Debbie, Michael Cronin, and Peader Kirby. 2009. *Transforming Ireland: Challenges, Critiques, Resources*. Manchester: Manchester University Press.

Gleeson, Jim, Patricia Conboy, and Aileen Walsh. 2003. *The Piloting of 'Exploring Masculinities' (1997–1998): Context, Implementation and Issues Arising*. Limerick: Gender Equality Unit.

Goldberg, Herb 1976 *The Hazards of Being Male: Surviving the Myth of Masculine Privilege*. New York: Nash.

Goleman, Daniel. 1996. *Emotional Intelligence*. London: Bloomsbury.

Goodwin, John. . 2002. Irish Men and Work in North County Dublin. *Journal of Gender Studies* 11 (2):151–166.

Gosine, Andil. 2007. Marginalisation Myths and the Complexity of Men: Engaging Critical Conversations about Irish and Caribbean Masculinities. *Men and Masculinities* 9 (3):337–357.

Gough, Brendan 1998. Men and the Discursive Reproduction of Sexism: Repertoires of Difference and Equality. *Feminism and Psychology* 8 (1):25–49.

Gough, Brendan, and Mark Conner. 2006. Barriers to Healthy Eating amongst Men: a Qualitative Analysis. *Social Science and Medicine* 62 (2):387–395.

Government of Ireland. 1937. *Bunreacht Na hÉireann (Constitution of Ireland)*. Dublin: Government Publications Office.

———. 2004. *Equal Status Acts 2000 and 2004*. Available at http://www.irishstatutebook.ie/ZZA8Y2000.html.

———. 2007. *National Women's Strategy 2007–2016*, edited by E. a. L. R. Department of Justice: The Stationery Office.

———. 2010. *Civil Partnership and Certain Rights and Obligations of Cohabitants Act*. Dublin: Government Publications Office.

Graham, Hilary. 1983. Caring: A Labour of Love. In *A Labour of Love: Women, Work and Caring*, edited by J. Finch and D. Groves. London: Routledge and Kegan Paul.

Gray, John. 1993. *Men Are from Mars, Women Are from Venus: A Practical Guide for Improving Communication and Getting What You Want in Your Relationships*. London: Thorsons.

Gray, Ross, Margaret Fitch, Karen Fergus, Eirc Mykhalovskiy, and Kathryn Church. 2002. Hegemonic Masculinity and the Experience of Prostrate Cancer: A Narrative Approach. *Journal of Aging and Identity* 7 (1):43–61.

Gregory, Abigail, and Susan Milner. 2009. Editorial: Work-Life Balance: A Matter of Choice? *Gender, Work and Organisation* 16 (1):1–13.

———. 2011. What Is '"New' about Fatherhood? The Social Construction of Fatherhood in France and the UK. *Men and Masculinities* 14 (5):588–606.

Grint, Keith. 2005. *The Sociology of Work*. Cambridge: Polity Press.

Grummell, Bernie, Dympna Devine, and Kathleen Lynch. 2009. Appointing Senior Managers in Education: Homosociality, Local Logics and Authenticity in the Selection Process. *Education Management Administration & Leadership* 37:329–349.

Guerrier, Yvonne, and Amel Adib. 2003. Work at Leisure and Leisure at Work: A Study of the Emotional Labour of Tour Reps. *Human Relations* 56 (11):1399–1417.

Hale, Susan, Sarah Grogan, and Sara Willott. 2010. Male Gps' Views on Men Seeking Medical Help: a Qualitative Study. *British Journal of Health Psychology* 15 (4):697–713.

Hall, Stuart. 2005. Who Needs Identity? In *Identity: A Reader*, edited by P. Du Gay, J. Evans and P. Redman. London: Sage.

Hanlon, Niall, and Kathleen Lynch. 2011. Care-free Masculinities in Ireland. In *Men and Masculinities around the World: Transforming Men's Practices*, edited by E. Ruspini, J. Hearn, B. Pease and K. Pringle. New York: Palgrave Macmillan.

Hanmer, Jalna 1990. Men, Power and the Exploitation of Women. In *Men, Masculinities and Social Theory*, edited by J. Hearn and D. Morgan. London: Unwin Hyman.

Hantover, Jeffrey P. 1998. The Boy Scouts and the Validation of Masculinity. In *Men's Lives*, edited by M. S. Kimmel and M. A. Messner. USA: Allyn and Bacon.

Harding, Sandra 1991. *Whose Science? Whose Knowledge?* Milton Keynes: Open University Press.

———. 1998. Can Men Be Subjects of Feminist Thought. In *Men Doing Feminism*, edited by T. Digby. London: Routledge.

———, ed. 1989. *Feminism and Methodology*. Bloomington: Indiana University Press.

———, ed. 2004. *The Feminist Standpoint Revisited: Intellectual and Political Controversies*. London: Routledge.

Harkim, C. 1991. Grateful Slaves and Self-Made Women: Fact and Fantasy in Women's Work Orientations. *European Journal of Sociology* 7 (2):101–121.

———. 1995. Five Feminist Myths about Women's Employment. *British Journal of Sociology* 46 (3):429–55.

Hartmann, Heidi. 1979. The Unhappy Marriage of Marxism and Feminism: Towards a More Progressive Union. *Capital & Class* 3 (2):1–33.

Hartstock, Nancy. 1998. *The Feminist Standpoint Revisited and Other Essays*. Boulder: Westview.

Harvey, David. 2005. *A Brief History of Neoliberalism*. Oxford: Oxford University Press.

Hausmann, Ricardo, Laura D. Tyson, and Saadia Zahidi. 2011. The Global Gender Gap Report 2011. Geneva: World Economic Forum.

Hayes, Nóirin, and Siobhan Bradley. 2006. The Childcare Question. In *Care and Social Change in the Irish Welfare Economy*, edited by B. Fanning and M. Rush. Dublin University College Dublin Press.

Hayward, Chris, and Máirtin Mac án Ghaill. 2003. *Men and Masculinities*. Buckingham: Open University Press.

Hearn, Jeff 1987. *The Gender of Oppression: Men, Masculinity and the Critique of Marxism*. Brighton: Wheatsheaf.

———. 1989. *Sociological Issues in Studying Men and Masculinities*. Manchester: University of Manchester.

———. 1999. A Crisis in Masculinity, or New Agendas for Men? In *New Agendas for Women*, edited by S. Walby. London: Palgrave Macmillan.

———. 2001. Men and Gender Equality: Resistance, Responsibilities and Reaching Out Orebro. Department of Applied Social Science, University of Manchester, UK and The Swedish School of Economics and Business Administration Helsinki, Finland.

———. 2004. From Hegemonic Masculinity to the Hegemony of Men. *Feminist Theory* 5 (1):49–72.

———. 2005. Autobiography, Nation, Postcolonialism and Gender Relations: Reflecting on Men in England, Finland and Ireland. *Irish Journal of Sociology* 14 (2):66–93.

Hearn, Jeff, and Keith Pringle. 2006a. Men, Masculinities and Children: Some European Perspectives. *Critical Social Policy* 26 (2):365–389.

———. 2006b. Violences. In *European Perspective on Men and Masculinities: National and Transnational Approaches*, edited by J. Hearn and K. Pringle. Hampshire, UK: Palgrave Macmillan.

———. 2009. *European Perspectives on Men and Masculinities: National and Transnational Approaches*. Houndsmills: Palgrave Macmillan.

Heath, Stephen. 1987. Male Feminism. In *Men in Feminism*, edited by A. Jardine and P. Smith. London: Routledge.

Held, Virginia, ed. 1995. *Justice and Care: Essential Readings in Feminist Ethics*. Boulder, CO: Westview Press.

Henwood, Karen, and Joanne Procter. 2003. The 'Good Father': Reading Men's Accounts of Paternal Involvement during the Transition to First-Time Fatherhood. *British Journal of Social Psychology* 42:337–355.

Hermans, Herbert, and Agnieszka Hermans-Konopka. 2010. *Dialogical Self Theory: Positioning and Counter-Positioning in a Globalizing Society*. Cambridge: Cambridge University Press.

Heymann, Jody 2007. *Forgotton Families: Ending the Growing Crisis Confronting Children and Working Parents in the Global Economy* Oxford: Oxford University Press.

Higgins, Michael D. 2012. *Renewing the Republic*. Portland: Dufour Editions.

Hillard, Betty. 2007. Family. In *Contemporary Ireland: A Sociological Map*, edited by S. O'Sullivan. Dublin: University of Dublin Press.

Hilliard, Betty, and Máire Nic Ghiolla Phádraig, eds. 2007. *Changing Ireland in International Comparision*. Dubliln: The Liffey Press.

Hirsch, Carl. 1996. Understanding the Influence of Gender Role Identity on the Assumption of Family Caregiving Roles by Men. *International Journal of Aging and Human Development* 42 (2):103–121.

Hobson, Barbara 2000. *Gender and Citizenship in Transition*. London: Palgrave Macmillan

Hochschild, Arlie. 1983. *The Managed Heart: Commercialization of Human Feeling*. London and Berkeley: University of California Press.

——. 1989. *The Second Shift: Working Parents and the Revolution at Home*. Middlesex: Penguin.

——. 1998. Sociology of Emotion as a Way of Seeing. In *Emotions in Social Life: Critical Themes and Contemporary Issues*, edited by G. Bendelow and S. J. Williams. London: Routledge.

Hochschild, Arlie, Will Hutton, and Anthony Giddens. 2000. Global Care Chains and Emotional Surplus Value. In *On the Edge Living with Global Capitalism*, edited by W. Hutton and A. Giddens. London: Jonathan Cape.

Hodges, Melissa J., and Michelle J. Budig. 2010. Who Gets the Daddy Bonus? *Gender & Society* 24 (6):717–745.

Holloway, Wendy, and Tony Jefferson. 2000. *Doing Qualitative Research Differently: Free Association, Narrative and the Interview Method*. London: Sage.

Holter, Oystein G. 1995. Family Theory Reconsidered. In *Labour of Love: beyond the Self-Evidence of Everyday Life*, edited by T. Borchgrevink and O. G. Holter. Aldershot, UK: Avebury.

Holter, Oystein G. 2007. Men's Work and Family Reconciliation in Europe. *Men and Masculinities* (9):425–456.

Holter, Oystein G., Catherine Egeland, and Helge Svare. 2009. *Gender Equality and Quality of Life: A Norwegian Perspective*. Oslo: Nordic Gender Institute.

Hook, Jennifer L. 2006. Care in Context: Men's Unpaid Work in 20 Countries, 1965–2003. *American Sociological Review* 71 (4):639–660.

hooks, bell. 2004. *The Will to Change: Men, Masculinity and Love*. New York: Washington Square Press.

Hopkins, Patrick D. 1998. How Feminism Made a Man Out of Me: The Proper Subject of Feminism and the Problem of Men. In *Men Doing Feminism*, edited by T. Digby London: Routledge.

Horney, Karen. 1932. The Dread of Woman: Obserations in the Specific Difference in the Dread Felt by Men and by Women Respectively for the Opposite Sex. *International Journal of Psycho-analysis* (13):348–60.

Howson, Richard. 2008. Hegemonic Masculinity Masculinity in the Theory of Hegemony *Men and Masculinities* 11 (1):109–113.

Hoyt, Michael A. 2009. Gender Role Conflict and Emotional Approach Coping in Men with Cancer. *Psychology & Health* 24 (8):981–996.

Hyde, Abbey, Jonathon Drennan, Etaoine Howlett, and Dympna Brady. 2008. Safer Heterosex: Perspectives from Young Men in Ireland. *Sexual Health* 5:25–30.

Hyde, Abbey, Etaoine Howlett, Jonathon Drennan, and Dympna Brady. 2005. Masculinities and Young Men's Sex Education Needs in Ireland: Problematising Client-Centred Health Promotion Approaches. *Health Promotion International* 20 (4):334–341.

Inglis, Tom. 1998a. From Sexual Oppression to Liberation. In *Encounters with Modern Ireland*, edited by M. Peillon and E. Slater. Dublin: Institute of Public Administration.

——. 1998b. *Moral Monopoly: The Rise and Fall of the Catholic Church in Modern Ireland.* 2nd edn. Dublin: University College Dublin Press.

——. 2006. Club Anabel. In *Uncertain Ireland: A Sociological Chronicle 2003–2004*, edited by M. Corcoran and M. Peillon. Dublin: Institute of Public Administration.

——. 2007. Individualisation and Secularisation in Catholic Ireland. In *Contemporary Ireland: A Sociological Map*, edited by S. O'Sullivan. Dublin: University of Dublin Press.

Irwin, Katherine, and Meda Chesney-Lind. 2008. Girls' Violence: Beyond Dangerous Masculinity. *Sociology Compass* 2 (3):837–855.

Isaacs, Dallas, and Marilyn Poole. 1996. Being a Man and Becoming a Nurse: Three Men's Stories. *Journal of Gender Studies* 5 (1):39–47.

Jackson, David 1990. *Unmasking Masculinity: A Critical Autobiography.* London: Unwin Hyman.

Jackson, Stevi. 1992. Towards a Historical Sociology of Housework: a Materialist Feminist Analysis. *Women's Studies International Forum* 15 (2):153–172.

——. 1993. Even Sociologists Fall in Love: An Exploration in the Sociology of Emotions. *Sociology* 27 (2):201–220.

Jackson, Stevi, and Amanda Rees. 2007. The Appalling Appeal of Nature: The Popular Influence of Evolutionary Psychology as a Problem for Sociology. *Sociology* 41 (5):917–930.

Jacobs, Jerry A., and Kathleen Gerson. 2004. *The Time Divide: Work, Family and Gender Inequality.* Cambridge MA: Cambridge University Press.

Jakupcak, Matthew, Matthew T. Tull, and Lizabeth Roemer. 2005. Masculinity, Shame, and Fear of Emotions as Predictors of Men's Expressions of Anger and Hostility. *Psychology of Men & Masculinity* 6 (4):275–284.

James, Nicky. 1989. Emotional Labour: Skills and Work in the Social Regulation of Feeling. *The Sociological Review* 37:15–42.

——. 1992. Care = Organisation + Physical Labour + Emotional Labour. *Sociology of Health and Illness* 14 (4):488–509.

Jamieson, Lynne. 2002. Intimacy Transformed? In *Gender: A Sociological Reader*, edited by S. Jackson and S. Scott. London and New York: Routledge.

Jenkins, Richard. 2004. *Social Identity.* 2nd edn. London: Routledge.

Johansson, Thomas. 2003. Fatherhood and Masculinity: Non-Resident Fathers' Construction of Identity. In *Among Men: Moulding Masculinities*, Volume 1, edited by S. Ervó and T. Johansson. Aldershot, UK: Ashgate Publishing.

Johnson, Martin. 2002. An Exploration of Men's Experience and Role at Childbirth. *The Journal of Men's Studies* 10 (2):165–182.

Johnson, Robert, A. 1986. *He: Understanding Masculine Psychology.* New York: Harper and Row.

Johnston, Cathal A. B., and Todd G. Morrison. 2007. The Presentation of Masculinity in Everyday Life: Contextual Variations in the Masculine Behaviour of Young Irish Men. *Sex Roles* 57:661–674.

Jones, Mark 1996. Men and Feminist Research. In *Gender and Qualitative Research*, edited by J. Pilcher and A. Coffey. Aldershot, UK: Avebury.

Jump, L. Theresa, and Linda Haas. 1987. Fathers in Transition: Dual Career Fathers Participating in Child-Care. In *Changing Men, New Directions in Research on Men and Masculinity*, edited by M. Kimmel. California: Sage.

Kahn, Jack. 2008. *An Introduction to Masculinities*. Waltham, MA: Blackwell Wiley.

——. 2010. Feminist Therapy for Men: Challenging Assumptions and Moving Forward. *Women & Therapy* 34 (1–2):59–76.

Kahn, Jack, Benjamin Brett, and Jessica Holmes. 2011. Concerns with Men's Academic Motivation in Higher Education: An Exploratory Investigation of the Role of Masculinity. *The Journal of Men's Studies* 19 (1):65–82.

Kahn, Jack, Jessica Holmes, and Benjamin Brett. 2011. Dialogical Masculinities: Diverse Youth Resisting Dominant Masculinity. *Journal of Constructivist Psychology* 24 (1):30–55.

Kaufman, Michael, ed. 1994. Men, Feminism, and Men's Contradictory Experience of Power. In *Theorising Masculinities*, edited by H. Brod and M. Kaufman. London: Sage.

Kee, John, and Kaye Ronayne. 2002. Partnership Rights of Same Sex Couples. Dublin: The Equality Authority.

Keenan, Marie. 2011. Researching the Lives of Irish Roman Catholic Clergy Who Have Sexually Abused Minors: Collaborative Inquiry. *Qualitative Social Work* 10 (2):2–17.

Kelly, Megan M., Audrey R. Tyrka, Lawrence H. Price, and Linda L. Carpenter. 2008. Sex Differences in the Use of Coping Strategies: Predictors of Anxiety and Depressive Symptoms. *Depression and Anxiety* 25 (10):839–846.

Kennedy, Finola. 2001. *Cottage to Crèche: Family Change in Ireland*. Dublin: Institute of Public Administration.

Kershaw, Paul. 2005. *Carefair: Rethinking the Responsibilities and Rights of Citizenship*. Vancouver: UBC Press.

——. 2006. Carefair: Choice, Duty, and the Distribution of Care. *Social Politics: International Studies in Gender, State & Society* 13 (3):341–371.

Kiely, Gabriel. 1998. Caregiving within Families. In *The Family: Contemporary Perspectives and Challenges*, edited by K. Matthijs. Belgium: Leuven University Press.

——. 2004. Individualisation. In *Theorising Irish Social Policy*, edited by B. Fanning, P. Kennedy, G. Kiely and S. Quin. Dublin: UCD Press.

Kiernan, Kathleen. 2004. Unmarried Cohabitation and Parenthood in Britain and Europe. *Law & Policy* 26 (1):33–55.

Kilkey, Majella. 2010. Men and Domestic Labor: A Missing Link in the Global Care Chain. *Men and Masculinities* 13 (1):126–149.

Kimmel, Michael. 1987. Rethinking Masculinity: New Directions in Research. In *Changing Men, New Directions in Research on Men and Masculinity*, edited by M. Kimmel. California: Sage.

——. 1990. After Fifteen Years: The Impact of Sociology of Masculinity on the Masculinity of Sociology. In *Men, Masculinity and Social Theory*, edited by J. Hearn and D. Morgan. London: Unwin Hyman.

——. 1993. Invisible Masculinity. *Society* (September/October).

——, ed. 1995. The Politics of Manhood: Profeminist Men Respond to the Mythopoetic Men's Movement (and the Mythopoetic Leaders Answer). Philadelphia: Temple University Press.

——. 1998. Who's Afraid of Men Doing Feminism. In *Men Doing Feminism*, edited by T. Digby. London: Routledge.

——. 2000. *The Gendered Society*. New York: Oxford University Press.

——. 2001. Male Victims of Domestic Violence: A Substantive and Methodological *Research Review*. Dublin: Department of Education and Science.

——. 2003. Masculinity as Homophobia. In *Privilege: A Reader*, edited by M. Kimmel, S. and A. Ferber, L. Boulder: Westview.

——. 2005. The Gender of Desire: Essays on Male Sexuality. New York: SUNY Press.

Kimmel, Michael, and Tom Mosmiller. 1992. *Against the Tide: Pro-Feminist Men in America, 1776–1990*. Boston: Beacon Press.

Kirby, Peader 2002. *The Celtic Tiger in Distress: Growth with Inequality in Ireland* New York: Palgrave Macmillan.

Kittay, Eva Feder. 1999. *Love's Labour*. New York: Routledge.

Kittay, Eva Feder, and Ellen K. Feder, eds. 2002. *The Subject of Care: Feminist Perspectives on Dependency*. New York: Rowman and Littlefield.

Klein, Melanie. 1928. Early Stages of the Oedipus Conflict. *International Journal of Psychoanalysis* 9:167–180.

Knights, David, and Maria Tullberg. 2011. Managing Masculinity/Mismanaging the Corporation. *Organization*. Published online before print. http://org. sagepub.com/content/early/2011/06/01/1350508411408170.abstract

Knudson-Martin, Carmen, and Anne Rankin Mahoney, eds. 2009. *Couples, Gender and Power: Creating Change in Intimate Relationships*. New York: Springer.

Korczynski, Marek. 2003. Communities of Coping: Collective Emotional Labour in Service Work. *Organization* 10 (1):55–79.

Korobov, Neill. 2009. Expanding Hegemonic Masculinity: The Use of Irony in Young Men's Stories about Romantic Experiences. *American Journal of Men's Health* 3 (4):286–299.

——. 2011. Young Men's Vulnerability in Relation to Women's Resistance to Emphasized Femininity. *Men and Masculinities* 14 (1):51–75.

Kraemer, Sebastian 1995. What Are Fathers For? In *Gender Power and Relationships*, edited by C. Burck and B. Speed. London: Routledge.

Kramer, Betty, J. 2005. Men Caregivers: An Overview. In *Men as Caregivers*, edited by B. Kramer, J. and E. Thompson, H. New York: Prometheus Books.

Kramer, Betty, J., and Edward Thompson, H., eds. 2005. *Men as Caregivers*. New York: Prometheus Books.

Kremer, Monique. 2007. *How Welfare States Care: Culture, Gender and Parenting in Europe*. Amsterdam: Amsterdam University Press.

Kullberg, Christian. 2003. Men's Lack of Family Orientation: Some Reflections on Scandinavian Research on Famililes. In *Among Men: Moulding Masculinities*, Volume 1, edited by S. Ervó and T. Johansson. Aldershot, UK: Ashgate Publishing.

Lanoix, Monique. 2007. Feminist Interventions in Democratic Theory: The Citizen in Question. *Hypatia* 22 (4):113–129.

Larrabee, Mary Jeanne, ed. 1993. *An Ethic of Care: Feminist and Interdisciplinary Perspectives*. New York and London: Routledge.

Leane, Maire, and Elizabeth Kiely. 1997. Single Lone Motherhood – Reality versus Rhetoric. In *Women and Irish Society*, edited by A. Byrne and M. Leonard. Dublin: Beyond Pale Publications.

Lee, Deborah 1997. Interviewing Men: Vulnerabilities and Dilemmas. *Women's Studies International Forum* 20 (4):553–564.

Leonard, Madeleine. 2004. Teenage Girls and Housework in Irish Society. *Irish Journal of Sociology* 13 (1):73–80.

Levin, Peter. 15th October 1996. *Standpoint and Masculinities: Standpoints, Situated Knowledge, and Masculinities.* Department of Sociology, University of Southern California 1996. Available at http://www-scf.usc.edu/~plevin/submit.html.

Lewis, Jane. 1992. Gender and the Development of Welfare Regimes. *Journal of European Social Policy* 2 (3):159–73.

——. 2001a. The Decline of the Male Breadwinner Model: Implications for Work and Care. *Social Politics* 8:152–169.

——. 2001b. Legitimising Care Work and the Issue of Gender Equality. In *Carework: The Quest for Security,* edited by M. Daly. Geneva: International Labour Office.

——. 2006a. Employment and Care: The Policy Problem, Gender Equality and the Issue of Choice. *Journal of Comparative Policy Analysis* 8 (2):103–114.

——. 2006b. Men, Women, Work, Care Policies. *Journal of European Social Policy* 16 (4):387–392.

Lewis, Jane, Mary Campbell, and Carmen Huerta. 2008. Patterns of Paid and Unpaid Work in Western Europe: Gender, Commodification, Preferences and the Implications for Policy. *Journal of European Social Policy* 18 (1):21–37.

Lewis, Jane, Trudie Knijn, Claude Martin, and Ilona Ostner. 2008. Patterns of Development in Work/Family Reconciliation Policies for Parents in France, Germany, the Netherlands, and the UK in the 2000s. *Social Politics: International Studies in Gender, State & Society* 15 (3):261–286.

Lewis, Pascall, and Ruth Simpson. 2007. *Gendering Emotions in Organisation.* London: Palgrave Macmillan.

Leyland, Joyce 1987. On the Conflicts of Doing Feminist Research into Masculinity. *Studies in Sexual Politics* 16: 38–47.

Lodge, Anne. 2005. Gender and Children's Social World: Esteemed and Marginalised Masculinities in the Primary School Playground. *Irish Journal of Sociology* 14 (2):177–192.

Lohan, Maria 2000. Extending Feminist Methodologies: Researching Masculinities and Technologies. In *(Re) Searching Women: Feminist Research Methodologies in the Social Sciences in Ireland,* edited by A. Byrne and R. Lentin. Dublin: Institute of Public Administration.

Lorber, Judith, and Susan Farrell. 1991. *The Social Construction of Gender.* London: Sage.

Lorentzen, JÃ¸rgen. 2010. On Fathers in Norwegian History 1850–1920. *Men and Masculinities* 14 (3):268–287.

Loseke, Donileen R. 2003. 'We Hold These Truths to be Self-evident': Problems in Pondering the Pedophile Priest Problem. *Sexualities* 6 (1):6–14.

Lovell, Terry. 2000. Thinking Feminism with and against Bourdieu. *Feminist Theory* 1 (1):11–32.

Lupton, Ben. 2000. Maintaining Masculinity: Men Who Do 'Women's Work'. *British Journal of Management* 11 (S1):33–48.

Lutz, Helma. 2008. *Migration and Domestic Work: a European Perspective on a Global Theme.* Aldershot, UK: Ashgate Publishing.

Lynch, Kathleen. 1989. Solidary Labour: Its Nature and Marginalization. *Sociological Review* 37 (1):1–14.

——. 2007. Love Labour as a Distinct and Non-Commodifiable Form of Care Labour. *Sociological Review* 55 (3):550–570.

Lynch, Kathleen, John Baker, Judy Walsh, and Maureen Lyons, eds. 2009. *Affective Equality: Who Cares? Love, Care and Injustice*. London: Palgrave Macmillan.

Lynch, Kathleen, Sara Cantillon, Judy Walsh, and John Baker. 2009. Which Equalities Matter? The Place of Affective Equality in Egalitarian Theory. In *Affective Equality: Who Cares? Love, Care and Injustice*, edited by K. Lynch, J. Baker, J. Walsh and M. Lyons. London: Palgrave Macmillan.

Lynch, Kathleen, and Maggie Feeley. 2009. Gender and Education (and Employment): Gendered Imperatives and Their Implications for Women and Men Lessons from Research for Policy Makers. Brussels: An independent report submitted to the European Commission by the NESSE networks of experts.

Lynch, Kathleen, and Maureen Lyons. 2008. The Gendered Order of Caring. In *Where Are We Now? New Feminist Perspectives on Women in Contemporary Ireland*, edited by U. Barry. Dublin: TASC.

———. 2009a. Care-less Citizenship? Public Devaluation and Private Validation. In *Affective Equality: Who Cares? Love, Care and Injustice*, edited by K. Lynch, J. Baker, J. Walsh and M. Lyons. London: Palgrave Macmillan.

———. 2009b. Gender, Social Class and Love and Caring: The Intersectionality of Inequaities. In *Affective Equality: Who Cares? Love, Care and Injustice*, edited by K. Lynch, J. Baker, J. Walsh and M. Lyons. London: Palgrave Macmillan.

———. 2009c. Love Labouring: Nurturing Rationalities and Relational Identities. In *Affective Equality: Who Cares? Love, Care and Injustice*, edited by K. Lynch, J. Baker, J. Walsh and M. Lyons. London: Palgrave Macmillan.

Lynch, Kathleen, Maureen Lyons, and Sara Cantillon. 2007. Breaking Silence: Educating Citizens for Love, Care and Solidarity. *International Studies in Sociology of Education* 19 (1/2):1–19.

———. 2009a. Love Labouring: Power and Mutuality. In *Affective Equality: Who Cares? Love, Care and Injustice*, edited by K. Lynch, J. Baker, J. Walsh and M. Lyons. London: Palgrave Macmillan.

———. 2009b. Time to Care: Care Commanders and Care Footsoldiers. In *Affective Equality: Who Cares? Love, Care and Injustice*, edited by K. Lynch, J. Baker, J. Walsh and M. Lyons. London: Palgrave Macmillan.

Lynch, Kathleen, and Eithne McLaughlin. 1995. Caring Labour, Love Labour. In *Irish Society: Sociological Perspectives*, edited by P. Clancy, S. Drudy, K. Lynch and L. O'Dowd. Dublin: Institute of Public Administration.

———. 1995 Caring Labour, Love Labour. In *Irish Society; Sociological Perspectives*, edited by P. Clancy, S. Drudy, K. Lynch and L. O'Dowd. Dublin: Institute of Public Administration.

Lyon, Margot. 1998. The Limitations of Cultural Constructionism in the Study of Emotion. In *Emotions in Social Life: Critical Themes and Contemporary Issues*, edited by G. Bendelow and S. J. Williams. London: Routledge.

Mac án Ghaill, Mairtin. 1994. *The Making of Men, Masculinities, Sexualities and Schooling*. Buckingham: Open University Press.

Mac án Ghaill, Máirtín, Joan Hanafin, and Paul F. Conway. 2004. Gender Politics and Exploring Masculinities in Irish Education: Teachers, Materials and the Media. Dublin: National Council for Curriculum and Assessment.

Mac án Ghaill, Máirtín, and Chris Hayward. 2007. *Gender, Culture and Society*. London: Palgrave Macmillan.

Mahalik, James R., Glenn E. Good, and Matt Englar-Carlson. 2003. Masculinity Scripts, Presenting Concerns, and Help Seeking: Implications for Practice and Training. *Professional Psychology: Research and Practice* 34 (2):123–131.

Mahoney, Rhona. 1995. *Breadwinning, Babies and Bargaining with Power*. New York: Basic Books.

Manning, Wendy D., Susan D. Stewart, and Pamela J. Smock. 2003. The Complexity of Fathers' Parenting Responsibilities and Involvement with Non-resident Children. *Journal of Family Issues* 24 (5):645–667

Marsh, Katy, and Gill Musson. 2008. Men and Work and at Home: Managing Emotion in Telework. *Gender, Work and Organisation* 15 (1):31–48.

Masciadrelli, Brian, Joseph H. Pleck, and Jeffrey Stueve, L. 2006. Fathers' Role Model Perceptions: Themes and Linkages with Involvement. *Men and Masculinities* 9 (1):23–34.

Mason, Jennifer, ed. 2002. Qualitative Interviewing: Asking, Listening, Interpreting. In *Qualitative Research in Action*. edited by T. May. London: Sage.

Maume, David J., Rachel A. Sebastian, and Anthony R. Bardo. 2010. Gender, Work-Family Responsibilities, and Sleep. *Gender & Society* 24 (6):746–768.

May, Larry. 1998. *Masculinity and Morality*. London: Cornell University Press.

May, Tim. 2001. *Social Research: Issues, Methods and Process*. 3rd edn. Berkshire: Open University Press.

Mc Evoy, Rachel, and Noel Richardson. 2004. Men's Health: A Report from the Men's Health Forum in Ireland. Belfast: Men's Health Forum in Ireland.

McClave, Henry. 2005. Education for Citizenship: A Capabilities Approach. Dublin: University College Dublin.

McCormack, Orla, and Gim Gleeson. 2010. Attitudes of Parents of Young Men towards the Inclusion of Sexual Orientation and Homophobia on the Irish Post-Primary Curriculum. *Gender and Education* 22 (4):1–16.

McCracken, Grant. 1988. *The Long Interview*. London: Sage.

McGinnity, Frances, and Helen Russell. 2007. Work Rich, Time Poor? Time-Use of Women and Men in Ireland. *The Economic and Social Review* 38 (3):323–354.

——. 2008. Gender Inequalities in Time Use: The Distribution of Caring, Housework and Employment among Women and Men in Ireland. In *Equality Research Series*. Dublin: The Equality Authority and the Economic and Social Research Institute.

McGinnity, Frances, Helen Russell, and Emer Smyth. 2007. Gender, Work-Life Balance and Quality of Life. In *Best of Times? The Social Impact of the Celtic Tiger*, edited by T. Fahey and C. Whelan. Dublin: Institute of Public Administration.

McGinnity, Frances, Helen Russell, James Williams, and Sylvia Blackwell. 2005. *Time Use in Ireland*. Dublin: Economic and Social Research Institute.

McKay, Jim, Michael A. Messner, and Don Sabo, eds. 2000. *Masculinities, Gender Relations, and Sport*. London: Sage.

McKegany, Neil, and Michael Bloor. 1991. Spotting the Invisible Man: The Influence of Male Gender on Fieldwork Relations. *British Journal of Sociology* 42 (2):195–210.

McKie, Linda, Susan Gregory, and Sophia Bowlby. 2002. Shadow Times: The Temporal and Spatial Frameworks and Experiences of Caring and Working. *Sociology* 36 (4):897–924.

McLeod, Julie. 2005. Feminists Re-Reading Bourdieu: Old Debates and New Questions about Gender Habitus and Gender Change. *Theory and Research in Education* 3 (1):11–30.

McMahon, Anthony. 1999. *Taking Care of Men: Sexual Politics in the Public Mind.* Cambridge: Cambridge University Press

McQueen, Anne C. H. 2004. Emotional Intelligence in Nursing Work. *Journal of Advanced Nursing* 47 (1):101–108.

Messner, Michael. 1990. Men Studying Masculinity: Some Epistemological Issues in Sport Sociology. *Sociology of Sport Journal* 7 (2).

———. 1998. Boyhood, Organised Sports, and the Construction of Masculinities. In *Men's Lives*, edited by M. S. Kimmel and M. A. Messner. USA: Allyn and Bacon.

———. 2001. Friendships, Intimacy, and Sexuality. In *The Masculinities Reader*, edited by S. M. Whitehead and F. J. Barrett. Cambridge: Polity Press.

———. 2002. *Politics of Masculinities: Men in Movements, The Gender Lens.* Oxford: AltaMira Press.

Metcalf, Andy, and Martin Humphries, eds. 1985. *The Sexuality of Men.* London: Pluto Press.

Meyer, Traute. 1998. Retrenchment, Reproduction, Modernisation: Pension Politics and the Decline of the Breadwinner Model. *Journal of European Social Policy* 8 (3):198–210.

Migrant Rights Centre. 2004. Private Homes, A Public Concern: The Experience of Twenty Migrant Women Employed in the Private Home in Ireland. Dublin: Migrant Rights Centre Ireland.

Milkie, Melissa A., Sarah M. Kendig, Kei M. Nomaguchi, and Kathleen E. Denny. 2010. Time with Children, Children's Well-Being, and Work-Family Balance among Employed Parents. *Journal of Marriage and Family* 72 (5):1329–1343.

Minister for Social Protection (Deputy Joan Burton). *Written Answers: National Carers Strategy.* Houses of the Oireachtas 2011. Available at http://debates. oireachtas.ie/dail/2011/06/07/00141.asp.

Minnotte, Krista, L., Daphne Stevens, P., Michael Minnotte, C., and Gary Kiger. 2007. Emotion-Work Performance among Dual-Earner Couples: Testing Four Theoretical Perspectives. *Journal of Family Issues* 28 (6):773–793.

Minton, Stephen J., Torunn Dahl, Mona O'Moore, and Tuck Donnely. 2008. An Exploratory Survey of the Experiences of Homophobic Bullying among Lesbian, Gay, Bisexual and Transgendered Young People in Ireland. *Irish Educational Studies* 27 (2):177–191.

Mitchell, Juliet. 1974. *Psychoanalysis and Feminism.* New York: Vintage Books.

Moane, Geraldine. 1999. The Concept of Liberation Psychology. *Thornfield Journal* 21:1–7.

Moi, Toril. 1991. Appropriating Bourdieu: Feminist Theory and Pierre Bourdieu's Sociology of Culture. *New Literary History* (22):1017–1049.

Möller-Leimkühler, Anne Maria. 2002. Barriers to Help-Seeking by Men: a Review of Sociocultural and Clinical Literature with Particular Reference to Depression. *Journal of Affective Disorders* 71 (1–3):1–9.

Monks, Kathy 2007. *The Business Impact of Equality and Diversity: The International Evidence*, edited by T. E. Authority. Dublin: The Equality Authority.

Morgan, David 1981. Men, Masculinity and the Process of Sociological Enquiry. In *Doing Feminist Research*, edited by H. Roberts. London: RKP.

———. 1996. *Family Connections*. Cambridge: Polity Press.

Morrell, Robert, and Rachel Jewkes. 2011. Carework and Caring: a Path to Gender Equitable Practices Among men in South Africa? *International Journal for Equity in Health* 10 (1):17.

Morrison, Ken. 2006. *Marx, Durkheim, Weber: Formations of Modern Social Thought*. London: Sage.

Mottier, Véronique. 2002. Masculine Domination: Gender and power in Bourdieu's writings. *Feminist Theory* 3 (3):345–359.

Munck, Ronaldo. 2007. Social Class and Inequality. In *Contemporary Ireland: A Sociological Map*. Dublin: University College Dublin Press.

Munro, Ian, and Karen-Leigh Edward. 2010. The Burden of Care of Gay Male Carers Caring for Men Living With HIV/AIDS. *American Journal of Men's Health* 4 (4):287–296.

Nepomnyaschy, Lenna, and Jane Waldfogel. 2007. Paternity Leave and Fathers' Involvement with Their Young Children. *Community, Work & Family* 10 (4):427–453.

NESF. 2001. Lone Parents: Forum Report No. 20. Dublin: National Economic and Social Forum.

Neufeld, Anne, and Margaret Harrison. 1998. Men as Caregivers: Reciprocal Relationships Or Obligation? *Journal of Advanced Nursing* 28 (5):959–968.

New, Caroline. 2001. Oppressed and Oppressors? The Systematic Mistreatment of Men. *Sociology* 35 (3):729–748.

Ní Laoire, Caitríona. 2002. Young Farmers Masculinities and Change in Rural Ireland. *Irish Geography* 35 (1):16–27.

———. 2005. 'You're Not a Man at All!': Masculinity, Responsibility and Staying on the Land in Contemporary Ireland. *Irish Journal of Sociology* 14 (2):94–114.

Nic Ghiolla Phádraig, Máire, and Betty Hillard. 2007. Socio-Economic Change in Ireland since the 1980s: The Tiger, The Transnational Corporation and the Peace Dividend. In *Changing Ireland in International Comparison*, edited by M. Nic Ghiolla Phádraig and B. Hillard. Dublin: The Liffey Press.

Nixon, Darren. 2009. 'I Can't Put a Smiley Face On': Working-Class Masculinity, Emotional Labour and Service Work in the 'New Economy'. *Gender, Work & Organization* 16 (3):300–322.

Nixon, Elizabeth, Pádraic Whyte, Joe Buggy, and Sheila Greene. 2010. Sexual Responsibility, Fatherhood and Discourses of Masculinity among Socially and Economicaly Disadvantaged Young Men in Ireland. Dublin: Crisis Pregnancy Agency.

Noonan, Mary, Sarah Beth Estes, and Jennifer L. Glass. 2007. Do Workplace Flexibility Policies Influence Time Spent on Domestic Labour? *Journal of Family Issues* 28 (2):263–288.

Nussbaum, Martha 1995a. Emotions and Women's Capabilities. In *Women, Culture and Development*, edited by M. Nussbaum and J. Glover. Oxford: Clarendon Press.

———. 1995b. Human Capabilities, Female Human Beings. In *Women, Culture and Development*, edited by M. Nussbaum and J. Glover. Oxford: Clarendon Press.

———, ed. 2000. *Women and Human Development: The Capabilities Approach*. Cambridge: Cambridge University Press.

O'Brien, Maeve. 2007. Mothers Emotional Care Work in Education and Its Moral Imperative. *Gender and Education* 19 (2):155–177.

O'Brien, Rosaleen, Kate Hunt, and Graham Hart. 2005. 'It's Caveman Stuff, But That Is to a Certain Extent How Guys Still Operate': Men's Accounts of Masculinity and Help Seeking. *Social Science & Medicine* 61 (3):503–516.

O'Connor, Pat. 2000. Ireland: A Man's World? *The Economic and Social Review* 31 (1):81–102.

———. 2008. The Elephant in the Corner: Gender and Policies Related to Higher Education. *Administration* 56 (1):85–110.

O'Neill, James, M. 1981. Patterns of Gender Role Conflict and Strain: Sexism and Fear of Femininity in Men's Lives. *The Personal and Guidance Journal* 203–210.

O'Sullivan, Eoin, and Mary Rafferty. 1999. *Suffer the Little Children: The Inside Story of Ireland's Industrial Schools*. Dublin: New Island Books.

O'Sullivan, Oriel. 2004. Changing Gender Practices within the Household: A Theoretical Perspective. *Gender & Society* 18 (2):207–222.

O'Sullivan, Sara. 2007. Gender and the Workforce. In *Contemporary Ireland: A Sociological Map*, edited by S. O'Sullivan. Dublin: University College Dublin Press.

———, ed. 2007. *Contemporary Ireland A Sociological Map*. Dublin University College Dublin Press.

O'Brien, Maeve. 2007 Mothers' Emotional Care Work in Education and Its Moral Imperative. *Gender and Education* 19 (2):139–157.

O'Connor, Orla, and Claire Dunne. 2006 Valuing Unpaid Care Work. In *Social Care in Ireland, Theory, Policy and Practice*, edited by T. O'Connor and M. Murphy. Cork: Cork Institute of Technology.

O'Higgins-Norman, James. 2008. Equality in the Provision of Social, Personal and Health Education in the Republic of Ireland: The Case of Homophobic Bullying? *Pastoral Care in Education* 26 (2):69–81.

———. 2009. Still Catching Up: Schools, Sexual Orientation and Homophobia in Ireland. *Sexuality and Culture* 13 (1):1–16.

O'Higgins-Norman, James, Michael Goldrick, and Kathy Harrison. 2010. Addressing Homophobic Bullying in Secondary Level Schools. Dublin Equality Authority.

Oakley, Ann. 1974 *The Sociology of Housework*. London: M. Robertson.

———. 1998. Gender, Methodology and People's Ways of Knowing: Some Problems with Feminism and the Paradigm Debate in Social Science. *Sociology* 32 (4):707–731.

———, ed. 2005. *Gender, Women and Social Science*. London: Polity Press.

Oliver, Michael. 1990. *The Politics of Disablement*. Basingstoke: Palgrave Macmillan.

Owens, David 1996. Men, Emotions and the Research Process: The Role of Interviews in Sensitive Areas. In *Qualitative Research: The Emotional Dimension*, edited by K. Carter and S. Delamont. Aldershot, UK: Ashgate Publishing.

Padgett, Deborah K. . 1998. *Qualitative Methods in Social Work Research: Challenges and Rewards*. London: Sage.

Palkovitz, Rob, Marcella Copes, and Tara Woolfolk. 2001. 'It's Like ... You Discover a New Sense of Being': Involved Fathering As an Evoker of Adult Development. *Men and Masculinities* 4 (1):49–69.

Parrott, Gerrod W. 2001. *Emotions in Social Psychology*. Philadelphia: Psychology Press.

Parsons, Talcott, and Robert Bales. 1953. *Family Socialisation and Interaction Process*. Glencoe, IL: Free Press.

Pascall, Gillian, and Jane Lewis. 2004. Emerging Gender Regimes and Policies for Gender Equality in a Wider Europe. *Journal of Social Policy* 33 (3):373–394.

Patton, Michael, Q. 1990. *Qualitative Evaluation and Research Methods*. 2nd edn. Newbury Park, CA: Sage.

Pease, Bob. 2000. Researching Pro-feminist Men's narratives: Participatory Methodologies in a Postmodern Frame. In Researching and Practicing in Social Work: Postmodern Feminist Perspectives, edited by B. Fawcett, B. Featherstone, J. Fook and A. Rossiter. London: Routledge.

——. 2002a. *Men and Gender Relations*. London: Tertiary Press.

——. 2002b. (Re)Constructing Men's Interests. *Men and Masculinities* 5 (2):165–177.

Percheski, Christine, and Christopher Wildeman. 2008. Becoming a Dad: Employment Trajectories of Married, Cohabiting, and Nonresident Fathers. *Social Science Quarterly* 89 (2):482–501.

Peterson, Alan 1998. *Unmasking the Masculine; 'Men' and 'Identity' in a Sceptical Age*. London: Sage.

Pettinger, Lynne, Jane Parry, Rebecca F. Taylor, and Miriam Glucksmann, eds. 2005. *A New Sociology of Work*. Oxford: Blackwell.

Pheonix, Anne, Anne Wollett, and Eva Lloyd. 1991. *Motherhood: Meanings, Practices, Ideologies*. London: Sage.

Philips, Angela 1993. *The Trouble with Boys*. London: Pandora.

Pierce, L. Jennifer. 1998. Rambo Litigators: Emotional Labour in Male Occupations. In *Men's Lives*, edited by M. S. Kimmel and M. A. Messner. USA: Allyn and Bacon.

Pitts, Margaret J., Craig Fowler, Matthew S. Kaplan, Jon Nussbaum, and John C. Becker. 2009. Dialectical Tensions Underpinning Family Farm Succession Planning. *Journal of Applied Communication Research* 37 (1):59–79.

Pleck, Joseph H. 1976. The Male Sex Role: Definitions, Problems and Sources of Change. *Journal of Social Issues* 3 (32):155–64.

——. 1981. *The Myth of Masculinity*. Cambridge, MA: MIT Press.

Pleck, Joseph H., and Jack Sawyer, eds. 1974. *Men and Masculinity*. Englewood Cliffs, NJ: Prentice-Hall.

Polce-Lynch, Mary, Barbara J. Myers, Christopher T. Kilmartin, Renate Forssmann-Falck, and Wendy Kliewer. 1998. Gender and Age Patterns in Emotional Expression, Body Image, and Self-Esteem: A Qualitative Analysis. *Sex Roles* 38 (11):1025–1048.

Prendergast, Shirley, and Simon Forrest. 1998. 'Shorties, Low-Lifers, Hardnuts and Kings': Boys, Emotions and Embodiment in Schools. In *Emotions in Social Life: Critical Themes and Contemporary Issues*, edited by G. Bendelow and S. J. Williams. London: Routledge.

Price, Linda. 2010. 'Doing It with Men': Feminist Research Practice and Patriarchal Inheritance Practices in Welsh Family Farming. *Gender, Place & Culture* 17 (1):81–97.

Pringle, Keith. 1995. *Men, Masculinities and Social Welfare*. London: UCL Press.

Puchert, R., M. Gärtner, and S. Höyng, eds. 2005. *Work Changes Gender: Men and Equality in the Transition of Labour Forms*. Opladen: Barbara Budrich.

Qayum, Seemin, and Raka Ray. 2010. Male Servants and the Failure of Patriarchy in Kolkata (Calcutta). *Men and Masculinities* 13 (1):111–125.

Rachel, Jewkes. 2002. Intimate Partner Violence: Causes and Prevention. *The Lancet* 359 (9315):1423–1429.

Ranson, Gillian. 2001. Men and Work: Change – or No Change? – in the Era of the 'New Father'. *Men and Masculinities* 4 (1):3–26.

Rantalaiho, Liisa, and Tuula Heiskanen, eds. 1997. *Gendered Practices in Working Life*. New York: St. Martins Press.

Reay, Diane. 2000. a Useful Extension of Bourdieu's Conceptual Framework?: Emotional Capital as a Way of Understanding Mothers' Involvement in Their Children's Education? *The Editorial Board of the Sociological Review* 48 (4):568–585.

Reay, Diane, Sarah Bignold, Stephen J. Ball, and Alan Cribb. 1998. 'He Just Had a Different Way of Showing It' Gender Dynamics in Families Coping with Childhood Cancer. *Journal of Gender Studies* 7 (1):39–52.

Reed, Richard K. 2005. *Birthing Fathers: The Transformation of Men in American Rites of Birth*. New Brunswick, NJ: Retgers University Press.

Remy, John 1990. Patriarchy and Fratriarchy as Forms of Androcracy. In *Men, Masculinities and Social Theory*, edited by J. H. a. D. Morgan. London: Unwin Hyman.

Reskin, Barbara. 1991. Bringing the Men Back In: Sex Differentiation and the Devaluation of Women's Work. In *The Social Construction of Gender*, edited by J. Lorber and S. Farrell. London: Sage.

Ricciardelli, Rosemary, Kimberley Clow, and Philip White. 2010. Investigating Hegemonic Masculinity: Portrayals of Masculinity in Men's Lifestyle Magazines. *Sex Roles* 63 (1):64–78.

Richard, Nelson-Jones. 1990. *Human Relationship Skills: Training and Self Help*. London: Cassell.

Richardson, Diane. 1996. XIII. Representing Other Feminists. *Feminism & Psychology* 6 (2):192–196.

———. 1998. Sexuality and Citizenship. *Sociology* 32 (1):83–100.

Richardson, Diane, and Victoria Robinson. 1994. Theorizing Women's Studies Gender Studies and Masculinity: The Politics of Naming. *European Journal of Women's Studies* 1 (1):11–27.

Richardson, Noel, and Paula C. Carroll. 2009. Getting Men's Health onto a Policy Agenda – Charting the Development of a National Men's Health Policy in Ireland. *Journal of Men's Health* 6 (2):105–113.

Rimmerman, Craig, and Clyde Wilcox. 2007. *The Politics of Same-Sex Marriage*. Chicago: University of Chicago Press.

Risman, Barbara J. 1987. Intimate Relationships from a Microstructural Perspective. *Gender & Society* 1 (1):6–32.

———. 1998. *Gender Vertigo: American Families in Transition*. New Haven, CT: Yale Univeristy Press.

Roberts, Brian. 2006. *Micro Social Theory*. Basingstoke: Palgrave Macmillan.

Robinson, Victoria. 2003. Radical Revisionings? The Theorizing of Masculinity and (Radical) Feminist Theory. *Women's Studies International Forum* 26 (2):129–137.

———. 2008. *Everyday Masculinities and Extreme Sport: Male Identity and Rock Climbing*. Oxford: Berg.

Robinson, Victoria, Alexandra Hall, and Jenny Hockey. 2011. Masculinities, Sexualities, and the Limits of Subversion: Being a Man in Hairdressing. *Men and Masculinities* 14 (1):31–50.

Romano, Andrew, and Tony Dokoupil. 2010. To Survive in a Hostile World, Guys Need to Embrace Girly Jobs and Dirty Diapers. Why It's Time to Reimagine Masculinity at Work and at Home. *Newsweek*, 20 September.

Rose, Kieran. 1994. *Diverse Communities: the Evolution of Lesbian and Gay Politics in Ireland.* Cork: Cork University Press.

Rowan, John. 1989. *The Horned God: Feminism and Men as Wounding and Healing.* London: London.

Rubin, Lillian, B. 1983. *Intimate Strangers: Men and Women Together.* New York: Harper Row.

Rush, Michael. 2004. Fathers, Identity and Wellbeing. In *Theorising Irish Social Policy*, edited by B. Fanning, P. Kennedy, G. Kiely and S. Quin. Dublin: UCD Press.

———. 2006. The Politics of Care. In *Care and Social Change in the Irish Welfare Economy*, edited by B. Fanning and M. Rush. Dublin: University College Dublin Press.

Rush, Michael, and Valerie Richardson. 2007. Welfare Regimes and Changing Family Attitudes. In *Changing Ireland in International Comparison*, edited by B. Hillard and M. Nic Ghiolla Phádraig. Dublin: The Liffey Press.

Rush, Michael, Valerie Richardson, and Gabriel Kiely. 2006. Family Policy and Reproductive Work. In *Care and Social Change in the Irish Welfare Economy*, edited by B. Fanning and M. Rush. Dublin: University College Dublin Press.

Russell, Helen, Emma Quinn, Rebecca King O'Rain, and Frances McGinnity. 2008. The Experience of Discrimination in Ireland: Analysis of the QNHS Equality Module. Dublin: The Equality Authority and the Economic and Social Research Institute.

Russell, Richard. 2007. The Work of Elderly Men Caregivers: From Public Careers to An Unseen World. *Men and Masculinities* 9 (3):298–314.

Rutman, Deborah. 1996. Caregiving as Women's Work: Women's Experiences of Powerfulness and Powerlessness as Caregivers. *Qualitative Health Research* 6 (1):90–111.

Ryan-Flood, Róisin. 2005. Contested Heteronormativities: Discourses of Fatherhood among Lesbian Parents in Sweden and Ireland. *Sexualities* 8 (2):189–204.

Ryan, Paul. 2006. Researching Irish Gay Male Lives: Reflections on Disclosure and Intellectual Autobiography in the Production of Personal Narratives. *Qualitative Research* (6):151–168.

Ryan, Sean. 2009. *Commission to Inquire into Child Abuse.* Dublin: Ryan Commission.

Ryle, Robyn. 2012. *Questioning Gender: A Sociological Exploration.* London: Sage.

Sarantakos, Stirios. 1988. *Social Research.* 2nd edn. New York: Palgrave Macmillan.

Sarti, Raffaella, and Francesca Scrinzi. 2010. Introduction to the Special Issue: Men in a Woman's Job, Male Domestic Workers, International Migration and the Globalization of Care. *Men and Masculinities* 13 (1):4–15.

Sattel, Jack, W. 1998. The Inexpressive Male: Tragedy or Sexual Politics? In *Men's Lives*, edited by M. S. Kimmel and M. A. Messner. USA: Allyn and Bacon.

Schippers, Mimi. 2007. Recovering the Feminine Other: Masculinity, Femininity, and Gender Hegemony. *Theory and Society* 36 (1):85–102.

Schneiders, Sandra M. 2004. *Beyond Patching: Faith and Feminism in the Catholic Church*. New Jersey: Paulist Press.

Schwalbe, Michael, and Michelle Wolkomir. 2001. The Masculine Self as Problem and Resource in Interview Studies of Men. *Men and Masculinities* 4 (1):90–103.

Scott, Jacqueline L., Rosemary Crompton, and Clare Lyonette. 2010. *Gender Inequalities in the 21st Century: New Barriers and Continuing Constraints*. Cheltenham: Edward Elgar.

Segal, Lynne. 1995. Feminism and the Family. In *Gender, Power and Relationships*, edited by C. Burck and B. Speed. London: Routledge.

———. 1997a. Sexualities. In *Identity and Difference*, edited by K. Woodward. London: Sage.

———. 1997b. *Slow Motion: Changing Masculinities, Changing Men*. 4th edn. London: Virago.

———. 2007. *Slow Motion: Men and Masculinities*. Houndmills: Palgrave Macmillan.

Seidler, Victor. 1988. Fathering, Authority and Masculinity. In *Male Order: Unwrapping Masculinity*, edited by R. Chapman and J. Rutherford. London: Lawrence and Wishart.

———. 1989. *Rediscovering Masculinity: Reason, Language and Sexuality*. London: Routledge.

———. 1991. *Recreating Sexual Politics*. London: Routledge.

———. 1997. *Man Enough, Embodying Masculinities*. London: Sage.

———. 1998. Masculinity, Violence and Emotional Life. In *Emotions in Social Life: Critical Themes and Contemporary Issues*, edited by G. Bendelow and S. J. Williams. London: Routledge.

———. 2003. Fathering, Masculinity and Parental Relationships. In *Among Men: Moulding Masculinities*, edited by S. Ervó and T. Johansson. Aldershot, UK: Ashgate Publishing.

———. 2006. *Transforming Masculinities: Men, Cultures, Bodies, Power, Sex and Love*. London and New York: Routledge.

———. 2007. Masculinities, Bodies, and Emotional Life. *Men and Masculinities* 10 (1):9–21.

Sevenhuijsen, Selma. 1998. *Citizenship and the Ethics of Care: Feminist Considerations on Justice, Morality and Politics*. London and New York: Routledge.

———. 2000. Caring in the third way: The Relation between Obligation, Responsibility and Care in Third Way Discourse. *Critical Social Policy* 20 (1):5–37.

Seward, Rudy, R., Daele Yeats, E., Iftekhar Amin, and Amy Dewill. 2006. Employment Leave and Father's Involvement with Children, according to Mothers and Fathers. *Men and Masculinities* 8 (4):405–427.

Shakespeare, Tom. 2000. The Social Relations of Care. In *Rethinking Social Policy*, edited by G. Lewis, S. Gewirtz and J. Clarke. London: Open University in association with Sage.

Sharma, Ursula, and Paula Black. 2001. Look Good, Feel Better: Beauty Therapy as Emotional Labour. *Sociology* 35 (4):913–931.

Sheppard, Roy, and Mary T. Cleary. 2007. *That Bitch: Protect Yourself against Women with Malicious Intent*. Bath: Centre Publishing.

Shilling, Chris. 1997. The Body and Difference. In *Identity and Difference*, edited by K. Woodward. London: Sage.

Shows, Carla, and Naomi Gerstel. 2009. Fathering, Class, and Gender: A Comparisson of Physicians and Emergency Medical Technicians. *Gender & Society* 23 (2):161–187.

Silverman, David. 2000. *Doing Qualitative Research: A Practical Handbook*. London: Sage.

Simonazzi, Annamaria. 2009. Care Regimes and National Employment Models. *Cambridge Journal of Economics* 33 (2):211–232.

Simpson, Ruth. 2004. Masculinity at Work: The Experiences of Men in Female Dominated Occupations. *Work, Employment and Society* 18 (2):349–368.

——. 2005. Men in Non-Traditional Occupations: Career Entry, Career Orientation and Experience of Role Strain. *Gender, Work & Organization* 12 (4):363–380.

——. 2009. *Men in Caring Occupations: doing gender differently* Houndsmills: Palgrave Macmillan.

Skeggs, Beverley. 2002. Techniques for Telling the Reflexive Self. In *Qualitative Research in Action*, edited by T. May. London: Sage.

——. 2008. The Dirty History of Feminism and Sociology: Or the War of Conceptual Attrition. *Sociological Review* 56 (4):670–690.

Smart, Carol. 1989. Power and the Politics of Child Custody. In *Child Custody and the Politics of Gender*, edited by C. Smart and S. Sevenhuijsen. London: Routledge.

Smart, Carol, and Bren Neale. 1999. *Family Fragments*. Cambridge: Polity Press.

Snyder, Karrie Ann. 2007. A Vocabulary of Motives: Understanding How Parents Define Quality Time. *Journal of Marriage and Family* 69 (2):320–340.

Somers, Margaret, R., and Gloria Gibson, D. 1994. Reclaiming the Epistemological 'Other': Narrative and the Social Constitution of Identity. In *Social Theory and the Politics of Identity*. Oxford: Blackwell.

Spade, Joan Z., and Catherine G. Valentine. 2007. *The Kaleidoscope of Gender: Prisms, Patterns, and Possibilities*. London: Sage.

Spector-Mersel, Gabriela. 2006. Never-Aging Stories: Western Hegemonic Masculinity Scripts. *Journal of Gender Studies* 15 (1):67–82.

Speer, Susan A. 2001. Reconsidering the Concept of Hegemonic Masculinity: Discursive Psychology, Conversation Analysis and Participants' Orientations. *Feminism & Psychology* 11 (1):107–135.

Springer, Kristen W., and Dawne M. Mouzon. 2011. 'Macho Men' and Preventive Health Care. *Journal of Health and Social Behavior* 52 (2):212–227.

Staden, Helene. 1998. Alertness to the Needs of Others: a Study of the Emotional Labour of Caring. *Journal of Advanced Nursing* 27 (1):147–156.

Standing, Guy. 2001. Care Work: Overcoming Insecurity and Neglect. In *Carework: The Quest for Security*, edited by M. Daly. Geneva: International Labour Office.

Stockard, Jean, and Miriam Johnson. 1992. *Sex and Gender in Society*. 2nd edn. New Jersey: Prentice Hall.

Stoltenberg, John. 1989. *Refusing to be a Man*. London: Fontana.

Stratigaki, Maria. 2004. The Cooptation of Gender Concepts in EU Policies: The Case of 'Reconciliation of Work and Family'. *Social Politics* 11 (1):30–56.

Strazdins, Lyndall, and Dorothy H. Broom. 2004. Acts of Love (and Work): Gender Imbalances in Emotional Work and Women's Psychological Distress. *Journal of Family Issues* 25 (3):356–378.

Stutcliff, Bob. 2001. *100 Ways of Seeing an Unequal World*. London: Zed Books.

Tanaka, Sakiko, and Jane Waldfogel. 2007. Effects of Parental Leave and Work Hours on Fathers' Involvement with Their Babies. *Community, Work & Family* 10 (4):409–426.

Taylor, Steve, and Melissa Tyler. 2000. Emotional Labour and Sexual Difference in the Airline Industry. *Work, Employment & Society* 14 (1):77–95.

The Equality Authority. 2005. *Implementing Equality for Carers*. Dublin: The Equality Authority.

———. 2006. *Traveller Ethnicity*. Dublin: The Equality Anthority.

The Gender Equality Project. 2012. *The Business Case for Gender Equality*. The Gender Equality Project: Equal Value, Equal Respect 2012 [cited 7 February 2012]. Available at http://www.genderequalityproject.com/?

Thébaud, Sarah. 2010. Masculinity, Breadwinning: Understanding Men's Housework in the Cultural Context of Paid Work. *Gender & Society* 24 (3):330–354.

Thomas, Alison 1990. The Significance of Gender Politics in Men's Accounts of Their 'Gender Identity'. In *Men, Masculinities and Social Theory*, edited by J. Hearn and D. Morgan. London: Unwin Hyman.

Thomas, Carol. 1993. De-Constructing Concepts of Care. *Sociology* 27 (4):649–669.

Thompson, Edward. 2000. Gendered Caregiving of Husbands and Sons. In *Aging in the Twenty-First Century: Issues and Inequalities in Social Gerontology*, edited by E. Markson and L. Hollis. Los Angelus: Roxbury.

———. 2005. What's Unique about Men's Caregiving. In *Men as Caregivers*, edited by B. Kramer, J., and E. Thompson, H. New York: Prometheus Books.

Thorpe, Holly. 2010. Bourdieu, Gender Reflexivity, and Physical Culture: A Case of Masculinites in the Snowboarding Field. *Journal of Sport and Social Issues* 34 (2):176–214.

Tong, Rosemarie P. 2009. *Feminist Thought: A More Comprehensive Introduction*. 3rd edn. Boulder, Colarado: Westview Press.

Tronto, Joan C. 1993. *Moral Boundaries: A Political Argument for an Ethic of Care*. New York Routledge.

Ungerson, Clare. 1983. Why Do Women Care? In *A Labour of Love: Women, Work and Caring*, edited by J. Finch and D. Groves. London: Routledge and Kegan Paul.

———, ed. 1990. *Gender and Caring*. New York: Havester Wheatsheaf.

Vachon, Marc, and Amy Vachon. 2010. *Equally Shared Parenting: Rewriting the Rules for a New Generation of Parents*. New York: Penguin.

Valentine, Gill. 2007. Theorizing and Researching Intersectionality: A Challenge for Feminist Geography. *The Professional Geographer* 59 (1):10–21.

Van den Berg, Bernard, Werner Brouwer, Job van Exel, Marc Koopmanschap, Geertrudis A. M. van den Bos, and Frans Rutten. 2006. Economic Valuation of Informal Care: Lessons from the Application of the Opportunity Costs and Proxy Good Methods. *Social Science & Medicine* 62 (4):835–845.

Wagner, Peter. 2001. *Theorising Modernity*. London: Sage.

Walby, Sylvia. 1997. *Gender Transformations*. London and New York: Routledge.
——. 2004. The European Union and Gender Equality: Emergent Varieties of Gender Regime. *Social Politics: International Studies in Gender, State & Society* 11 (1):4–29.
Wall, Glenda, and Stephanie Arnold. 2007. How Involved Is Involved Fathering? An Exploration Of the Contemporary Culture of Fatherhood. *Gender & Society* 21 (4):508–527.
Walsh, Judy, and Fergus Ryan. 2006. *The Rights of DeFacto Couples*. Dublin: Irish Human Rights Commission.
Walter, Natasha. 2010. *Living Dolls: The Return of Sexism*. London: Vigaro.
Warren, Carol. 1988. *Gender Issues in Field Research*. London: Sage.
Warren, Tracey, Gillian Pascall, and Elizabeth Fox. 2010. Gender Equality in Time: Low-Paid Mothers' Paid and Unpaid Work in the UK. *Feminist Economics* 16 (3):193–219.
Way, Niobe 1997. Using Feminist Research Methods to Understand the Friendships of Adolescent Boys. *Journal of Social Issues* 53 (4):703–726.
Weeks, Jeffrey. 1985. *Sexuality and Its Discontents: Meanings, Myths and Modern Sexualities*. London Routledge.
——. 1994. The Body and Sexuality. In *The Polity Reader in Gender Studies*, edited by Polity. Cambridge: Polity Press.
——. 2007. *Sexuality*. 2nd edn. London: Routledge.
Weinland, Jo Ann. 2009. The Lived Experience of Informal African American Male Caregivers. *American Journal of Men's Health* 3 (1):16–24.
West, Candace, and Don Zimmerman, H. 1991. Doing Gender. In *The Social Construction of Gender*, edited by J. Lorber and S. A. Farrell. London: Sage.
Westwood, Sallie. 1990. Racism, Black Patriarchy and the Politics of Space. In *Men, Masculinities and Social Theory*, edited by J. Hearn and D. Morgan. London: Unwin Hyman.
Wetherell, Margaret, and Nigel Edley. 1999. Negotiating Hegemonic Masculinity: Imaginary Positions and Psycho-Discursive Practices. *Feminism & Psychology* 9 (3):335–356.
Whitehead, Antony. 2005. Man to Man Violence: How Masculinity May Work as a Dynamic Risk Factor. 44:411–422.
Wilcox, Clyde. 1991. Support for Gender Equality in West Europe: A Longitudinal Analysis. *European Journal of Political Research* 20:127–147.
Wilkes, Julie, ed. 1995. *The Social Construction of a Caring Career*. In *Gender Power and Relationships*, edited by C. Burck and B. Speed. London: Routledge.
Wilkinson, R., and K. Pickett. 2010. *The Spirit Level: Why Equality Is Better for Everyone*. London: Penguin Books Ltd.
Williams, Christine, L. 1992. The Glass Escalator: Hidden Advantages for Men in 'Female' Professions. *Social Problems* 39 (3):253–267.
——. 1995. *Still a Man's World: Men Who Do Women's Work*. Berkeley: University of California Press.
——. ed. 1993. *Doing Women's Work: Men in Non-Traditional Occupations*. London: Sage.
Williams, Christine L., and Joel Heikes, E. 1993. The Importance of Researcher's Gender in the In-Depth Interview: Evidence of Two Case Studes of Male Nurses. *Gender and Society* 7 (2):280–291.

Williams, Claire. 2003. Sky Service: The Demands of Emotional Labour in the Airline Industry. *Gender, Work & Organization* 10 (5):513–550.

Williams, Fiona. 2004. *Rethinking Families*. London: Central Books.

Williams, Malcolm. 2002. Generalisation in Interpretive Research. In *Qualitative Research in Action*, edited by T. May. London: Sage.

Williams, Simon J., and Gillian Bendelow. 1998. Introduction: Emotions in Social Life: Mapping the Sociological Terrain. In *Emotions in Social Life: Critical Themes and Contemporary Issues*, edited by G. Bendelow and S. J. Williams. London: Routledge.

Willott, Sara, and Christine Griffin. 1997. 'Wham Bam, am I a Man?': Unemployed Men Talk about Masculinities. *Feminism & Psychology* 7 (1):107–128.

Witz, Anne, and Barbara L. Marshall. 2003. The Quality of Manhood: Masculinity and Embodiment in the Sociological Tradition. *The Sociological Review* 51 (3):339–356.

Woodward, Kath. 1997a Concepts of Identity and Difference. In *Identity and Difference*, edited by K. Woodward. London: Sage.

———. 1997b. Motherhood, Identities, Meanings and Myths. In *Identity and Difference*, edited by K. Woodward. London: Sage.

Yates, Simeon, Stephanie Taylor, and Margaret Wetherell. 2001. *Discourse as Data: a Guide for Analysis*. London: Sage.

Young, Iris 1990. *Justice and the Politics of Difference*. Princeton, NJ: Princeton University Press.

———. ed. 1984. Is Male Gender Identity the Cause of Male Domination? *In Mothering; Essays in Feminist Theory*, edited by J. Trebilcot. USA: Rowman and Allenheld.

Zaretsky, Eli. 1994. Identity Theory, Identity Politics: Psychoanalysis, Marxism, Post-Structuralism. In *Social Theory and the Politics of Identity*, edited by C. Calhoun. Oxford: Blackwell.

Zeidner, Moshe, Gerald Matthews, and Richard D. Roberts. 2004. Emotional Intelligence in the Workplace: A Critical Review. *Applied Psychology* 53 (3):371–399.

Zimmerman, Mary K., Jacquelyn S. Litt, and Christine E. Bose, eds. 2006. *Global Dimensions of Gender and Care Work*. Stanford, CA: Stanford University Press.

Zwicker, Amy, Anita DeLongis, Joan C. Chrisler, and Donald R. McCreary. 2010. *Gender, Stress, and Coping. Handbook of Gender Research in Psychology*. New York: Springer.

Index

CPSIA information can be obtained at www.ICGtesting.com
Printed in the USA
LVOW10*1615160514

386132LV00011B/323/P